Radical work on the labour process had tended to concentrate on the economic exploitation embodied in it, and assumed that it is the objective determinant of society and state — where what is normally understood as global politics is carried on. *The Politics of Production* challenges this easy separation of economic 'base' and political 'superstructure'. Burawoy argues that the production process must be seen as an inseparable combination of its economic, political and ideological aspects.

Viewing the labour performed in transforming nature as a relational process permits us to see that the reproduction of social relations at work is structured by *production apparatuses* or *factory regimes*. The way in which surplus is both obscured and secured within the work-place, Burawoy argues, is guaranteed by specific institutions that regulate struggles over pay, conditions and status. The importance of differing 'factory regimes' in determining class consciousness, and indeed the form of politics in the wider arena of the state, is explored through a series of comparative studies focusing on early capitalism, advanced capitalism, state socialism and post-colonialism.

Michael Burawoy has lived or worked in each of the zones he analyses. A Mancunian by origin, he has been an ordinary factory operative in the American Midwest and Hungary and has carried out extensive fieldwork on the Copperbelt of Zambia. These case studies give *The Politics of Production* an unusual range of international comparisons and empirical depth. They are preceded by reflections on Marxist theories of the labour process, particularly those of Braverman, and a conclusion sets out the implications for political thought of this fresh theorization of production.

MICHAEL BURAWOY teaches at the University of California, Berkeley. His earlier books include *The Colour of Class on the Copper Mines* and *Manufacturing Consent*.

Michael Burawoy

Verso

The Politics of Production

Factory Regimes Under Capitalism and Socialism

Verso is the imprint of **New Left Books**

**British Library
Cataloguing in Publication Data**

Burawoy, Michael
   The politics of production: factory regimes
   under capitalism and socialism.
   1. Factory system — Political aspects
   I. Title
   338.6'5   HD2351

First published 1985
© Michael Burawoy 1985

Verso
15 Greek Street London WIV 5LF

Filmset in Imprint by
PRG Graphics Ltd
Redhill, Surrey

Printed in Great Britain by
The Thetford Press Ltd
Thetford, Norfolk

ISBN 0 86091 096 2
     0 86091 804 1 pbk

To Jaap

Contents

Preface

The origins of this book go back to 1968, when I became a research officer in the Zambian Copper Industry Service Bureau. For one and a half years I watched two multinational mining corporations respond to the new Zambian regime, installed four years earlier. I was able to observe managerial decisions made in relation to both the union and the government. I was also able to study what was going on in the mines themselves when I fielded a large social survey of the labour force with Zambian personnel officers as interviewers. I subsequently moved to the University of Zambia, where for two and a half years I undertook the research that forms the empirical basis of Chapter Five of this book. During the summer of 1971 I was joined by Abel Pandawa, Nat Tembo and Tony Simusokwe.

While at the University of Chicago I again took a job in industry, this time as a machine operator in the engine division of a multinational corporation that I called Allied. Although management knew of my research interest, I was treated like any other worker. This was 1974, and I held the job for ten months. I told my fellow-workers that I was doing this for my PhD thesis, but they either didn't care or didn't believe me. This was certainly not their idea of a university education.

By a stroke of fortune I had followed in the footsteps of one of the most astute and experienced field workers to have passed through the University of Chicago. Donald Roy had been a radial drill operator in the same plant thirty years earlier. His studies of 'Geer' were not only a base of comparison but also an inspiration to my own work. Don Roy died in 1980, just as he was putting together thirty years of studying union organizing in North Carolina. He was one of the few sociologists who managed to straddle the world of the industrial worker and the world of the academic — although at considerable personal cost. The comparison of my own study with Don's is more fully worked out in *Manufacturing Consent*. Here, in Chapter Three, I am more concerned to compare my study with that of another industrial sociologist with close connections to the working class. Tom Lupton's *On the Shop Floor*, a study of two Manchester factories, was as important for British industial sociology as Don Roy's work was for American industrial sociology.

My interest in Hungary was first stimulated by Miklós Haraszti's book, whose English title is *A Worker in a Worker's State*. Like Don Roy and myself, Haraszti was a machine operator — a mill operator in 1971 in a Budapest tractor factory. His book is a remarkable literary piece, vividly capturing the trials and tribulations of a new machine operator. But the book generates a paradox: life at Red Star appears much more despotic than what Don Roy, Tom Lupton or I found in our shops. And this flies in the face of conventional wisdoms about work in Soviet societies, where the absence of significant unemployment, the difficulty of firing, and the common interests binding workers and managers together in opposition to central administration have supposedly made for a more relaxed tempo on the shopfloor. I have been going to Hungary to find out how the system Haraszti describes is possible, and how widespread it is. In the fall of 1983 I worked in a champagne factory and a small textile factory, and in the summer of 1984, for two months, I worked as a radial drill operator in a machine shop similar to the ones at Allied and Red Star. My experiences there inform my resolution of Haraszti's paradox in Chapter Four.[1]

The essays in this book begin from working-class experiences inside the factory. As an academic who would be returning to the university after serving his time on the shopfloor, it has not always been easy to interpret those experiences. Without the workers who were willing to allow me to enter their lives as well as show me the ropes, the accounts that follow would never have been possible. I cannot say that my life on the shopfloor was a permanent joy, but that it was at all bearable and at times amusing was due to the social inventiveness of my companions.

I have also accumulated debts outside the mines and factories. Apart from introducing me to anthropology and sociology, Jaap van Velsen was the first to impress upon me the importance of studying actually existing socialism instead of postulating some utopia in which all the evils attributed to capitalism miraculously disappear. At Chicago I had the fortune of continuing dialogue, friendship and teaching of Adam Przeworski. For good or evil, he turned my Fanonite Marxism into a more respectable structuralism. Since coming to Berkeley I have become more sceptical of structuralist claims. The strains of critical Marxism, originally due to Margaret Cerullo, are most apparent in Chapter One. Whenever I veered too far in the humanist direction, Erik Wright was always on hand to try and set me on the scientific path once again. Throughout the last six years he has been a source of unfailing encouragement and criticism. He has read and commented on all parts of this book, not just once but many times.

Students at Berkeley have had to endure a lot. A number tolerated my reduction of Marxism to a silence — a silence about the politics of production. Undoubtedly, much that I have learned from them has found its way into this book. In particular, Tom Long has been my patient guide in theory and philosophy for the last eight years. During 1982-83 I benefited from discussions in the 'Class Analysis and Historical Change Program' at the University of Wisconsin, Madison. Three institutions have sponsored my research. The Southern African Research Program at Yale provided me with a semester's support in 1980. The Institute of International Studies at Berkeley financed a six-month trip to Hungary and Poland in 1983. In Hungary I was a guest of the Institute of Sociology at the Hungarian Academy of Sciences. There László Cseh-Szombathy, Elemér Hankiss, Laci Bruszt, Csaba Makó, János Lukács, Péter Galasi and Gábor Kertesi all helped to make my stays in Hungary fruitful and enjoyable. Ivan Szelényi and Robi Manchin started it all, and they continue to provide encouragement as well as intellectual and practical guidance.

Apart from those mentioned above, a number of people have commented on different parts of this book: David Plotke, Ruth Milkman, Leonard Thompson, Stanley Greenberg, Amy Mariotti, Colin Leys, Mahmood Mamdani, Jeff Haydu, Carol Hatch, Steve Frenkel, Vicki Bonnell, Isaac Cohen, Reggie Zelnik, Chuck Tilly, Ron Aminzade, Maurice Zeitlin, Perry Anderson, Mike Davis, John Myles, Leo Panitch and Wally Goldfrank. I am grateful to them all, and to Gretchen Franklin, whose political criticisms never interfered with her immaculate editing and typing. I am indebted to anonymous referees of the *American Journal of Sociology* and the *American Sociological Review* as well as the editorial boards of *Politics and Society* and *Socialist Review*. Finally, I should like to pay tribute to the late Alvin Gouldner. In large part, this book is an extended dialogue with his *Patterns of Industrial Bureaucracy*. Although I never met him, he more than any other contemporary theorist captivated my interest in sociology. In whatever directions my studies lead, I always discover that he's been there before me.

4

Notes

1. An ethnographic account, 'Piece Rates, Hungarian Style', written as a counterpoint to Haraszti's study, will appear in *Socialist Review* (January, 1985).

Introduction: Bringing Workers Back In

This is an unfashionable book. It defends an unfashionable thesis about an unfashionable class formed in an unfashionable place. The class is the industrial proletariat.[1] The place is the point of production. And the thesis has two parts. First, I argue that the industrial working class has made significant and self-conscious interventions in history. Second, I argue that these interventions were and continue to be shaped by the process of production. This thesis is in contention with contemporary trends, both within and beyond Marxism, which either abandon the working class for new social movements or consider it to be just one of a number of collective actors formed in the public sphere. Found on both sides of the Atlantic, the "newer left", as it has been called, challenges two central Marxist propositions: the privileged status of the working class, and the primacy of production. Can one recognize what underlies these critiques and still be a Marxist? My answer is yes.

Within these emerging political and intellectual currents, the postulate of the revolutionary working class is held to be theoretically and philosophically overburdened.[2] From the beginning the working class could only give lie to the mission, assigned by Marxists, of emancipating itself and therewith the whole of humanity. 'Marxism has been the greatest fantasy of our century.'[3] We must cry farewell to the working class, embracing the new social movements which spring from civil society, understood as the forgotten space between state and economy.[4] From here community struggles, the feminist movement, the ecology movement, the civil rights movement and the peace movement burgeon forth as the progressive movements of the 1980s.[5] If they have a limited vision this is all to the good, since transcendental tasks, such as the one that Marxists assigned to the working class, are the back door or even the front door to totalitarianism.

If messianic radicalism is now philosophically, theoretically and politically unacceptable, why can we not simply reduce the burden on the working class to one appropriate to its real rather than imagined interventions in history? The answer, it seems, is that the working class not only has lost its revolutionary temper, if it ever had one, but also is a dying class.[6] The post-industrial society ushers in 'deindustrialization' and with it a shrinking, weakening industrial working class. In its place new classes, such as intellectuals, emerge as agents for alternative visions of the future.[7] Another strategy is to reduce socialism to social democracy, and social democracy to a question of numbers. On careful investigation it now turns out that there were never enough proletarians for socialist parties to become effective forces through electoral means.[8] Coalition politics between the working class and allied classes, and therefore the compromise of socialist goals, were always and inevitably part of capitalist democracy. This provides the basis for a movement to the right in the name of electoral politics.

Contemporary historical studies reproduce this drift. Marxism is fleetingly raised from the floor only to be knocked out of the ring. Marx mistakenly projected the model of a revolutionary bourgeoisie onto the working class, which could never achieve the transformative power of its overlord.[9] Paradoxically, the peasantry — which Marx, at least in conventional interpretations, condemned to the proverbial sack of potatoes — is resurrected as the last heroic class capable of fuelling revolution.[10] Revolutions become a thing of the past, save perhaps in the beleaguered Third World. Certainly the working class plays no leading role in them.[11] Instead the state becomes an actor in its own right with its own interests, something to be not transformed or destroyed but manipulated and bargained with. States are here to stay, so we must learn to live with them.

Equally damning for the postulate of a revolutionary proletariat are the studies of workers in their brief moments of heroism. These studies have unearthed the swan songs of artisans in their battle to defend their skills against the encroachment of capital — a battle they seemed destined to lose, but which momentarily threw up radical visions.[12] We are left rescuing the pristine artisans of the past in those moments of tragedy and ecstasy, as an exhortation to the hollow walls of the present. Now we face an atomized, fragmented, objectified working class.[13] Labour historian and prophet of work degradation join hands in orchestrating the proletariat's last dance — in a conspiracy upset only by the authors' refusal to be implicated and by their surges of utopianism.

This, then, is the polemical context of this book — the emergence of perspectives that conjure away the working class. A pathos has engulfed Marxist and 'post-Marxist' thought, reconstructing history in its own image and projecting those reconstructions into the future. It would be foolhardy to place oneself outside the course of history, to swim directly against a tide which is dashing the revolutionary proletariat onto the rocks of history or sweeping it out to sea, never to be seen again. I am not, therefore, going to restore the working class to its messianic role, but nor do I intend to abandon it to the vicissitudes of some putative logic of history. I am not going to replace one metaphysical imputation (the working class as saviour of humanity) with its opposite (the working class as incapable of shaping its own destiny). As we shall see when we undertake sociological analyses in comparative and historical dimensions, the record of the industrial working class is not as insignificant as its detractors would lead us to believe. As to the question of deindustrialization, I do not deny its importance in advanced capitalist countries: it might indeed be happening on a world scale too. Of greater significance, however, is the international *recomposition* of the industrial working class — which entails that the conditions for the renewal of working-class radicalism are to be found in the industrially advancing areas of Latin America, Africa and Eastern Europe. In other words, the quiescence of industrial workers in some of the most advanced capitalist countries should not be projected into the past and the future or generalized to other countries. Just as revolutionary impulses are not innate characteristics of the working class, so resignation to the status quo is neither natural nor inevitable but is produced by specific conditions.

In the following chapters I argue that the lurches which have plagued the history of Marxism — lurches between a voluntarism in which anything seems possible and a determinism in which nothing seems possible, between a naive workerism and bleak prognostications — can be brought into line with reality if we expand our understanding of production beyond its purely economic moment and explicitly include politics. It is an ironic fact that political economy has conspired in the separation of economics and politics, never attempting to theorize a politics of production. But although I align myself with contemporary critiques of economic determinism, this does not lead me to argue that the working class does or does not become a historical actor outside production. Instead I defend the thesis that the process of production decisively shapes the development of working-class struggles. This thesis can be sustained only if the process of production is seen to have two political moments. First, the organization of work has political and ideological *effects* — that is, as men and women transform raw materials into useful things, they also reproduce particular social relations as well as an experience of those relations. Second, alongside the organization of work — that is, the *labour process* — there are distinctive political and ideological *apparatuses of production* which regulate production relations. The notion of *production regime* or, more specifically, factory regime embraces both these dimensions of production politics.

Studying the industrial working class may be unfashionable, but it is neither anachronistic nor irrelevant. The framework of production politics lends new interest to the study of an old class, offering an alternative understanding not only of that class but also, by extension, of the new social movements. This should be clear from the rationales for the study of traditional proletarians. First, let me consider the methodological rationale. The thesis of this book requires that real workers be examined in their productive circumstances in periods of turbulence as well as of passivity. It will also be necessary to investigate the various forms of factory regime, and the conditions of their existence and transformation. In order to demonstrate that the factory regime has effects for the mobilization of the working class, independent of the labour process, we shall have to undertake comparisons between countries and over time in which the labour process is more or less the same but the factory regime varies. In order, then, to examine labour processes that are commonly found in different countries in different periods, the essays that follow focus on textile workers, machine operators and miners.

Closely related to this methodological rationale for studying such traditional industrial workers is a theoretical rationale. For the industrial working class is at once the most fundamental and the most suspect link in the Marxian schema. The reconstruction of Marxism must examine how the process of production shapes the industrial working class not only objectively — that is, the type of labour it carries out — but also subjectively — that is, the struggles engendered by a specific experience or interpretation of that labour. Or, in my own terms, it must examine the political and ideological as well as the purely economic moment of production. Moreover, as we shall see, this reconceptualization of production also recasts some of the anomalies and contradictions in theories of underdevelopment, of the state, of state socialism, of the reproduction of labour power and, more generally, of the development of capitalism on a world scale.

The reconceptualization can also illuminate problems in other areas, not least the study of social movements. There are too few theoretically informed attempts to explain why certain groups become movements at certain times while others do not, to understand the effects of apparatuses of domination on struggles. Just as the abandonment of the working class proceeds from the fact of rather than the reason for its passivity, so the embrace of social movements often stems from the fact of rather than the reason for their struggles. In this respect, by re-examining the historical interventions and abstentions of the industrial proletariat from the standpoint of production apparatuses, we can learn not only about the working class but also from it. All of which is *not* to say that there is nothing to learn from social movements — quite the contrary. The very concept of production politics owes much to the feminist movement: to its critique of the distinction between public and private, and to its notion of the personal as political. There are, in other words, politics outside the state. Nor do I think these movements are unimportant in their own right. Yet too often that importance is mystified by a certain impatience to discover an actor here and now without examining its basis in micro-apparatuses of domination, the relationship of the latter to state apparatuses, and the barriers that capitalism poses to the transformation of these forms of domination.

In the last instance the reason for studying the industrial working class or any other oppressed group must be political. The industrial working class still represents the most fundamental point of critique, both of advanced capitalism, dominated by private appropriation of the product of direct producers, and of state socialism, dominated by central appropriation of the product of direct producers. The standpoint of the direct producer embodies an alternative to expropriation of one class by another — namely, the principle according to which the producers (considered singularly or collectively) control their product. However, any failure of the working class to realize this principle in no way invalidates its suffering, nor does it free us of the responsibility of examining the forms of its oppression.

I am not denying the existence of other forms of oppression, such as gender or racial oppression. Nor do I believe that any transition from capitalism to socialism would automatically eliminate these. While gender and racial domination may have a greater tenacity than class domination, class is the more basic principle of organization of contemporary societies. This means two things. First, class better explains the development and reproduction of contemporary societies. Second, racial and gender domination are shaped by the class in which they are embedded more than the forms of class domination are shaped by gender and race. Therefore, any attempts to eliminate non-class forms of domination must acknowledge the limits and character of change within capitalism and state socialism, considered as class societies.

At this point, it may assist the reader if I trace the genesis of the concept of production politics. It first emerged while I was machining parts of diesel engines at the South Chicago division of the multi-national corporation Allied. During my ten-month stint as a miscellaneous machine operator, from June 1974 to April 1975, Harry Braverman published his path-breaking *Labour and Monopoly Capital*. At the time it failed to speak to my experiences on the shopfloor, to get at what work meant to me and my fellow operators. We were constructing a shopfloor life of our own that took for granted what Braverman bemoaned: the separation of conception and execution. Our jobs may have had little skill in Braverman's sense, but they involved ingenuity enough. They absorbed our attention and sometimes even left us too much autonomy. Uncertainty could be as nerve-wracking as it was seductive. Objectification of work, if that is what we were experiencing, is very much a subjective process — it cannot be reduced to some inexorable laws of capitalism. We participated in and strategized our own subordination. We were active accomplices in our own exploitation. That, and not the destruction of subjectivity, was what was so remarkable.

It was not Braverman who offered insights into my daily life but, curiously, the abstract theories of politics and ideology found in Gramsci, Poulantzas and Althusser — very much in fashion at the time. Their analyses of hegemony — the presentation of the interests of the dominant classes as the interests of all, the constitution of the popular class state, the construction of the power bloc, the disorganization of the subordinate classes, the relative autonomy of the law, and so forth — all appeared as germane to the factory as to the sphere of public power. Thus, collective bargaining concretely coordinated the interests of workers and management, the grievance machinery constituted workers as industrial citizens with rights and obligations, and the internal labour market produced a possessive individualism right there on the shopfloor. These institutions materialized a balance of power, which first and foremost set limits on workers' struggles but also restrained management from its authoritarian impulses. The regulating institutions afforded an arena of self-activity, free from managerial depredations, that gave workers the opportunity to construct effective working relations and drew them into the pursuit of capitalist profit. Cooperation revolved around 'making out', a 'game' in which the goal was to make a certain quota, and whose rules were recognized and defended by workers and management alike. Originally constructed to alleviate boredom and to introduce some meaning into eight hours of drilling, milling or turning, this 'making out' had the effect of generating consent to its rules and of obscuring the conditions that framed them. Coercion was applied only when the rules were violated, and even then within bounds that were themselves part of a larger game. In short, as we slaved away on our machines trying to make our quotas we manufactured not only parts of diesel engines, not only relations of cooperation and domination, but also consent to those activities and relations.

I christened the regulating institutions that embodied and guaranteed this hegemonic order the 'internal state', underlining the analogies with the 'external state'. However, once the central point had been made that there was a politics outside the state — that is, a production politics as well as a state politics — the concept of 'internal state' was of limited analytical use. It had to go for at least two reasons. First, it blurred the essential association of the state with the monopoly of the means of organized coercion, guaranteed by armed bodies of men and women. The state remains the decisive nucleus of power in capitalist societies in that it guarantees the constellations of power outside the state, in the family, the factory, the community, and so on. In this sense state politics is 'global' politics; it is the politics of politics. The second reason for abandoning the concept of 'internal state' was its unjustified focus on the factory. There was no obvious warrant for referring to factory apparatuses as an 'internal state' while denying such a designation for family apparatuses. I therefore stuck to the idea of politics of production, whose locus and object were not an 'internal state' but simply the political apparatuses of production. The concept of factory regime encompasses these apparatuses and the political effects of the labour process.

The similarities and differences between workplace and state apparatuses led inexorably to the question of their interrelationship. Allied turned out to be the same plant that Donald Roy, a famous industrial sociologist, had studied in meticulous detail while he was a radial drill operator thirty years earlier. I was therefore able to map changes in the factory regime during the post-war period, but I never succeeded in isolating secular changes due to the development of new forms of state regulation of production apparatuses from changes specific to the enterprise, particularly its changing market context. Indeed, I tended to stress the absorption of Roy's Geer Company into the multinational Allied — that is, the firm's passage from the competitive to the corporate sector — as the major explanation for the movement along the axis from despotic to hegemonic regimes.

Undoubtedly the major inspiration for linking production politics

and state politics came from Miklós Haraszti's extraordinary socio-
graphy of Red Star Tractor Factory in Budapest, where he worked as
a mill operator in 1971. The same stroke of luck that had landed me in
Donald Roy's factory also landed me in a machine shop which, in
terms of work organization, technology and payment system, bore a
remarkable resemblance to the one at Red Star. And yet the production politics could not have been more different. Whereas the hegemonic regime at Allied relied on the relative autonomy of the factory
apparatuses, restricting managerial interventions while regulating
working-class struggles, the despotic regime at Red Star gave management a coercive instrument of untrammelled domination over the
workforce. The importance of the relationship between state and
factory was immediately obvious. At Allied, the factory apparatuses
and state apparatuses were institutionally separated; at Red Star they
were fused. To be sure, the state intervened to shape the form of
factory apparatuses at Allied, but it was not physically present at the
point of production. At Red Star, management, party and trade union
were arms of the state at the point of production.

I called the regime at Red Star despotic because coercion prevailed
over consent. I called it bureaucratic despotism because it was constituted by the administrative hierarchy of the state. Market despotism,
by contrast, is constituted by the economic whip of the market, and
the state regulates only the external conditions of market relations —
that is, the state protects market relations and labour mobility among
firms. Under market despotism, Marx's prototypical factory regime
for modern industry, the state is separated from and does not directly
shape the form of the factory regime; whereas, under the hegemonic
regime, the state and factory apparatuses are also institutionally separated but the state shapes the factory apparatuses by stipulating, for
example, mechanisms for the conduct and resolution of struggle at the
point of production. Our three types of regime may be presented in
the following table.

		Institutional Relationship between Apparatuses of Factory and of State	
		Separation	*Fusion*
Intervention of State in Factory Regime	*Direct*	HEGEMONIC	BUREAUCRATIC DESPOTIC
	Indirect	MARKET DESPOTIC	COLLECTIVE SELF-MANAGEMENT

The fourth cell — collective self-management — combines a different form of state-factory relations, in which factory apparatuses are managed by workers themselves. However, the state, or at least some central administrative organ, stipulates the conditions under which factories become self-regulating — that is, it stipulates what is to be produced with what materials obtained from what source. Moreover, this central planning agency is subject to influence from below through institutionalized mechanisms of participation by factory councils.

The above table provides the point of departure for this book. What significance can we attach to four types of factory regime inferred from a study of just two machine shops?! In particular, is there any relationship between market despotism, hegemonic systems and bureaucratic despotism on one side and early capitalism, advanced capitalism and state socialism on the other? If so, what is it? What other types of factory regime can be found under capitalism and socialism in both core and peripheral countries? What are the conditions of their reproduction and transformation? What are the consequences, in particular for class struggles, of the different regimes? Can we isolate their effects from those of other institutions? And what can we say about the transition from one system of politics (combination/articulation of production politics and state politics) to another? How much is this shaped by tendencies inherent to those systems, and how much by political and economic factors of an international character? We can begin to answer these questions only by situating regimes in their historical contexts of specific economies and states.

Before proceeding to these questions, we must be careful not to detach the political apparatuses of production from their material base — from the labour process. The first part of this study will therefore attempt, through a detailed examination of Braverman's work, to establish the premises for theorizing the concept of factory regime and production politics. For Braverman, the generic notion of the labour process involves a combination of two sets of activities: mental and manual labour. The hallmark of capitalism is their separation, which appears to the worker as domination. Here we shall pursue a slightly different course, defining the labour process by the social relations into which men and women enter in order to produce useful things. I call these social relations between and among workers and managers *relations in production*. These must be distinguished from the *relations of exploitation* between labour and capital. Whereas the former refer to the organization of tasks, the latter refer to the relations through which surplus is pumped out of the direct producer.

It should be noted that relations of exploitation are part of the *relations of production*, which also include the relations among the units which organize exploitation. Thus, relations of production include both the appropriation and the distribution of surplus. Whereas the relations of production uniquely define a mode of production, the same relations in production — the same labour process — may be found in different modes of production. Hence we refer not to the capitalist labour process but to the labour process in capitalist society.

Once a notion of the labour process as the unity/separation of conception and execution is replaced with a relational notion, the emphasis shifts from a question of *domination* to one of *reproducing* social relations. This is precisely the theoretical inspiration behind the concept of production apparatuses, although there is no one-to-one correspondence between institution and function. Thus, state apparatuses also reproduce relations in production and relations of exploitation, just as production apparatuses can reproduce relations of domination, such as gender and race relations, originating outside production.

Whereas my discussion of Braverman's work stresses the directly political and ideological *effects of the labour process*, the succeeding parts of the book deal with struggles as they are also shaped by different types of *production apparatuses*. I will be at pains to demonstrate that the labour process is only one of a number of factors that condition their form. The other factors emerge through a series of historical case studies. Thus, Chapter Two examines Marx's prototypical factory regime — market despotism. By returning to the site of Marx's analysis, the Lancashire cotton industry, we discover that market despotism, far from being the tendential form of regime, is quite exceptional. During the nineteenth century the Lancashire cotton industry moved from a company state to a patriarchal regime to a paternalistic regime, reflecting changes not only in the labour process but also in the market structure among firms. Moving further afield, to the United States cotton industry, we discover the importance of the mode of reproduction of labour power, or, what amounts to the same thing, the mode of expropriation of the direct producers from the means of subsistence, in the transition from a paternalistic regime to market despotism. Finally, comparisons with Russia suggest the importance of the precise interrelationship between apparatuses of the state and those of the workplace.

In effect, Chapter Two shows how problematic, contingent and indeed rare are the conditions of market despotism, conditions that Marx either took for granted or assumed would emerge with the development of capitalism. Chapter Three continues to elaborate the actual historical variability, in order to illuminate the development of what I call hegemonic regimes. Here the most crucial factor is the active role of the state in the reproduction of labour power: workers are no longer at the mercy of the overseer's arbitrary rule, and management must strike a new balance between consent and coercion, in which the former rather than the latter prevails. Of course, the extent of state support for the reproduction of labour power varies among countries, being stronger in Sweden and England than in the United States and Japan. Nor should the attempt to develop a scheme of national systems of production and state politics blind one to the considerable variation within countries, occasioned by market factors, the labour process and the differential relations of factories and their employees to the state. Finally, I discuss the emergence of a new despotic production politics in the contemporary period, one that bears the marks of the pre-existing hegemonic regime. This hegemonic despotism is rooted in the accelerated mobility of capital which threatens labour as a collectivity and forces concessions from it in the same way that labour extracted concessions from capital in the previous period.

Studies of the 'capitalist labour process' presume the existence of a distinctive socialist organization of work. But the presumption is rarely put to any serious empirical test. In fact, all the evidence we have from state socialist societies suggests a striking similarity between their labour processes and those in capitalist societies. If there is no obvious 'socialist labour process', I argue in Chapter Four that there is a distinctive state-socialist mode of *regulating* the labour process. The existence of such a distinctive production politics can be explained through a comparison of the political economies of capitalism and state socialism. Instead of the private appropriation and distribution of surplus through a market, the state socialist enterprise faces central appropriation and redistribution. Instead of competition among firms in the pursuit of profit, state socialist firms bargain with central planning agencies. Enterprises have greater or lesser capacity to extend concessions to their employees according to their bargaining power with the centre, linked to their monopoly of the production of key goods. The more centralized the economic system, the more important is the bargaining and the more there develops a dualism of factory regimes: bureaucratic despotism in the weaker sectors producing low-priority goods (for example, consumer durables, clothes, food); and bureaucratic bargaining in the stronger sectors producing high priority goods (for example, fuel, such as coal, steel, machinery).

State socialism also generates a second tendency, toward political dualism *within* the enterprise. Whereas capitalist firms operate under stringent profit constraints — hard budget constraints — state-socialist enterprises are protected by the state, and operate under soft budget constraints. They continually seek out resources with which to expand or maintain production, if only to enhance their bargaining power with the state. They face shortages, not overproduction, and this leads to searching, queuing and, most important, continual substitution of inputs and outputs. Production is therefore subject to a rhythmical change, requiring constant improvisation. As a result there are pressures toward the bifurcation of the labour force into a core and a periphery. The former, composed of skilled and experienced workers (who are also more likely to be party members or trade union officials), manage the exigencies of continually changing production requirements, while the latter, composed of subordinate groups of unskilled or semi-skilled workers and often peasant workers, perform jobs that are more easily routinized. Management becomes dependent on the core, which is able to extract concessions but only at the expense of the peripheral workers. Bureaucratic bargaining in the core and bureaucratic despotism in the periphery reproduce each other.

Differential bargaining strength of enterprises leads to a dualism between sectors, while indeterminacy of supply relations among firms leads to dualism within enterprises. With a more centralized system of appropriation and redistribution, bargaining with the centre becomes more important and hence the dualism between sectors more pronounced, while management has less autonomy to respond to supply constraints by developing an internal dualism. In Hungary we find dualism more developed within the firm, whereas in Poland it is more developed between firms; as we shall see, this in part explains the different trajectories of class struggles in the two countries.

Just as in capitalism the increasing independence of the reproduction of labour power from the individual firm, guaranteed by the state, leads from despotic to hegemonic regimes, a similar transition can be observed in state socialist societies during the shift from extensive to intensive development. Increasingly workers obtain the conditions for the reproduction of labour power independently of the enterprise, as a result of the distribution of housing and social benefits independent of performance at work but also through the development of the so-called second economy. Whereas under capitalism the state cushions workers against the economic whip of the market, under state socialism the opening up of the market cushions workers against the political whip of the state.

In the study of early capitalism, advanced capitalism and state socialism we discovered a constellation of determinants of factory regime: labour process, enterprise relations to state and market, the mode of reproduction of labour power. This constellation is itself shaped by wider political and economic forces of an international character. This becomes particularly clear in the study of Third World countries. Chapter Five examines how international forces shaped a particular form of primitive accumulation in colonial Zambia. A non-interventionist colonial state generated and reproduced labour supplies, while a company state regulated the miners' work and leisure during their period of employment. I call the regime of regulation in the mines 'colonial despotism', based on the colonial character of the apparatuses of production. There emerged a distinctive labour process which presupposed the existence of colonial despotism. The transformation of state politics in the post-colonial period called forth corresponding changes in production politics, generating tensions for the labour process which for technical reasons could not be altered so easily. In other words, once a certain 'colonial' technology had been adopted, often it could not be changed without overhauling mining techniques and excavation; at the same time, its effectiveness depended on a form of production regime that had been swept away with the colonial state.

Our study of Zambian copper mining, as well as the experience of other peripheral economies, indicates that the relationship between the form of production politics is limited on one side by the labour process and on the other by international political and economic forces. It suggests further that we consider the development of factory regimes in different countries as an interconnected international process, governed by the combined and uneven development of capitalism and indeed of socialism. Bureaucratic despotism at Red Star is as much a product of international economic and political forces as is the colonial regime in Northern Rhodesia. Equally, the anarchic character of English production politics is the result not only of the country's history as a pioneer industrial nation, but also of the appropriation of surplus from peripheral and semi-peripheral societies. The exploration of the international determinations of factory regimes is attempted in a preliminary fashion in the conclusion of this book.

Inevitably my critics will wonder how I can draw any conclusions from particular case studies. They will point to the exceptional character, and even bias, of my sample of factories. For biased it certainly is! The cases were chosen not for statistical representativeness but for theoretical relevance. Nineteenth-century cotton spinning, Geer Company, Allied Corporation, Jay's, Red Star and the Zambian mining industry can hardly be regarded as a representative sample. They are not even 'typical' of the societies in which they are embedded. Indeed, the very idea of a typical factory is a sociological fiction. It is the artificial construction of those who see only one mode of generalization — the extrapolation from sample to population. There is, however, a second mode of generalization, which seeks to illuminate the forces at work in society as a totality rather than to reflect simply on the constancy and variation of isolated factory regimes within a society. This second mode, pursued here, is the extension from the micro context to the totality which shapes it. According to this view every particularity contains a generality; each particular factory regime is the product of general forces operating at a societal or global level. It is the purpose of my analysis to expose those forces as they impinge on quite specific and unique factory regimes.

Thus, we discover that the various factory despotisms found in nineteenth-century cotton spinning are a product of the labour process, market forces, patterns of labour force reproduction and state interventions. Just as the more bureaucratic hegemonic regime at Allied is peculiar to the corporate sector of the United States economy, so the more anarchic regime at Jay's is distinctive of a similar sector of the British economy. Haraszti writes his book, *A Worker in a Worker's State*, as though it is a portrait of a typical worker in a typical state-socialist factory. In fact it is the portrait of an intellectual's experiences as a peripheral worker in a Hungarian enterprise suffering from the withdrawal of subsidies at the time of the economic reforms. Thus, Chapter Four deliberately entitled 'Workers in Workers' States', underlines the specificity of Haraszti's experiences and the variety of factory regimes in state-socialist societies. Equally, the despotism of the early Zambian mining regimes was a product of distinctive form of primitive accumulation and state abstentionism — a complex of conditions that we may call colonialism. In each case I seek to extract the general from the particular.

Of course, the facts do not speak for themselves. This process of induction from the concrete situation can be carried through only with the aid of a theoretical framework which already points to critical forces at work. Without the Marxist theory that I critically analyse and elaborate in Chapter One and elsewhere, I could never carry through the connection between the micro and the macro. A theoretical framework also leads us beyond what is, beyond verification, to what could be. We have already observed this in the formulation of a system of politics I have called collective self-management, species of which have only been realized for fleeting moments under very unusual circumstances. The analysis of realized — past or present — political systems draws out the importance of the labour process, the mode of reproduction of labour power, relations among enterprises, and the relationship of enterprises to the state for the reproduction of production regimes. The salience of these same factors must be brought to bear in the examination of the feasibility and potential instabilities of collective self-management.

For all its dependence on an elaborate theoretical framework, the extended case method roots our analyses in the day-to-day experiences of workers. I have tried throughout to connect the most abstract and most global analyses to what it means to be a worker under early capitalism, advanced capitalism, state socialism or colonialism. Intellectuals who exchange ideas over the heads of those whose interests they claim to defend, without founding their work on the lived experience of those people, run the risk of irrelevance and elitism.

Notes

1. Strictly speaking, the industrial proletariat is a class fraction. Here I take the working class to include all wage earners who do not exercise control over production. I follow Erik Wright's formulations in chapter 2 of *Class, Crisis and the State* (London 1978) as well as his most recent reformulations in *Classes* (London 1985, forthcoming). What distinguishes different fractions of the working class is not the character of the labour process but what I call the political regime of production. Although this book is about the industrial working class, the ideas can be extended to other fractions of the working class, such as state workers, and I do return to this question in the conclusion.

2. The most powerful and cogent critique of Marx along these lines is Jean Cohen's *Class and Civil Society* (Amherst, Massachusetts 1982). I can accept much of her argument but not the conclusion, which jettisons Marxism for a systems analysis of state and civil society abstracted from the economic context. As we shall see, the concept of production politics is an attempt at Marxist reconstruction partly designed to meet Cohen's criticisms.

3. Leszek Kolakowski, *Main Currents of Marxism*, London 1978, vol. 3, p. 523.

4. Again Cohen is very relevant here. A more popular formulation is André Gorz's *Farewell to the Working Class*, London 1982.

5. One of the best examples of this is Manuel Castells's *The City and the Grassroots* (Berkeley 1983). Castells's comparative and historical analysis of urban social movements is a theoretically rooted attempt to move away from the context of production and the working class while retaining some allegiance to a Marxist framework.

6. See, for example, Fred Block, 'The Myth of Reindustrialization', *Socialist Review*, no. 73, January-February 1984, pp. 59-76.

7. There are many theories of the 'new class', but one of the most interesting and novel is still Alvin Gouldner's *The Future of Intellectuals and the Rise of the New Class*, New York 1979.

8 See Adam Przeworski, 'Social Democracy as a Historical Phenomenon', *New Left Review*, no. 122, 1980. Przeworski and John Sprague's forthcoming study of European voting patterns during the last century underlines the dilemmas of socialist electoral strategy as shaped by a changing class structure.

9. See, for example, Cornelius Castoriadis, 'On the History of the Workers' Movement', *Telos*, no. 30, Winter 1976-77, pp. 3-42.

10. Teodor Shanin's 'Marx and the Peasant Commune' (*History Workshop*, no. 12, Autumn 1981, pp. 108-28) is a sign of the times. For some time Marxists have been interested in peasant revolts, but only now do we have a serious attempt to construct a Marx who actually anticipated the radical potential of the peasantry. In the 1960s and 1970s debates raged over the existence of an 'epistemological break' between a Hegelian Marx and a scientific Marx. In the 1980s debates have begun to rage over Marx's evaluation and reevaluation of historical change and its agents.

11. Skocpol (*States and Social Revolution*, Cambridge 1979) deliberately excludes the working class from a significant role in the Russian revolution because it was not central to the Chinese and French revolutions. The argument rests on the tenuous assumption that all three revolutions were essentially the same and therefore had to be caused by the same forces.

12. The most celebrated work here is E.P. Thompson's *The Making of the English Working Class* (Harmondsworth 1968), but there is now a burgeoning literature on craft workers' resistance to the encroachment of capitalism (see Chapter 2 of this book).

13. The best example of this tendency is Harry Braverman's *Labour and Monopoly Capital* (New York 1974). Thus, the contradictory perspectives of the working class as maker of history and victim of history can be cast in evolutionary terms in which early radicalism gives way to later quiescence. Throughout this book, but most explicitly in Chapter Two, I suggest the inadequacy of such a resolution, substituting one that underlines the centrality of factory regime in shaping the interests and capacities of the working class.

1
The Labour Process
in Capitalist Society

It is one of the interesting paradoxes in the history of Marxism that Marx's analysis of the labour process, as formulated in *Capital,* had until recently remained largely unchallenged and undeveloped. Whereas there had been debates over the reproduction schema in Volume 2 of *Capital* and over the falling rate of profit in Volume 3, Marxists had taken Volume 1 for granted. Harry Braverman, whose *Labour and Monopoly Capital* reflected and then instigated a resurgence of interest in Marxist theories of the labour process, wrote:

> The extraordinary fact is that Marxists have added little to his body of work in this respect. Neither the changes in productive processes throughout this century of capitalism and monopoly capitalism, nor the changes in the occupational structure of the working population have been subjected to any comprehensive Marxist analysis since Marx's death. . . . The answer probably begins with the extraordinary thoroughness and prescience with which Marx performed his task.[1]

Indeed, *Labour and Monopoly Capital* is a monument to the prophetic power of Marx's analysis.

But we should beware of Braverman's humility before Marx. We should not be deceived by his easy flow between the emergent features of monopoly capitalism and the pages of *Capital.* Indeed, Braverman goes beyond Marx in constructing a theory of social structure from the analysis of the capitalist labour process. His argument is elegant, simple, all-embracing, and above all convincing. He begins with the distinctive feature of the capitalist mode of production: that the direct producers sell to the capitalist neither themselves nor labour services but their labour power — their capacity to labour. The definitive problem of the capitalist labour process is therefore the translation of labour power into labour. This is the managerial problem of control that Braverman reduces to the alienation of the labour process from the labourer — that is, to the separation of manual and mental

labour, or more precisely, using his terms, the separation of conception and execution. Around this idea Braverman weaves the tendencies of both the capitalist labour process and the capitalist social
structure.

Within the labour process itself the division of labour brought
about by scientific management, and in particular Taylorism, epito-
mizes this separation of conception and execution. It is a means
through which skill and knowledge are expropriated from the direct
producer and placed in the hands of management. The introduction
of more advanced forms of machinery, whereby science is harnessed
to the labour process, both compounds and complements Taylorism
in the development of the separation of conception and execution.
Thus, the tendencies of the labour process under the guiding principle of managerial control are toward the deskilling and fragmentation of work on one hand and the creation of an apparatus of 'conception' on the other. Following his own logic, Braverman proceeds to
show that conception — the planning, coordination and control of
work — is itself a labour process and is therefore subject to the same
separation of conception and execution. Hence, along with the few
managers and technical personnel created by the development of the
intervention of science, there also appear armies of clerical workers.
This is one strand of his argument — the historical development of
the capitalist labour process. He combines this with a second strand
concerning the expansion of capital into ever new arenas of life. Thus,
Braverman documents the movement of capital into service industries, transforming domestic work, for example, into an arena of
capitalist relations. The proliferation of such service industries is, of
course, subject to the same process of separation of conception and
execution. As capital conquers one sphere after another and as it is
itself transformed within the spheres it has already conquered, old
jobs are destroyed and new jobs created. The movement of labour,
and thus the shaping and reshaping of the occupational structure,
follow the laws of capital.

Braverman's analysis is exclusively from the side of the object. This
is no oversight; it is quite deliberate. Braverman repeatedly stresses
the mechanisms through which subjectivity is destroyed or rendered
ineffectual and through which individuals lose their individuality. In
this he follows a powerful tradition within Marxism, most clearly
represented by Georg Lukács in *History and Class Consciousness*.[2] Like
Lukács, Braverman presents capitalism as a process of becoming, of
realizing its own inner essence, of moving according to its immanent
tendencies, of encompassing the totality, of subordinating all to itself,

and of destroying all resistance. Unlike Lukács, however, Braverman does not call upon the miraculous appearance of a messianic subject — the revolutionary proletariat — which, through the agency of the party, would conquer history and turn capitalism on its head. Whereas at the time Lukács was writing such a vision could present itself as reality, today in the United States it would present itself as a utopia. Not surprisingly, there are utopian elements in Braverman's analysis, although they do not appear in the guise of a party. Despite disclaimers, Braverman offers traces of a romantic utopianism.

It is clear, however, that a critique of Braverman cannot simply replace a one-sided view that emphasizes the objective aspects of capitalism with an equally one-sided view emphasizing the subjective aspects. To the contrary, Braverman pushes the subject-object framework as far as it will go and thereby lays bare its limitations. Thus, within the Lukács tradition, *Labour and Monopoly Capital* is a memorable study. It is the work of a lifetime — the result of sifting and resifting, reading and rereading, interpreting and reinterpreting Marx through a continuous dialogue with the concrete world. Not for nothing have we had to wait over a century for a comprehensive reassessment of Marx's theory of the labour process. Its place in the Marxist tradition is secure. If I do not continually harp on Braverman's remarkable achievement, it is because I am trying to come to terms with it and, at the same time, to draw upon alternative Marxisms to go beyond it.

1. Introduction

In *Capital* Marx accomplishes the rare feat of combining an evaluation and an analysis of the operation of the capitalist mode of production. Critique and science are here two moments of the same study. They develop together and in harmony. In *Labour and Monopoly Capital*, the two moments have come unstuck. They interfere with and impede each other's development. In this chapter I try to show how critique *can* set limits on the penetration of the working of capitalism.[3]

In section 2, I will argue that the essence of capitalist control can be understood only through comparison with a non-capitalist mode of production. By contrast, Braverman takes his standpoint from within capitalism, alongside the craft worker — the embodiment of the unity of conception and execution. While capitalism continually creates new skills and new craft workers,[4] it also systematically destroys them by taking, in Bill Haywood's words, 'managers' brains' away from 'under the workman's cap.'[5]

The separation of hand and brain is the most decisive single step in the division of labour taken by the capitalist mode of production. It is inherent in that mode of production from its beginnings, and it develops, under capitalist management, throughout the history of capitalism, but it is only during the past century that the scale of production, the resources made available to the modern corporation by the rapid accumulation of capital, and the conceptual apparatus and trained personnel have become available to institutionalize this separation in a systematic and formal fashion.[6]

However, it is not altogether clear why the separation of mental and manual labour is a principle inherent in the capitalist mode of production rather than one that cuts across all class-divided modes of production. Braverman does not penetrate the specific form of the separation of conception and execution to reach the essence of the capitalist labour process. He mystifies his analysis with unexamined assumptions concerning 'antagonistic social relations' and 'control', without revealing the specific meanings they assume under the capitalist mode of production. So long as he insists on focusing on variations within capitalism, Braverman is prevented from arriving at the structure of the capitalist labour process and thus of its relationship to the separation of conception and execution.

What 'external' perspectives can one adopt? Braverman, it is true, develops some of his notions by reference to the animal world.[7] For animals the separation of conception and execution is impossible. For humans, because they engage in purposive behaviour, the separation is always possible. But this sheds no light on the specificity of that separation under capitalism. An alternative point of departure is some notion of a socialism, but since this is deduced for Braverman by inverting a picture of capitalism taken from within, it tells us nothing new about the capitalist labour process.[8] Instead, I suggest taking feudalism as a point of departure.

In section 3, I will examine Braverman's theoretical framework. 'This is a book about the working class as a class *in itself*, not a class *for itself* . . . (There is a) self-imposed limitation to the "objective" content of class and the omission of the "subjective". . . .'[9] I try to show that an understanding of capitalist control cannot, almost by definition, be reached without due attention to the 'subjective' components of work. However, the problem lies not only in the dislocation of the 'subjective' from the 'objective' but also in the very distinction itself.[10] The economic 'base' cannot be considered as defining certain 'objective' conditions — 'class in itself' — which are then activated by the 'super-structure' — the so-called subjective aspects — to form or not to form a 'class for itself'. Rather the productive process must itself be seen as an inseparable combination of its economic, political and ideological aspects.

The 'class in itself/class for itself' scheme allows Braverman to ignore all those day-to-day responses that yield the secrets of how and why workers acquiesce in 'building for themselves more "modern", more "scientific", more dehumanized prisons of labour' and of workers' 'willingness to tolerate the continuance of an arrangement so obviously destructive of the well-being and happiness of human beings'.[11] Ironically, Braverman dismisses the very studies that might illuminate the nature of capitalist control and consent as the preserve of the 'conventional stream of social science' and assimilates them to 'the petty manipulations of personnel departments'.[12] While industrial sociology may conceal much, may offer at best a limited critique, and may present what exists as necessary and immutable, it nonetheless reveals the concrete forms through which labour is enlisted in the pursuit of profit.

Just as reliance on the 'objective' aspects of the labour process prevents Braverman from understanding the day-to-day impact of particular forms of 'control', and specifically Taylorism, so the same one-sided perspective leads him to compound Taylorism as ideology and Taylorism as practice. The same focus also precludes an explanation of the historical tendencies and variations in the labour process. Rather, Braverman assimilates cause and consequence in elevating a description of the tendency toward the separation of conception and execution into its explanation. In the process, he makes all sorts of assumptions about the interests of capitalists and managers, about their consciousness, and about their capacity to impose their interests on subordinate classes.

In section 4, I suggest that Braverman's conception of socialism is limited by his critique of capitalism. His exclusive focus on the relationship between conception and execution frequently leads him to attribute to machinery and technology a neutrality they may not possess and to turn romantic notions of early capitalism into restricted visions of a socialist future.

In section 5, I turn to the way Braverman links the labour process to the rest of society. Here, as in section 3, I note his collapsing of cause and consequence as the irresistible forces of degradation and commodification penetrate the furthest corners of social life. This is the essence of his critique: to emphasize the domination of capital over society, rather than the problematic character of the conditions presupposed by that domination.

Finally, in section 6, I argue that Braverman's analysis is a product of a specific time and place. His work expresses the apparently un-trammelled dominance of capital in the United States — its capacity to absorb or repel alternatives, to incorporate change and criticism, and when necessary to eliminate resistance. Mistaking appearances for essence stems not only from Braverman's expressive totality and concomitant teleological view of history but also from the absence of any comparative framework that might offer some notion of alternative patterns'of development. I draw upon the work of Gramsci as an example of a comparative approach that examines the limits of the possible. I then speculate on the causes of variations in the labour process, both within and between capitalist societies. In other words, it is because *Labour and Monopoly Capital* is so closely tied to the social and historical context in which it was produced that Braverman clings to critique all the more desperately.

2. Capitalist Control: Essence and Appearance

If there is a single concept that has served to generate ahistorical accounts of organizations and to mystify their operation, it is the concept of control. By virtue of its use as a general concept — and by incorporating an imprecision as to whom or what is being controlled, for what ends, how, and by whom — modern social science has successfully obfuscated the working of capitalism.[13] Despite his important efforts to specify its meaning, Braverman's use of the term is not without its flaws and unstated assumptions. He too fails to come to terms with the specificity of capitalist control over the labour process — that is, the manner in which the capacity to labour is translated into the expenditure of labour, or the translation of labour power into labour.

Control and Interests

Braverman derives his notion of control from the destruction of crafts. The 'degradation of work' through expropriation of skill and knowledge refers to what changes rather than to what is constant under capitalism, to the varieties of organization of work rather than to the underlying structure that identifies the labour process as a labour process in capitalist society. One can approach the latter only by comparing the capitalist mode of production to a non-capitalist mode of production.

But first let us specify the problem: why is control necessary at all? Braverman argues as follows. In the early period of capitalism, when putting out and subcontracting still prevailed, the entrepreneur's task was to eliminate uncertainty over the amount and method of work. Labourers were therefore brought together under a single roof and paid a daily wage for their 'labour power'. But in reducing one form of uncertainty a new form was created: the uncertainty in the realization of labour power in the form of labour. This new problem inaugurated capitalist management.

> When he (the capitalist) buys labour time, the outcome is far from being either so certain or so definite that it can be reckoned in this way, with precision and in advance. This is merely an expression of the fact that the portion of his capital expended on labour power is the 'variable' portion, which undergoes an increase in the process of production; for him the question is how great that increase will be. It thus becomes essential for the capitalist that control over the labour process pass from the hands of the worker into his own. This transition presents itself in history as the progressive *alienation of the process of production* from the worker; to the capitalist, it presents itself as the problem of *management*.[14]

The task of management has been to reduce or eliminate the uncertainty in the expenditure of labour while at the same time ensuring the production of profit. But why the need to reduce uncertainty? Why can labour not be left to its own devices? Why must it be reduced to a machine? In short, why is control necessary? The answer, of course, lies in the presumption that capitalist social relations are 'antagonistic'.[15] But what are these antagonistic relations? More specifically, what is antagonistic about them? And what is specifically capitalist? Braverman does not provide complete answers to these questions.

Let us begin with the issue of the opposition of the objective interests of labour and capital. 'The labour process has become the responsibility of the capitalist. In this setting of antagonistic relations of production, the problem of realizing the "full usefulness" of the labour power he has bought becomes exacerbated by the opposing interests of those for whose purposes the labour process is carried on, and those who, on the other side, carry it on.'[16]

But why the opposed interests? There are many passages in the works of Marx where he declares or presumes a fundamental opposition of interests between labour and capital. Moreover, Marx implies that this antagonism will become increasingly transparent over time. The material basis for the opposition of interests lies in the increase of unpaid labour relative to paid labour, of surplus labour to necessary labour. This is a tendency inscribed in the capitalist mode of production. In short, the economic relationship of capital to labour is zero-sum — the gains of capital are always at the expense of labour.

But how does labour come to recognize that its interests are opposed to those of capital? What determines the short-term, every-day interests, and how shall these turn into labour's long-term, imputed or fundamental, interests? Marx's answer can be found in his political texts, most clearly in *Class Struggles in France*. The proletariat will come to understand its opposition to capital, will recognize its historic role only through class struggle. Thus, the bloody defeat that the proletariat suffered in June 1848 was necessary to the evolution of a class consciousness, to the movement from a 'class in itself to a class for itself'.[17] In addition, Marx argues that the maturity of the working class hinges on the development of the forces of production that is coterminous with their homogenization and socialization, preparing the ground for revolutionary combination against capital.[18]

History suggests, however, that the outcome of class struggle mollifies the opposition of interests and frequently coordinates the interests of labour and capital. Thus, universal suffrage, the object of considerable struggle in Europe, turned into a means of incorporating the working class into the capitalist order and became a fetter on proletarian consciousness. How all this has happened is not the object of the present discussion. Suffice it to say that whereas in terms of exchange value, relations between capital and labour may be zero-sum, in terms of use value those relations are non-zero-sum. That is, capital has been able to extend concessions to labour without jeopardizing its own position. Marx did not pay much attention to this possibility, although he did sometimes recognize it: 'To say that the worker has an interest in the rapid growth of capital is only to say that the more rapidly the worker increases the wealth of others, the richer will be the crumbs that fall to him, the greater is the number of workers that can be employed and called into existence, the more can the mass of slaves dependent on capital be increased.'[19] Thus, even if the 'value' of wages — that is, the amount of labour time socially necessary for the reproduction of labour power — falls, the commodities that the wage can fetch can increase owing to productivity advances. And it is not in exchange-value terms that workers understand their interests and act in the world but in terms of the actual commodities they purchase with their wage. Through the concessions and higher living standards associated with an advanced capitalist economy, the interests of capital and labour are concretely coordinated.[20]

The crucial issue is that the interests that organize the daily life of workers are not given irrevocably; they cannot be imputed; they are produced and reproduced in particular ways. To assume, without further specification, that the interests of capital and labour are opposed leads to serious misunderstandings of the nature of capitalist control, if only because it provides an excuse to ignore the ideological terrain on which interests are organized.[21] Rather, we must begin to develop a theory of interests. We must investigate the conditions under which the interests of labour and capital actually become antagonistic. In short, we must go beyond Marx.

So, if we cannot take interests as given, what becomes of Braverman's notion of control? Why is control so necessary? What is its function? We can begin to answer these questions only by tracing the specificity of capitalist control from the perspective of a non-capitalist mode of production, in our case, feudalism.

From Feudalism to Capitalism

The portrait of feudalism that I am about to offer does not correspond to any historically concrete feudal social formation. Rather, it represents the feudal mode of production as a pure form, something that never existed in reality. The purpose here, as it was for Marx, is to use the notion of the feudal mode of production not to help us understand feudalism but to illuminate the essence of the capitalist mode of production.

A mode of production can be defined generally as the social relations into which men and women enter as they transform nature.[22] Each mode of production is made up of a combination of two sets of social relations, or as Balibar calls it a 'double connection'.[23] First, there are the social relations of 'men and women to nature': the relations of productive activity and of the labour process, sometimes known as the technical division of labour. I shall refer to these as the *relations in production*.[24] Second, there are the social relations of 'men and women to one another': the relations of distribution and consumption of the product of labour and the relations through which surplus is pumped out of the direct producers, sometimes known as the social division of labour. I shall refer to these as the *relations of production*.

At the most general level, and as a first approximation, we can regard the feudal relations *of* production as defined by particular mechanisms designed to expropriate surplus through rent, while the feudal relations *in* production are characterized by the ability of direct producers to set the instruments of production in motion autonomously. We can discover essentially three types of rent: labour rent,

rent in kind, and money rent. We shall confine ourselves to the first, which Banaji analyses as the fully developed or crystallized form of feudalism.[25] The essential cycle of production is as follows. For a portion of the work-week, say four days, serfs work on land that they 'possess' or hold at the will of the lord; during the remaining two days they work on the land of the lord, the lord's demesne. While the former labour is necessary to meet the subsistence needs of the serf's family, the latter constitutes surplus labour in the form of rent, which is appropriated by the lord.

Five features of this 'pure' form of feudalism should be noted. First, necessary and surplus labour are separated in both time and space. Labourers work for themselves on their own land and then for the lord in a different area. Second, serfs are in immediate possession of the means of their subsistence as they engage in production. They grow and consume their own crops. Third, serfs possess and set in motion the instruments of production independently of the lord.[26] Fourth, at the same time, the lord actually organizes the labour process, particularly on his own land, through the specification of labour services in the manorial courts. Here, too, we find the separation of conception and execution. Struggles over the amount of surplus to be produced occur through the political-legal apparatus of the estate. Finally, serfs find themselves working for the lord because ultimately they can be compelled to carry out customary services. This is presented in the realm of ideology as fair exchange for the right to hold land and the right to military protection.

In summary, under the feudal mode of production surplus is transparent. Furthermore, it is produced neither automatically nor simultaneously within the cycle of subsistence production. It is produced outside this cycle. As a result, the lord has to appropriate surplus through extra-economic means. This has many implications for the nature of feudal law, politics, religion and so forth, since it is in these realms that we discover the mechanisms for ensuring the continuous appropriation of surplus. However, the contrast with the capitalist mode of appropriation is what is important here. In capitalism, workers are dispossessed of access to their own means of production. For reasons of survival they have no alternative but to sell their labour power to a capitalist, in return for a wage with which they can then purchase the means of their existence. Whereas it appears that workers are paid for the entire time they work for the capitalist, say eight hours each day, in reality their wage is equivalent to only a portion of the working day, say five hours. These five hours constitute necessary labour time (necessary for the reproduction of labour power), while the remaining three hours are appropriated by the capitalist as unpaid or surplus labour time and later realized as profit through the sale of commodities on the market.

Five points should again be noted. First, there is no separation either in time or in space between necessary and surplus labour time. This distinction, to which Marx draws our attention, does not appear as such in the organization of production. It is invisible (and possibly implausible) to both worker and capitalist. We experience only its effects — the production of surplus value and therefore of the capitalist on the one hand, and the production of wage-equivalent and therefore of the labourer on the other. Second, labourers are never in possession of the means of subsistence during the production process. One cannot live by pins alone; there is no possibility that workers will run off with the means of their existence. The only way a worker can gain access to the means of subsistence is by working the full eight hours and receiving a wage equivalent to, say, five hours. In other words, workers are dependent on selling their labour power in a market, just as capitalists, if they are to remain capitalists, are dependent on selling their products in a market. Third, workers cannot set the means of production into motion by themselves. They are subordinated to, and largely controlled by, the labour process. On the other hand, and this is the fourth point, the amount of surplus or, more accurately, the tasks they have to accomplish are not specified as they are under feudalism. Rather than political struggles in the manorial courts, we now find 'economic' struggles over the control of work or, as some have referred to it, over the 'effort bargain' either on the shopfloor or in negotiations between management and labour.[27] Finally, workers are compelled to go to work not so much through the threat or activation of extra-economic mechanisms but through the very need for survival. The wage offers means of existence, and the worker's appearance at the factory gates has to be renewed each day if he or she is to survive.

In summary, we find that under the capitalist mode of production the very act of production not only contributes to the making of a commodity (a use value), but also produces on one side the capitalist (surplus value) and on the other side the labourer (necessary value). The transformation of nature as defined by the labour process — that is, by the relations in production — reproduces the relations of production and at the same time conceals the essence of those relations. By contrast, feudal relations in production neither reproduce nor conceal the relations of production between lord and serf. To the contrary, the relations in production are such as to throw into relief the exploitative relationship between lord and serf and to necessitate the intervention of some extra-economic element to ensure the reproduction of that relationship. On the other hand, just because surplus is transparent and well specified, the lord always knows when he has obtained it. Under capitalism, because of the absence of a separation, either temporal or spatial, between necessary and surplus labour time, the capitalist is never sure whether he has indeed recovered a surplus. The expenditure of labour on the shopfloor occurs between the time when a capitalist makes a wage commitment and the time when he realizes the value of the product in the market. Whereas the lord knows he has pumped surplus out of serfs, because for two days each week he can see them working in his fields, the capitalist is cast in an ambiguous position since he cannot see surplus or its absence until it is too late. Surplus is obscured in the process of production not only for the worker but also for the capitalist. The dilemma of capitalist control is thus to secure surplus value while at the same time keeping it hidden.[28]

Obscuring and Securing Surplus Value

What can the Marxist literature tell us about the specific mechanisms of obscuring and securing surplus value? Let us begin with the obscuring of surplus. As we have already discussed, the wage-labour contract mystifies the existence of unpaid labour, since wages are paid as if for the entire working day. In Volume 3 of *Capital* Marx writes about two other sources of the mystification of the origins of profit. On one hand he shows how profit appears to be the return to constant capital, to the investment in machinery. On the other hand, he demonstrates how the market also appears to be the source of profit, how the realization of profit obscures its origin in unpaid labour.

But how does the organization of the labour process itself, the relations *in* production, conceal the existence of surplus, the relations *of* production? First, the relations in production are dislocated from the relations of production. The reproduction of labour power and of capital are the external effects of the expenditure of labour. The one takes place within and the other outside the factory. At the point of production workers interact only with one another and with managers who *appear*, like themselves, to sell their labour power for an income (although they may in fact appropriate a share of the surplus value). Capitalists are generally invisible. This separation of relations in and of production, of course, corresponds directly to the institutional separation of 'ownership and control'.[29]

Second, rather than the emergence of a collective consciousness due to interdependence and homogenization of labour, we discover that the relations in production have the effect of fragmenting and individuating life on the factory floor. As Lukács notes: 'In this respect, too, mechanization makes of them isolated abstract atoms whose work no longer brings them together directly and organically; it becomes mediated to an increasing extent exclusively by the abstract laws of the mechanism which imprisons them.'[30] A number of studies have documented the creation of skill hierarchies that pit workers against one another,[31] or shown how rules can be used to diffuse conflict.[32] Moreover, as Braverman notes, workers can no longer grasp the totality; they can no longer see beyond their immediate fractionalized job, let alone beyond the labour process to the relations of production. 'A necessary consequence of the separation of conception and execution is that the labour process is now divided between separate sites and separate bodies of workers. . . . The physical processes of production are now carried out more or less blindly, not only by the workers who perform them, but often by the lower ranks of supervisory employees as well. The production units operate like a hand, watched, corrected, and controlled by a distant brain.'[33]

Finally, there are those who argue that bourgeois ideology penetrates the consciousness of the proletariat and obstructs its capacity to recognize itself as a class opposed to capital. Thus, Lukács talks of the 'insidious effects of bourgeois ideology on the thought of the proletariat' and of the 'devastating and degrading effects of the capitalist system upon its (the proletariat's) class consciousness'.[34] A similar view is to be found in Lenin: 'But why, the reader will ask, does the spontaneous movement, the movement along the line of least resistance, lead to the domination of bourgeois ideology? For the simple reason that bourgeois ideology is far older in origin than socialist ideology, that it is more fully developed, and that it has at its disposal *unmeasurably* more means of dissemination. . . . The working class spontaneously gravitates towards socialism; nevertheless, most widespread (and continuously and diversely revived) bourgeois ideology spontaneously imposes itself upon the working class to a still greater degree.'[35]

This is not very helpful, but it is the best Lenin has to offer. Each class has its own ideology (given spontaneously), and these ideologies then engage in a battle with one another. As in all the writings to which we have referred, there is no attempt to come to terms with the production of a specific type of consciousness or ideology at the point of production — one whose effect is to obscure surplus value and relations of production.

What about the securing of surplus? Following Marx, Marxist theory has taken the existence of surplus for granted and therefore focused on its quantity.[36] As Braverman writes: 'It is known that human labour is able to produce more than it consumes, and this capacity for "surplus labour" is sometimes treated as a special mystical endowment of humanity or of its labour. In reality it is nothing of the sort, but is merely a prolongation of working time beyond the point where labour has reproduced itself, or in other words brought into being its own means of subsistence or their equivalent.'[37]

This is a transhistorical generalization that may, in fact, not hold under all circumstances. But, what is more important, it is one thing to speak of a potential to produce more than one consumes; it is quite another matter to realize that potential.[38] And that precisely is the problem of 'control', which faces all dominant classes and assumes different forms according to the mode of production. Under feudalism the potential is realized through the intervention of an extra-economic element. Under capitalism not only is this possibility ruled out, but in addition surplus itself is concealed.

Thus, Braverman is mistaken in applying the logic of 'feudal control' to the capitalist labour process. Commenting on Taylor's notion of a 'fair day's work', Braverman writes: 'Why a "fair day's work" should be defined as physiological maximum is never made clear. In attempting to give concrete meaning to the abstraction "fairness", it would make just as much if not more sense to express a fair day's work as the amount of labour necessary to add to the product a value equal to the worker's pay; under such conditions, of course, profit would be impossible.'[39]

But workers do not first produce for themselves and then for the capitalist, as occurs between feudal peasants and the lord. Necessary and surplus labour time are indistinguishable at the level of experience.

The notion of a fair day's work as equivalent to a wage does not make sense for another reason — namely, the individual labourer's dependence on capital. Proletarian existence rests not merely on today's wage but also on tomorrow's and the next day's. Unlike feudal serfs, who produce and consume their own surplus independently of the lord, capitalist labourers depend on the production of profit. Their future interests, as organized under the capitalist mode of production, lie in the production of surplus value.[40] Here rests the material basis for capitalist hegemony, according to which the interests of capital are presented as the interests, both present and future, of all.[41]

Let me summarize the argument so far. In adopting a standpoint within capitalism Braverman is unable to uncover the essence of the capitalist labour process. Instead he assimilates the separation of conception and execution to the fundamental structure of capitalist control. In so doing he treats what is but a single expression of capitalist control as its essence. By taking an alternative mode of production as point of departure, I have tried to construct the features common to all forms of the capitalist labour process. I have defined these in terms of what has to be accomplished — namely, the obscuring and securing of surplus value. In the section that follows I propose to show that 'obscuring and securing' surplus value can be understood only with reference to the ideological and political as well as 'economic' realms of work. In other words, Braverman's restricted attention to the 'objective' elements of work does not allow us to understand the nature of control — for, by definition, control involves what Braverman would refer to as 'subjective' aspects of work and what I will refer to as political and ideological processes. Only when these processes are understood can we proceed to examine the variety of forms of the capitalist labour process, the transition from one to another, and the relationship between the separation of conception and execution and the obscuring and securing of surplus.

3.   Class: In Itself or For Itself?

In this section I will begin to establish a framework in which we can pose the problem of capitalist control, that is, of securing and obscuring surplus. But first it will be necessary to show why Braverman's concepts, and not merely the way he uses them, are inadequate to the task.

The Economic, Political and Ideological Moments of Work

Braverman's 'critique' is directed to the degradation of work, to the factory as a prison. By portraying workers as 'general purpose machines' and 'abstract labour', and by asserting that the scientific-technical revolution removes the 'subjective factor of the labour process . . . to a place among its inanimate objective factors',[42] Braverman is clinging to the critical moment in *Capital*: 'Labour in the form of standardized motion patterns is labour used as an interchangeable part, and in this form comes ever closer to corresponding, in life, to the abstraction employed by Marx in analysis of the capitalist mode of production.'[43] In the resolute retention of critique, therefore, he refuses to countenance the human side of work — the adaptation to degradation. For such are the concerns of the 'conventional stream of social science'.[44] Industrial sociology, claims Braverman, rather than condemning deprivation inherent in industrial work, seeks to understand and, if possible, to assist workers in coping with that deprivation — a deprivation portrayed as inevitable and more or less necessary.[45] 'This leaves to sociology the function, which it shares with personnel administration, of assaying not the nature of the work but the degree of adjustment of the worker. Clearly, for industrial sociology the problem does not appear with the degradation of work, but only with the overt signs of dissatisfaction on the part of the worker. From this point of view, the only important matter, the only thing worth studying, is not work itself but the reaction of the worker to it, and in that respect sociology makes sense.'[46]

Perhaps Braverman's dismissal is a little too hasty, a little too easy.[47] For, if there is one issue on which both Marx and Mayo agree, it is the importance of consciousness as mediating the control exercised by the 'objective' factors of the organization of work, particularly technology.[48] Throughout the three volumes of *Capital*, Marx insists that the capitalist mode of production is not just the production of things but simultaneously the production of social relations and of *ideas about those relations*, a lived experience or ideology of those relations. That insight stretches from the discussion of fetishism in the first chapter of Volume 1 to the discussion of the trinity formula in the conclusion of Volume 3.[49] The Western Electric studies offered similar conclusions: namely, the importance of the creation of relations in production (the informal group) and the production of a certain consciousness (cooperation, fear, non-logical codes, etc.) as men and women manufactured things.[50] The point is that capitalist control, even under the most coercive technology, rests on an ideological structure that frames and organizes 'our lived relationship to the world' and thereby constitutes our interests. To be sure, industrial sociology interprets 'responses', 'informal groups' and 'games' in terms of its own concerns — that is, generally in terms of *marginal* changes in output, cooperation or whatever — whereas we will be concerned with relevance to the constant and common features of capitalist control, that is, the obscuring and securing of surplus value.

Since the range of excellent studies is so wide, I will confine myself to the implications of a single mode of adaptation applicable to a large variety of work contexts. Perhaps the most general formulation can be found in William Baldamus's *Efficiency and Effort*. Baldamus argues that industrial labour can be defined in terms of certain 'work realities' that represent inherent forms of deprivation or what he calls effort. Thus, physical conditions give rise to 'impairment', repetitiveness to 'tedium', and coercive routines to 'weariness'. To the extent that these forms of effort are viewed as unavoidable, workers attempt to compensate through the achievement of corresponding 'relative satisfactions'. Impairment — the experience of physical discomfort due to working conditions such as long hours, heat, cold, noise, bad lighting — loses some of its effects over time as a result of 'adaptation', 'acclimatization' or 'inurement'. Tedium — the experience of repetitive or monotonous work — may be partially relieved through rhythm and the feeling of being pulled along by the inertia inherent in the particular activity, which Baldamus calls traction. Weariness or fatigue due to the coerciveness of industrial work finds its compensation in attitudes that express 'being in the mood to work', which Baldamus calls contentment. While inurement corresponds to specific working conditions, contentment corresponds to the coerciveness of work in general. But what is crucial to these compensating mechanisms is that 'they are feelings of temporary relief from the discomfort of certain work realities, feelings which arise when these factors have become part of the worker's customary interpretation of his situation. They are, to this extent, only apparent satisfactions, which are actually derived from deprivation.'[51]

Baldamus's insights about the emergent relations of workers to work can be extended to the creation of relative satisfactions in the social sphere. There are few work contexts, for example, in which labourers do not construct 'games', with respect to technology and to one another. Even on the assembly line workers manage to secure spaces for themselves in which to introduce uncertainty and to exercise a minimal control.[52] These games are modes of adaptation, a source of relief from the irksomeness of capitalist work. In the literature of industrial sociology there is some ambivalence about the significance of games. On one hand they provide a way of absorbing hostility and frustration, diffusing conflict and aggression, and in general facilitating 'adjustment to work'.[53] On the other hand, they tend to undermine managerial objectives, reduce productivity, and waste time. William Foot Whyte expresses the dilemma admirably when he asks: 'Can the satisfaction involved in playing the piecework game be preserved in our factories at the same time that the attendant conflicts are reduced?'[54] Those who are interested in 'output restriction' or 'soldiering' tend to emphasize the negative effects. Crozier ests that games assume the form of power struggles wherever there is uncertainty in the labour process. He implies, therefore, that management should eliminate that uncertainty if work is to be more efficient.[55] In his commentary on the bank wiring-room experiment, George Homans suggests that games are an expression of informal sentiments that spring up in opposition to management.[56] What all these perspectives share is their concern with the *marginal* effects of games, the effects on increasing or decreasing output, on the distribution of power, or on the release of frustration. They take the existence of surplus, the conditions of accumulation, and so on, for granted, and their analyses revolve around quantitative concerns of how much surplus is appropriated.

I wish to take a different approach, in which games will be examined as providing the ideological preconditions for the obscuring and securing of surplus. More specifically, I will suggest that participation in games has the effect of concealing relations of production while coordinating the interests of workers and management. A game is defined by a set of rules, a set of possible outcomes, and a set of outcome preferences.[57] The seductiveness of a game rests on a combination of outcome uncertainty and a semblance of control over the outcomes through a 'rational' or 'calculating' choice among alternative strategies. Naturally the amount of control exercised, and the actual variation in permissible outcomes, are narrowly circumscribed. Yet, and this is what is important, they come to loom very large in everyday life on the shopfloor when everything else appears irrevocable. Indeed, the ideological effect of playing the game is to take 'extraneous' conditions (such as having to come to work) as unchangeable and unchanging, together with a compensatory emphasis on the little choice and uncertainty offered in the work context. That is, the game becomes an ideological mechanism through which necessity is presented as freedom.[58]

Let me explain! The very act of playing a game produces and reproduces consent to the rules and to the desirability of certain outcomes. Thus, one cannot play chess and at the same time question the rules and objectives. Playing the game generates the legitimacy of the conditions that define its rules and objectives.[59] What are those conditions in the context of capitalist work if not the relations of production — having to come to work, the expropriation of unpaid labour, and so on? Workers, moreover, develop a stake in those rules and objectives, as can be seen when management intervenes to change them or somehow infringes on them.

But who establishes the game, its rules and its objectives, in the first place? This is a matter of struggle, to be sure, and when the objectives genuinely threaten production, as sometimes occurs when workers double up on assembly lines, then management steps in and un-ambiguously outlaws the game.[60] For the most part, however, shop management (if not higher levels) becomes actively engaged in organizing and facilitating games on the shopfloor, particularly where they revolve around output. It is through their common interest in the preservation of work games that the interests of workers and shop management are coordinated. The workers are interested in the rela-tive satisfactions games can offer while management, from super-visors to departmental superintendents, is concerned with securing cooperation and surplus.

The point of this digression has been to show how the *day-to-day adaptations*[61] *of workers create their own ideological effects that become focal elements in the operation of capitalist control.* Not only can one not ignore the 'subjective' dimension, but the very distinction between 'objec-tive' and 'subjective' is arbitrary. Any work context involves an economic dimension (production of things), a political dimension (production of social relations), and an ideological dimension (pro-duction of an experience of those relations). These three dimensions are inseparable. Moreover, they are all 'objective' inasmuch as they are independent of the *particular* people who come to work, of the particular agents of production.

These formulations pose an alternative to the problematic that continues to have strong roots in the Marxist tradition and is the cornerstone of Braverman's work. According to the traditional view, class as a historical force — class for itself — can emerge only from a particular intervention of certain 'superstructural' (political and ideo-logical) or 'subjective' factors, situated outside the economic realm, on a pre-existing 'class in itself' defined in 'objective' economic terms. But, as we have seen, there is no such thing as a class in itself defined in 'objective' 'economic' terms. The so-called economic realm is in-separable from its political and ideological effects, and from specifi-cally political and ideological 'structures' of the workplace.[62] There is no 'objective' notice of class prior to its appearance on the stage of history. Acting on the historical stage has to be conceived of as a moment in the constitution of class.[63] Thus, class becomes the com-bined *effect* of a set of economic, political and ideological structures found in all arenas of social activity.[64] Edward Thompson makes the same point:

> Even if 'base' were not a bad metaphor we would have to add that, whatever

it is, it is not just economic but human — a characteristic human relationship entered into involuntarily in the productive process. I am not disputing that this process may be broadly described as economic, and that we may thus agree that the 'economic movement' has proved to be the 'most elemental and decisive'. But my excursion into definition may have more than semantic interest if two points are borne in mind. First, in the actual course of historical or sociological (as well as political) analysis it is of great importance to remember that social and cultural phenomena do not trail after the economic at some remote remove: they are, at their source, immersed in the same nexus of relationship. Second, while one form which opposition to capitalism takes is in direct economic antagonism — resistance to exploitation whether as producer or consumer — another form is, exactly, resistance to capitalism's innate tendency to reduce all human relationships to economic definitions. The two are inter-related, of course; but it is by no means certain which may prove to be, in the end, more revolutionary.[65]

In the following sections I hope to trace the significance of these two responses, to which I have referred as adaptation and struggles for understanding changes in the labour process, particularly those that revolved around Taylorism and the scientific-technical revolution.

Taylorism in Practice

Braverman distinguishes between Taylorism and the 'scientific-technical revolution' in that the former does not involve changes in technology. At points he implies that fundamental alterations in the labour process, the relations in production, were also part of Taylorism.[66] However, Taylor's own examples do not warrant such a conclusion. In the handling of pig iron at Bethlehem, in the machine shop at Midvale, in the inspection of bicycle balls, in Grant's analysis of brick-laying, and in the research on metal cutting, the intervention of scientific management perfected tasks already defined rather than reorganizing the division of labour. Braverman summarizes the principles of scientific management as follows: 'Thus, if the first principle is the gathering and development of knowledge of labour processes, and the second is the concentration of this knowledge as the exclusive province of management — together with its essential converse, the absence of such knowledge among the workers — then the third is the use of this monopoly over knowledge to control each step of the labour process and its mode of execution.'[67] To be sure, Taylor's *description* of his successes, say at Bethlehem and Midvale, follows these principles, but there are good reasons to be sceptical about their accuracy, particularly since Taylor was an interested party.

I have no quarrel with the first principle. There is no doubt that scientific management gathered together knowledge about tasks and decided the 'best way' to perform them. But it is by no means clear that this constituted a monopoly of knowledge of the labour process (after all, Taylor obtained his knowledge about the lathes from being a lathe operator himself), or that the new rulings could be enforced. Missing from the picture are the workers' responses and their ability to resist the specification of tasks.[68] It is one thing for management to appropriate knowledge; it is another thing to monopolize it. Braverman himself says, 'since the workers are not destroyed as human beings but are simply utilized in inhuman ways, their critical, intelligent, conceptual faculties, no matter how deadened or diminished, always remain in some degree a threat to capital'.[69] Rather than a separation of conception and execution, we find a separation of workers' conception and management's conception, of workers' knowledge and management's knowledge. The attempt to enforce Taylorism leads workers to recreate the unity of conception and execution, but in opposition to management rulings. Workers show much ingenuity in defeating and outwitting the agents of scientific management before, during and after the 'appropriation of knowledge'.[70] In any shop there are 'official' or 'management-approved' ways of performing tasks, and there is the workers' lore devised and revised in response to any management offensive. Not only does management fail to appropriate these 'trade secrets' but, as I shall suggest in the next section, it is not necessarily to its advantage to appropriate them. Shop management usually knows this.

Unlike changes in the division of labour and the scientific-technical revolution, Taylorism, defined by the specification of task performance, cannot be identified with the separation of conception and execution. What then is its relationship to capitalist control? It has been resisted by trade unions the world over and has promoted struggles by organizing labour and capital into hostile camps.[71] On a day-to-day basis workers attempt to sabotage Taylorism, while at a broader level unions join in struggles to defend 'output' clauses in rules. Thus, scientific management may have undermined capitalist controls over the obscuring of surplus and of the relations of exploitation between capital and labour. With respect to the securing of surplus there can be no definitive answer.[72] Insofar as Taylorism fostered antagonism between capital and labour, the coordination of interests became less feasible and the reliance on coercive measures more necessary.

As a practical tool of increasing capitalist control, Taylorism was a failure. In a recent historical study of scientific management, Daniel Nelson concludes:

> If the rather modest effect of scientific management on the wage-earners in these factories is surprising, its apparent failure to end the workers' traditional restrictive practices is not. Subsequent studies have documented the persistence of informal production norms and the employees' ability to defy the supervisor and the time study expert. That Taylor, his followers, and their clients believed scientific management would end 'soldiering' was another indication of how little they understood the foreman's functions and the workers' outlook. If the foreman, with his combination of threats and persuasion, could not change the workers' behaviour, what hope was there for an outside expert equipped with only a stopwatch and an incentive plan? Obviously there were limits to the manager's authority just as there were to the foreman's empire.[73]

So what is the significance of Taylorism? One might argue that it lay precisely in its limited capacity to enhance capitalist control over the labour process, thus necessitating the transition to a new type of labour process inaugurated by the scientific-technical revolution. Was Taylorism then the expression of a transition from one labour process, which had developed its greatest potential in a detailed division of labour, to a labour process that incorporated 'capitalist control' within the very form of its technology?

Taylorism as Ideology

Braverman's exclusive concern with the 'objective' features of work blinds him not only to the *import* of Taylorism as a means of capitalist control — the fact that, by sowing the seeds of its own destruction, it necessitates its own supersession — but also to its significance as a purely ideological movement. Indeed, as I suggest below, his failure to distinguish between Taylorism as managerial practice and Taylorism as a mode of legitimation prevents him from understanding a crucial aspect of domination under advanced capitalism, namely the appearance of ideology in the guise of science.

Writing of the United States, Bendix argues that Taylorism was harnessed to the managerial cause in the open-shop movement. At the turn of the twentieth century managerial ideology was still linked to the social philosophy of Spencer and Smiles, whose emphasis on initiative and independence had the unwelcome effect of encouraging the growth of trade unions. Taylorism, on the other hand, with its emphasis on compliance and obedience to management in the pursuit of the common interest, could be mobilized as an *ideological* attack on the nascent trade-union movement. 'But the major point is that American employers did not regard Taylor's methods as an effective answer to the challenge of trade unionism, even when they decided to adopt these methods to solve some of the managerial problems. In their struggle against trade unions employers made use of weapons which differed strikingly from the tests and measurements that were the hallmark of scientific management. Yet the principal ideas in Taylor's work were widely accepted: the social philosophy rather than the techniques of scientific management became a part of prevailing ideology.'[74]

Maier takes Bendix's argument much further in his examination of the receptiveness of different nations to Taylorism or scientific management. He shows how Taylorism was most strongly embraced in those nations faced with a political crisis. During the early post-war years, it became an important plank in the ideology of national syndicalists and fascists in Italy, 'revolutionary conservatives' and 'conservative socialists' in Germany, the new leadership in the Soviet Union, and the Industrial Workers of the World and the Socialist parties in the United States.[75] Disparate though these social movements were, they all shared in the attempt to transcend immediate political institutions by mobilizing scientism in the projection of a utopian image of a harmonious society where 'politics' becomes superfluous. The combination of technology and what Maier refers to as 'irrationalism' offered a cooperative vision of the present or future society in the context of, and as a reaction to, the intensifying class struggle of the period.[76]

But why was Taylorism embraced so enthusiastically during the crises of that particular period? What was peculiar about those crises? What was it about Taylorism that made it acceptable to such a wide audience? The crises of the first three decades of this century were bound up with the transition from competitive to monopoly ('advanced' or 'organized') capitalism.[77] The market became increasingly ineffective as a mechanism for regulating relations among capitalists, between capital and labour, and among different segments of the labour force. At the same time, the state was assuming a larger role in the organization of these relations. The political and economic became increasingly intertwined. The prevailing ideology of 'free and equal' exchange, based as it was on the dominance of the market, could not legitimate the new relations of capitalism.

From where would a new ideology appear to legitimate the state's growing involvement in the organization of the economy? How would the political aspects and implications of state interventions be obscured or made acceptable to the public? Habermas and Marcuse argue that under advanced capitalism political problems are no longer masked by the 'natural' working of the market but are projected as problems of science and technology. Thus the application of science to the labour process not only led to the 'expansion of the forces of production' but simultaneously laid the basis for a new ideology in which the preservation of capitalist relations was presented as a technical matter to be removed from political discourse.[78] The pursuit of 'efficiency' became the basis of a new ideology, a new form of domination. Rationality was turned on its head and became irrationality.[79] Or, as Habermas puts it, rationality from below (science as the pursuit of efficiency) merges with rationality from above (science as ideology) and in this way both obscures capitalist relations of production and legitimates state interventions as non-political because scientific.[80] In failing to distinguish clearly between Taylorism as practice and Taylorism as ideology, Braverman is merely giving expression to appearances. And this, as I have argued, is because his theoretical framework allows him to discount ideology as a factor essential to the study of capitalism. In short, because he ignores ideology he becomes its prisoner.

The Rise of Taylorism

Thus far we have seen how, in assessing the *effects* of Taylorism as practised, Braverman makes all sorts of erroneous assumptions about the ideological dimension of the labour process, while at the same time missing the import of Taylorism as part of a wider ideological shift reflecting a critical transition in the development of capitalism. The problem is not only that Braverman ignores the 'subjective' dimension of work or 'super-structural elements', but that his very conceptual scheme — subjective/objective (base/superstructure) — leads him to a misleading formulation of the problem. Braverman runs into similar problems when writing about the *causes* of change in the labour process, of Taylorism, of the separation of conception and execution, and of the scientific-technical revolution, in that he makes certain assumptions about the consciousness of managers and capitalists and continues to ignore resistance and struggle.[81]

Let us first confine our attention to Taylorism. Here the functionalist logic of Braverman's analysis is particularly clear. 'Modern management came into being on the basis of these principles. It arose as theoretical construct and as systematic practice, moreover, in the very period during which the transformation of labour from processes based on skill to processes based upon science was attaining its most rapid tempo. Its role was to render conscious and systematic, the formerly unconscious tendency of capitalist production. It was to ensure that as craft declined, the worker would sink to the level of general and undifferentiated labour power, adaptable to a large range of simple tasks, while as science grew, it would be concentrated in the hands of management.'[82]

According to Braverman, then, the presumed effect (increased control over the labour process) is also the cause of scientific management. He is therefore forced to assert that Taylor's formulations on control were part and parcel of managerial consciousness: 'What he (Taylor) avows openly are the now-unacknowledged private assumptions of management.'[83] Braverman's focus on outcomes rather than causes parallels his concern with the objective circumstances of labour and their critique rather than with how Taylorism works, whether it works at all, or how people put up with it or change it.

Further, why was it that Taylorism appeared when and where it did? Why did it follow its particular historical trajectory? If 'the dictation to the worker of the precise manner in which work is to be performed' is an 'absolute necessity for adequate management',[84] then why did we have to wait until the end of the nineteenth and the early twentieth century before Taylorism was applied? Not surprisingly, Braverman's explanation focuses on ecological factors, in particular the 'growth of the size of the enterprise'.[85] 'Taylorism cannot become generalized in any industry or applicable in particular situations until the scale of production is adequate to support the efforts and costs involved in "rationalizing" it. It is for this reason above all that Taylorism coincides with the growth of production and its concentration in ever larger corporate units in the latter part of the nineteenth and in the twentieth centuries.'[86] In limiting his attention to such factors, Braverman imports three major and possibly questionable assumptions into his argument. First, the interests of managers and capitalists lay in the implementation of Taylorism. Second, managers and capitalists shared and understood those interests.[87] Third, managers and capitalists had the power to impose these interests on the working class. Let us look at each assumption in turn.

With regard to the first, as I have already suggested, Taylorism as a managerial practice was not always in the interests of capital. Rather, it often promoted resistance and struggle and in so doing undermined the extraction of surplus. Thus, it is difficult to argue that Taylorism's consequences were also its causes. In turning to the second assumption, however, we must pose the question of the intentions of managers and capitalists in their endeavours to introduce scientific management. One might want to examine changes in the conscious-ness of managers and capitalists during the period 1880 – 1920 in an attempt to account for interest in (and also opposition to) Taylorism. Thus, Hobsbawm emphasizes how with the growth of trade unions, operatives were learning the rules of the game — that is, to manipu-late market factors in adjusting effort to reward. This brought about new employment practices that would utilize labour time more effi-ciently.[88] Montgomery argues that it was after immigrants to the United States had accustomed themselves to the discipline of indus-trial work and had learned the rules of the game that scientific management gained widespread appeal among managerial classes, even if it failed to eliminate 'restrictive practices'.[89]

As both Hobsbawm and Montgomery recognize in their tentative explorations, the issues are complex. One must ask, for example, what impact the growth of the corporation, and in particular the institu-tional separation of ownership and control had upon the conscious-ness of managers. Could it not be argued that the specialization of the managerial function led to attempts to introduce scientific manage-ment? Moreover, if management's consciousness can be seen apart from that of capitalists, can it not be argued that managers themselves do not form a monolithic group? Variations might appear not only between different fractions of capital but also within the firm itself. Thus, one might speculate that different levels of management will be preoccupied with different aspects of the labour process. Lower-level management, in daily contact with the worker, might oppose the introduction of Taylorism in an attempt to prevent conflict, while middle levels of management might be responsible for instigating such changes with a view to cheapening the cost of labour power. The highest levels might be concerned only with profits and efficiency and express little interest in how these are realized. They would be more concerned with mobilizing Taylorism as ideology. Equally significant are the diverse concerns of different fractions of management within the single firm, that is, among different departments: engineering, quality control, manufacturing, maintenance, and so on. Any change in the labour process will therefore emerge as the result not only of competition among firms, not only of struggle between capital and labour, but also of struggle among the different agents of capital.

Whatever the answers to these questions, it is clear that one cannot *assume* the existence of a cohesive managerial and capitalist class that automatically recognizes its true interests. Rather, one must examine how that class is organized and how its interests emerge historically through competition and struggle. This brings me to the third assumption: that agents of capital were sufficiently powerful to enforce their interests over those of other classes. Braverman relegates workers' resistance to Taylorism to an essentially derivative role, an impotent expression of their helpless subordination to capital.[90] The fact of the matter is that many unions in the United States were able to resist Taylorism.[91] In other countries resistance was even more effective.[92] What must be explained is the specific balance of power between capital and labour that led to effective resistance here and capitulation there. Was Taylorism an offensive of capital against a weak proletariat, or a defensive measure taken in the face of a strengthening proletariat? Perhaps the significance of large corporations lay not only in their size but also in the power they bestowed upon capital to impose its will on labour. What was the relationship between the emergence of the corporate liberal state and the struggles between capital and labour? Can changes in the balance of power account for shifts in the trade unions' position vis-à-vis Taylorism?[93]

The Scientific-Technical Revolution

Whereas Braverman may express a certain ambiguity about the stimulus to scientific management, his views on the source of the scientific-technical revolution are unequivocal. Like Marx, Braverman argues that competition among capitalists leads to increasing productivity through mechanization.[94] Control becomes a secondary feature in the organization of work, while the pursuit of efficiency becomes its primary feature. Relations in production are fashioned by a concern for the separation of conception and execution only after machinery has been determined by productivity drives. But Braverman presents another view, based on the Babbage principle, according to which control is inseparable from the pursuit of efficiency.[95] 'The design which will enable the operation to be broken down among cheaper operators is the design which is sought by management and engineers who have so internalized this value that it appears to them to have the force of natural law or scientific necessity.'[96]

We shall return to a discussion of the relationship between 'efficiency' and 'control' in section 4. For the moment let us assume that management invests in order to increase the productivity of labour. The question of timing remains. *When* does management introduce new machines? When they are available on the market? When there is pressure of competition? Or as a response to struggle? Indeed, can the concept of efficiency be examined independently of struggle? An interesting contemporary example is the mechanization of field work in agribusiness. Technology has been available or could always have been developed, but so long as growers could draw on a reservoir of cheap labour there was no urgency. With the growth of unionism and the end of the Bracero programme, mechanization has proceeded rapidly in tomato picking and promises to dominate lettuce harvesting.[97] The advance of mechanization must be seen as a response not just to increasing costs of labour but also to labour's increasing power. Hand picking was acceptable so long as an ample labour supply was available, but with the growth of the United Farm Workers the availability of large quantities of gang labour became problematic. The move toward capital-intensive harvesting is therefore an attempt to undercut the union's strength by reducing labour requirements. All of this indicates that the advance of the scientific-technical revolution hinges not only on competition but also on struggle. Braverman cannot justifiably reduce resistance from labour to 'internal friction'.[98] Struggle is not merely derivative but is also determinative of capitalism's development.[99]

Historical Tendencies of the Capitalist Labour Process

Can we extend our discussion of the growth of mechanization to its emergence? What is the relationship between scientific management and mechanization (scientific-technical revolution)? Braverman states categorically: 'Scientific management and the "movement" for the organization of production on its modern basis have their beginnings in the last two decades of the last century. And the scientific-technical revolution, based on the systematic use of science for the more rapid transformation of labour power into capital, also begins . . . at the same time. In describing these two facets of the activity of capital, we have therefore been describing two of the prime aspects of monopoly capital. Both chronologically and functionally, they are part of the new stage of capitalist development, and they grow out of monopoly capitalism and make it possible.'[100]

Of course, such an assertion requires a good deal of documentation.[101] By collapsing Taylorism and the scientific-technical revolution as two aspects of monopoly capitalism, Braverman squeezes all the dynamics out of the transition from competitive to monopoly capitalism. Earlier I suggested an alternative hypothesis. Just as Marx described how class struggle, through the enforcement of the factory acts in England, led to the transition from 'absolute surplus value' (extending the working day to enhance profits) to 'relative surplus value' (increasing productivity to enhance profits), so at a later time class struggle fostered by Taylorism led to the transition from scientific management to the scientific-technical revolution.[102] Moreover, I would suggest that this transition at the level of the labour process may have corresponded to the transition from competitive to monopoly capitalism. According to such an argument Taylorism, rather than being the handmaiden of monopoly capitalism, was its midwife.

However, we might ask whether the systematic development of the separation of conception and execution constitutes the only or even the most appropriate demarcation of competitive from monopoly capitalism, with regard to the process of production. To make an argument of this type requires at least a minimal examination of the labour process under competitive capitalism, that is, in the United States prior to 1880. But Braverman systematically fails to do this. Instead he presents a false comparison of the realities, as he sees them, of twentieth-century capitalism, based on the expropriation of skill, with an idealization of nineteenth-century capitalism, based on the craft worker.[103] It does not require a great deal of historical knowledge to appreciate the extreme forms of deskilling prevalent during the early years of capitalism. A cursory glance through Engels's survey of the various branches of industry in the first half of nineteenth-century Britain makes it clear that few workers had much control over the labour process.[104] In short, it is difficult to link the separation of conception and execution to the periodization of capitalism. An alternative way of characterizing changes in the production process would be to focus on the emergence of particular ideological and political structures at the point of production that serve to obscure and secure surplus by organizing consent on the shop floor, displacing struggles, and thus guaranteeing the reproduction of the relations *in* production.[105]

Finally, we must return to the question we posed earlier concerning the relationship between capitalist control and the separation of conception and execution. I would suggest that capitalist control — the simultaneous obscuring and securing of surplus — sets limits on the form of the separation of conception and execution. Too little separation threatens to make surplus transparent, while too much threatens the securing of surplus. The capitalist labour process — in all its phases — is confined within these historically variable limits. Economic crises, global or local, are inaugurated when those limits are traversed. Thus, job enrichment, job enlargement and job rotation signify the existence of upper limits on the separation of conception and execution. While they may not actually reverse the trend, these marginal adjustments to the labour process may nevertheless act as a buffer to further deskilling. They are a warning light: do not go beyond this point. If only for this reason, the new human relations of corporate management must be taken very seriously and not dismissed as so many 'petty manipulations of personnel departments and industrial psychology and sociology'.[106] We must now turn to the question of how much manipulation is actually possible under capitalism, and of the extent to which such changes are limited by purely technical imperatives on one hand and social imperatives on the other.

4.   Technology: Innocent or Tainted?

Given his leaning toward 'critique', Braverman naturally devotes much space, implicitly if not always explicitly, to the nature of the labour process under socialism. Indeed, in this respect Marxism has been the only major social theory that neither marks capitalism as the end of history nor regards the labour process under capitalism as eternal or inevitable. On this turns the debate between Marx and Weber and, more recently, between Marcuse and Habermas.[107] Is the rationality that Weber spends so much space delineating a capitalist rationality that embodies, albeit in veiled form, a specific form of capitalist domination? Or is it somehow innocent, neutral, and destined to be with us in its essentials for ever more? Do 'technology' and 'efficiency' have a momentum and determinism of their own that carry society with them? Or are they relative to the mode of production in which they appear, and in this sense determined by the corresponding set of relations of production?

Braverman naturally takes a position against crude technological determinism and views the shaping of the labour process as specific to a mode of production. Thus, he argues that the same 'technology' can in fact appear as part of two different labour processes corresponding to two different modes of production — for example, steam power under feudal and capitalist modes of production. Furthermore, each mode of production creates its own technology: 'Thus if steam power "gives us" the industrial capitalist, industrial capitalism "gives us", in turn, electric power, the power of the internal combustion engine, and atomic power.'[108] Just as feudal relations of production give us one type of technology and capitalist relations of production give us another, so presumably socialism will give us a third. However, actually to anticipate its form in a positive rather than negative manner would be like asking a feudal journeyman to anticipate capitalist atomic power. The question, then, is not whether socialist technology is *possible* but whether it is *necessary*. That is, can socialism operate with capitalist machines, or do the machines impose constraints on relations of and in production that make socialism impossible?[109]

The issue is not abstract, as can be seen in current debates on the nature of the Soviet Union. We all know, if only because we have been told so countless times, that Lenin enthusiastically embraced Taylorism and the capitalist machines that went along with it. Braverman writes: 'Whatever view one takes of Soviet industrialization, one cannot conscientiously interpret its history, even in its earliest and most revolutionary period, as an attempt to organize labour processes in a way fundamentally different from those of capitalism — and thus as an attempt that came to grief on the rocks of Clark Kerr's eternal verities. One would be hard put to demonstrate that any of the successive Soviet leaderships has ever claimed that such an attempt should be made at this stage of Soviet history.'[110]

A crucial question emerges: to what extent can we attribute the failure of the socialist experiment in the Soviet Union to the continuity of what is, for all intents and purposes, a capitalist labour process? Lenin's position was to assume that in its advanced form — and in 1917 Taylorism was an advanced form — capitalist technology provides the basis for socialism. He saw his task as grafting socialist relations of production, which he tended to reduce to the political superstructure — 'the dictatorship of the proletariat' — onto capitalist forces of production. In so doing he denied the specifically capitalist character of the labour process: fragmented work, alienation, exploitation, separation of manual and mental activities, the simultaneous obscuring and securing of surplus value. But equally important, he also denied that this capitalist organization of the labour process imposed limits on the form of the corresponding relations of production and therefore on the mode of production as a whole.[111]

Social and Technical Relations in Production

For Braverman the transformation of the relations in production is a sine qua non for establishing socialism, but what is less clear is whether the socialist project also involves a new technology — a socialist technology. The problem can be formulated as follows. Capitalist relations in production are at least partly shaped by capitalist relations of production (obscuring and securing of surplus, or for Braverman the separation of conception and execution). This aspect of the labour process we can call the *social relations in production*. At the same time, the very instruments of production may embody their own imperatives for the organization of the labour process. That is, machines, irrespective of the relations of production under which they are used, may place certain limits on the organization of work, which I will call the *technical relations in production*.[112] There are then two aspects to the question of the necessity of socialist machines. First, do capitalist machines generate technical relations in production? Second, if so, are these relations compatible with socialism? In other words, does the assembly line or the numerically controlled lathe *require* certain forms of hierarchy, alienation and so on, at odds with socialism? If capitalist machines do impose such limitations, then the inauguration of socialism also requires socialist machines.

Braverman generally argues that there are no technical relations in production and that capitalist machines can be used under socialism. 'Machinery comes into the world not as the servant of "humanity", but as the instrument of those to whom the accumulation of capital gives the ownership of the machines. The capacity of humans to control the labour process through machinery is seized upon by management from the beginning of capitalism as the prime means whereby production may be controlled not by the direct producer but by the owners and representatives of capital. Thus, in addition to its technical function of increasing the productivity of labour — which would be a mark of machinery under any social system — machinery also has in the capitalist system the function of divesting the mass of workers of their control over their own labour.'[113]

Even more clearly: '(I)n the factory it is not the machines that are at fault but the conditions of the capitalist mode of production'; 'it is not the productive strength of machinery that weakens the human race, but the manner in which it is employed in capitalist social relations.'[114] However, at other points Braverman is more hesitant about the neutrality of machines: 'These necessities are called "technical needs", "machine characteristics", "the requirements of efficiency", but *by and large* they are the exigencies of capital and not of technique' (italics mine).[115] Moreover, some capitalist machines would indeed be inconceivable under socialism because of the technical constraints they impose. One such example is the assembly line, which Braverman considers a 'barbarous relic'. Significantly, he writes, 'from a technological point of view it is extraordinarily primitive and has little to do with "modern machine technology".'[116] The upshot is that for

Braverman 'advanced' capitalist technology gives rise to only insignificant technical relations in production, and capitalist machines therefore do not present an obstacle to the implementation of socialism.[117]

Socialist Machines and Capitalist Efficiency

But one can only argue that the technical relations in production are insignificant by reference to some explicit notion of socialism. For Braverman 'socialist socialization' of the workplace seems to mean the reunification of conception and execution.[118] 'In reality, machinery embraces a host of possibilities, many of which are systematically thwarted, rather than developed, by capital. An automatic system of machinery opens up the possibility of the true control over a highly productive factory by a relatively small corps of workers, providing these workers attain the level of mastery over the machinery offered by engineering knowledge, and providing they then share out among themselves the routines of the operation, from the most technically advanced to the most routine. This tendency to socialize labour, and to make of it an engineering enterprise on a high level of technical accomplishment, is, considered abstractly, a far more striking characteristic of machinery in its fully developed state than any other. Yet this promise, which has been repeatedly held out with every technical advance since the Industrial Revolution, is frustrated by the capitalist effort to reconstitute and even deepen the division of labour in all of its worst aspects, despite the fact that this division of labour becomes more archaic with every passing day.'[119]

Few would disagree that the reunification of conception and execution is a *necessary* condition for the advent of socialism or communism, and to be sure, given Braverman's analysis of how the occupational structure rests on this principle, its elimination would involve a major transformation of society. Nevertheless for many, in particular the leading members of the Frankfurt School, the impediments to socialism cannot be reduced to the separation of conception and execution but enter into the very constitution of capitalist technology.[120] No matter how advanced, machines built for capitalist efficiency may be incompatible with socialism. There is an argument in *Labour and Monopoly Capital* that could be mobilized against the innocence of capitalist machines, and it rests on the Babbage principle. The expropriation of skill does not merely enhance the control of the capitalist but also cheapens the labour power he employs: 'In a society based upon the purchase and sale of labour power, dividing the craft cheapens its individual parts', and 'therefore, both in order to ensure management control and to cheapen the worker, conception and execution must be rendered separate spheres of work.'[121] In other words, the type of machine that is designed to increase efficiency under capitalism is the very machine that enhances control; efficiency becomes domination.[122]

While this position may be found in Braverman, he more usually argues that efficiency and domination are distinct aspects of the labour process, and capitalist machines are uncorrupted by the needs of capitalist control. 'While the forms of utilization of machinery — the manner in which labour is organized and deployed around it — are dictated by the tendencies of the capitalist mode of production, the drive to mechanize is itself dictated by the effort to increase the productivity of labour.'[123] Machines themselves are innocent; they are instruments of increasing the productivity of labour, of incorporating 'ever smaller quantities of labour time into ever greater quantities of product';[124] increasing the productivity of labour under capitalism is therefore the same as increasing its productivity under socialism.[125]

This brings us back to the problem we discussed earlier, the nature of capitalist control. Capitalism can and did survive under conditions of the unification of conception and execution. Their separation is not at the core of the capitalist labour process per se but is something that emerges and disappears in an uneven fashion as capitalism develops. The craft worker was, and indeed in some places still is, a part of capitalism. Thus, to identify the reunification of conception and execution with socialism is to confuse job control with workers' control,[126] relations in production with relations of production. It risks not going far enough and, in the process, mistaking a nostalgia for the past for a nostalgia for the future.

5. Totalities: Expressive or Structured?

In section 2, we saw how Braverman mistakes appearances for essence in the projection of the separation of conception and execution as the definitive feature of the capitalist labour process; in section 3, how he sets the separation of conception and execution in motion, marching it through the history of capitalism and casting resistance to the winds; and in section 4 how, pushed to its furthest limits, the separation of conception and execution must eventually bring forth its own negation and, like Odysseus, return home to the restoration of the craft worker as the principle of socialism. Braverman's capitalist totality, then, is constructed out of the penetration of the entire social structure by the commodification of social life and with it the degradation of work as manifested through the separation of conception and execution. Like a cancerous growth commodification and degradation appear with a momentum of their own, as they are expelled from the centre of the capitalist economy into its furthest corners. They cannot rest until they have subordinated the entire fabric of social life to themselves. A concern with specific causes, bringing them about here rather than there, now rather than later, is irrelevant in the broad sweep of history. Since commodification and degradation are the defining principle of capitalist society, its essence, its true self, an irresistible force, so cause and effect are indeed one.

The Destruction of the Bourgeois Individual

What Braverman describes with seductive clarity and imagination is an expressive totality in which each part becomes the expression of a single dominant principle, of the whole. 'It is not the primacy of economic motives in historical explanation that constitutes the decisive difference between Marxism and bourgeois thought, but the point of view of the totality, the all-pervasive supremacy of the whole over the parts that is the essence of the method Marx took over from Hegel.'[127]

Parallels with Weber's conception of rationalization as the emergent and pervasive essence of capitalism are instructive. Although Weber makes rationalization a principle of all future societies, while Braverman and Lukács confine their expressive totalities to capitalism, all three fail to spell out the mechanism that drives society forward. It is presumed by Weber that industrialism seeks ever greater heights of efficiency, that this efficiency embodies its own irreversible momentum, and that rationalization is its inevitable and only mode of realization. There is little concern to examine for whom, by whom, and how it will be carried out, the struggles it may engender, or the different forms it may take.

But Weber is also sensitive to the other side of rationality: domination. 'This (modern economic) order is now bound to the technical and economic conditions of machine production which today determine the lives of all the individuals who are born into this mechanism, not only those directly concerned with economic acquisition, with irresistible force. Perhaps it will so determine them until the last ton of fossilized coal is burnt. In Baxter's view the care for external goods should only lie on the shoulders of the "saint like a light cloak, which can be thrown aside at any moment." But fate decreed that the cloak should become an iron cage.'[128]

Weber's individuals are Braverman's workers, who 'work every day to build for themselves more "modern", more "scientific", more dehumanized prisons of labour.'[129] The craft worker is destroyed, converted into a disembodied appendage of capital. The same theme dominates critical theory: 'The original fruitfulness of the bourgeois organization of the life process is thus transformed into a paralyzing barrenness, and men by their own toil keep in existence a reality which enslaves them in ever greater degree.'[130] This convergence is no coincidence. Braverman as the dispossessed craft worker, Weber as the disenchanted liberal, and Horkheimer as the isolated and despairing Marxist intellectual, each mourns the eclipse of the bourgeois individual, if in different incarnations.[131] In the name of the future, they ressurrect a mythical past as the basis for refusing the iron cage, the prisons of labour, and the paralyzing barrenness, for resisting the capitalist totality — totalitarianism in its various guises. But of the three, Braverman offers the richest concretization of the expressive totality, and it is to this that we now turn.

Braverman's Totality

Like its forerunners, Braverman's analysis is no crude historicism: it is both subtle and compelling. Far from suggesting a smooth linear tendency, Braverman demonstrates how the degradation of work continuously creates its own countertendencies — barriers it casts aside as surely as it sets them up. Thus capitalism, as it expands and subordinates ever greater regions of social life, creates new skills and with them new craft workers embodying the unity of conception and execution. But with equal consistency, capitalism proceeds to fragment the craft, doling it out again in minute and deskilled tasks.[132]

Braverman develops his 'expressive totality' in its purest form when describing the penetration of capital into the family and community. Here he is at his most explicit in adopting the metaphors of critical theory: the disintegration, destruction, atomization, irrationality of everyday life outside the factory and office; the eclipse of neighbourly feelings and affective ties. The family must 'strip for action in order to survive and succeed in the market society.'[133] 'It is only in its era of monopoly that the capitalist mode of production takes over the totality of individual, family and social needs and, in subordinating them to the market, also reshapes them to serve the needs of capital. It is impossible to understand the new occupational structure — and hence the modern working class — without understanding this development. How capitalism transformed all of society into a gigantic marketplace is a process that has been little investigated, although it is one of the keys to all recent social history.'[134]

Rosalyn Baxendall, Elizabeth Ewen and Linda Gordon extend the notion of separation of conception and execution to domestic life.[135] At the same time, the functions hitherto carried out in the family are appropriated by capital in the formation of new industries such as cleaning, health, personal, food and protective services. 'The conquest of the labour processes formerly carried on by farm families, or in homes of every variety, naturally gave fresh energy to capital by increasing the scope of its operations and the size of the "labour force" subjected to its exploitation.'[136] The story is repeated — capital destroys old occupations, creates new ones, and then subjects these to the separation of conception and execution.

From where do people emerge to fill these new occupations? Here Braverman makes imaginative use of Marx's 'general law of accumulation'.[137] Accumulation involves not only the expansion of surplus value and the conquest by capital of new branches of production, but also the creation of a relative surplus population. The penetration of capital into domestic and agricultural work sets free a hitherto untapped reservoir of labour power, which enters the working class in large numbers. In addition, labour is pushed out of highly mechanized industries and piles up in the less developed, less mechanized service and retail sectors. The movement and creation of living labour obey the marching orders of dead labour. 'But since, in its [the working class's] permanent existence, it is the living part of capital, its occupational structure, modes of work and distribution through the industries of society are determined by the ongoing processes of the accumulation of capital. It is seized, released, flung into various parts of the social machinery and expelled by others, not in accord with its own will or self-activity, but in accord with the movement of capital.'[138]

Here then, in summary form, we have Braverman's expressive totality. The capitalist mode of production in its aspect of relations of production (the appropriation and distribution of surplus value) propels capital into family and community life, releasing labour power and creating new industries. In its aspect of forces of production (relations in production, mechanization, labour process) the capitalist mode of production propels labour power from one sector to another and simultaneously spreads the degradation of work through the separation of conception and execution. The rise and fall of new industries and occupations is not uniform through time or space, but follows a law of combined and uneven development.

Its uneven development notwithstanding, Braverman appears to assume that the labour process of monopoly capital will eventually conquer the entire economy. Competitive capital with its own distinctive labour process inevitably succumbs to monopoly capital. In practice, however, monopoly capital continually recreates competitive capital as a condition for its own expansion. Thus, market uncertainties that cannot be controlled through increases in size are contracted out or otherwise externalized and made the basis of competitive capital, as, for example, is true for the garment industry. Inasmuch as this picture of competitive and monopoly capital reproducing each other is empirically well founded, it is misleading to equate, as Braverman tends to do, the period in which monopoly capital is dominant — that is, monopoly *capitalism* — with monopoly *capital*.

Mistaking the part for the whole is, of course, a consequence of the adoption of an expressive totality. In this light it would be of interest to examine the changes in the labour process of some competitive industry during the period of monopoly capitalism. In what ways have these changes been shaped by functional relations of interdependence among capitals mediated through the market, and in what ways by new forms of capitalist control pioneered in the monopoly sector and adopted in response to struggles or in the pursuit of efficiency? While the labour processes in both competitive and monopoly sectors of the economy have been changing over the last century, are they tending to diverge or converge in the forms they assume? What is the direction of development in the state sector? Again such studies would have to consider the political and ideological institutions that have grown up around the labour process.

It becomes clear from the above that Braverman has exposed for us only one aspect of capitalist society, namely, how the economic increasingly dominates the social structure, the totality. But what is this totality? In what does it consist? What determines it? Because he takes for granted the existence of the totality, Braverman leaves us in the dark on these issues. And possibly for a good reason. For to pose these questions would carry him into a very different type of analysis, one that would aim to discover the preconditions of domination: how it all works; how in fact labour power, capital, and needs for new commodities coincide spatially and temporally; how under advanced capitalism it just so happens that the commodities produced are also consumed, and so on. In the endeavour to see how capitalism actually works, how it is at all possible, it is necessary to cast off the simple functionalist logic that underlies much of *Labour and Monopoly Capital*, and historicist analysis in general — that is, we must unlock the identification of cause and consequence, of intention and effect, of purpose and outcome.[139]

The peculiarity of the capitalist mode of production, from a Marxist point of view, is that the economic realm *both dominates the parts of the social structure and determines the form of existence of, and the relations among, those parts*. Whereas in general the economic determines that aspect of the social structure that is dominant, only under capitalism does the economic determine that it itself is dominant. As Marx wrote: 'The mode of production determines the character of (read 'dominates') the social, political, and intellectual life generally; all this is very true for our own times, in which material interests preponderate, but not for the middle ages, in which Catholicism, nor for Athens and Rome, where politics reigned supreme. . . . This much, however, is clear, that the middle ages could not live on Catholicism, nor the ancient world on politics. On the contrary, it is the mode in which they gained a livelihood that explains why here politics, and there Catholicism, played the chief part.'[140]

Thus, by confining his attention to the dominance of the economic, Braverman succumbs to appearances and ignores the conditions that determine that dominance and make it possible.

The Structured Totality

I will now develop an alternative notion of totality. We will begin with a notion of history conceived of, at the most general level, as a succession of modes of production. How is it that any one mode of production can survive over time without collapsing or being superseded by a different mode? In other words, what are the conditions of reproduction of a given mode of production, or what are the conditions of reproduction of the combination 'relations of and in production' that define a mode of production?

In section 2, I established that feudal relations of production can be reproduced only through the intervention of an extra-economic element. This extra-economic element — say, religion — then becomes dominant because it is necessary for the reproduction of the feudal mode of production. By contrast, under the capitalist mode of production, since the relations of and in production reproduce themselves of themselves (in principle), political, legal and ideological intervention is limited and the economic itself becomes dominant.[141] Moreover, because the political, legal and ideological instances are not implicated in the mode of production itself, we can talk about the political, legal and ideological as separate spheres of activity. We can even talk about their relative autonomy. The legal structure, for example, has a coherence and dynamic of its own, and its precepts cannot be arbitrarily changed by external forces. Moreover, it performs a 'legitimating' function by masking the relations of production, in particular by *creating* distinctions between people and things, by blurring the distinctions between different types of things (things consumed productively — machines — and things consumed unproductively — shirts) and different types of people (those who must sell their labour power and those who own the means of production), and by reconstituting agents of production as 'free and equal' citizens.[142] Similar arguments can be made concerning the political and ideological realms.

Suffice it to say that by attempting to construct a social structure out of the reproduction requirements of the capitalist mode of production, one arrives at a totality composed of different parts, each with its own structure that both expresses and conceals economic relations, each moving with its own dynamics of 'history' in relative independence of the economic. Brief though this digression has been it nonetheless lays the basis for a very different type of totality — a structured rather than an expressive totality. As I shall suggest below, both notions of totality are necessary, but the structured totality must be regarded as prior to the expressive totality.[143]

First let me concretize the issues with a few examples that highlight the differences between the two types of totality. What I said above is true only at a very general level. In practice, even though the political, legal and ideological instances are not implicated within the capitalist mode of production, they are nonetheless necessary for the reproduction of the relations of production. Thus, James O'Connor discusses the market-supplementing functions of the state, how it organizes relations among capitalists by the provision of social investment (infrastructure that individual capitalists cannot afford, such as highways and research) and social consumption (items that reduce the costs of reproducing labour power — that is, wages — through state education, subsidized housing, and so forth).[144] The state functions to provide conditions not only of accumulation but also of legitimation. The latter involve social expenses such as welfare and social security. O'Connor also shows how it is both *necessary* and problematic to combine the functions of legitimation and accumulation. But Braverman does not find much that is problematic about the survival of capitalism, and not surprisingly devotes only six pages to 'the role of the state'.[145]

However, a serious examination of the capitalist state would reveal the problematic nature of what Braverman regards as unproblematic, and show that contradictions frequently become crystallized in the state. Thus, Claus Offe and Volker Ronge see a major crisis tendency for advanced capitalism in the *inability* of surplus capital to meet up with surplus labour power.[146] Only by state intervention, through what they call administrative recommodification, can idle capital be joined to unemployed labour. Thus, too, Habermas locates the distinctive features of advanced capitalism as the breakdown of the market and the 'legitimation' crises this calls forth.[147] With the declining significance of the market, the distribution of commodities, rather than appearing natural and inevitable, becomes the object of political struggle. The state must seek new ways to justify the existing patterns of distribution, and we discover the emergence of price and income policies. For Ernest Mandel, as for Marx in *Capital* Volume 2, the problem is to *match* the production of exchange value and the production of use value.[148] How is it that under advanced capitalism, operating on the logic of exchange value, capitalists produce use values in accordance with society's capacity to consume? Again the state is invoked to ensure that correspondence. Braverman explicitly assumes the correspondence to be unproblematic.

André Gorz points to the tensions between the expansion and content of education on one hand and the very processes of deskilling to which Braverman refers on the other. Poulantzas and Gramsci are concerned with a different problem, but the logic is the same. Given the history of class struggles in Western and Mediterranean Europe, how is it that capitalism has consistently managed to absorb or repel those struggles? Both writers, in their different ways, attempt to understand how class struggles are organized within the confines of capitalism, how the state relates to different classes, and how different classes are organized in the political arena.[149] Braverman, on the other hand, takes for granted the capacity of capitalism to survive class struggles, and dismisses these as ineffectual outbursts signifying capitalism's inhumanity.

For Braverman, then, the expressive totality designates the subordination of society to capital, so that everything appears functional to capital. There are no dysfunctional elements, tensions or crises, only a widening gap between what *is* and what is possible.[150] It is true that the contrary analyses cited above have a mechanical air: a 'contradiction' is discovered, a crisis tendency unveiled, and the state is called in, like the plumber, to seal the functional gap. Yet even they are a major advance on the functional automatism of the expressive totality, which asserts the identity of cause and outcome. Poulantzas,

Habermas, Offe and O'Connor all uncouple cause and outcome by suggesting that certain outcomes are problematic, that they are by no means natural and inevitable under capitalism, and that they can be ensured only by the activation of certain mechanisms located in the state.

Future research could attempt to develop this essentially functionalist paradigm in four ways. First, a more careful analysis is required of actual tendencies of the capitalist mode of production — the contradictions and crises it promotes. We already have a choice — for example, the falling rate of profit, the absorption of surplus, the matching of exchange and use values. Second, the mechanisms have to be identified which stabilize, contain, control, absorb or cushion the proposed crisis tendencies or contradictions. Third, it has to be shown under what conditions those mechanisms will be activated to counteract the developing crises or contradictions — a problem that intimately involves struggle and the way it is shaped by politics and ideology. Fourth, we have to elucidate the circumstances under which these mechanisms in fact have the capacity to offset crises or contradictions. Obviously this is no easy agenda! But it is a sine qua non if we are to understand the potential for change, for bridging the chasm between what is and what could be.

Now, it may be objected that Braverman only rewrote the first volume of *Capital*, not all three. Yet one cannot avoid drawing political implications from Braverman's exclusive concern with an expressive totality. For this leaves out, as I have repeatedly stated, a consideration of the conditions of existence of that domination, and therefore the *possibility* that the domination may be precarious.[151] Ironically (or paradoxically) we note here the *convergence* of critical and 'traditional' theory. Critical theory, inasmuch as it embraces an expressive totality, offers only a partial view of the world and, for the very reasons Lukács and Horkheimer elaborate in connection with traditional theory or bourgeois science, cannot but conclude that the world of capitalism is essentially durable. Both types of theory ignore the presuppositions of that world, the linkages of the structured totality.[152]

But critical theory distinguishes itself from traditional theory, in this connection at least, in that the one applauds what the other condemns. Critique therefore involves the assertion that the domination of capital systematically creates the potential for an alternative society only to the extent that it equally systematically prevents its realization. However, this formulation, and all the pessimism, fatalism and despair that go along with it, are embedded in the very partiality of the standpoint it adopts. It is a matter of taking the standpoint not just of the totality, but of two totalities, of domination *and* the conditions of domination, of essence *and* determination — in short, of the *expressive totality and the structured totality*.

Let Gramsci have the last words on the importance of penetrating the *appearances* of inevitability and durability to reach their *conditions*: 'One may say that no real movement becomes aware of its global character all at once, but only gradually through experience — in other words, when it learns from the facts that nothing which exists is natural (in the non-habitual sense of the word), but rather exists because of the existence of certain conditions, whose disappearance cannot remain without consequences. Thus, the movement perfects itself, loses its arbitrary, "symbiotic" traits, becomes truly independent, in the sense that in order to produce certain results it creates the necessary preconditions, and indeed devotes all its forces to the creation of these preconditions.'[153]

Thus the strength, the plausibility of *Labour and Monopoly Capital* is an eloquent testimony to the power of ideology: in normal times it is more convincing to negate appearances than to explain them. Clearly these are not separate tasks.

6. The Specificity of the United States

In pointing to the shortcomings of Braverman's analysis, I have also proposed an alternative approach. In section 2, it was suggested that the simultaneous obscuring and securing of surplus, rather than the separation of conception and execution, constitutes the essence of the capitalist labour process. In section 3 it was proposed that the object–subject framework was inappropriate for the examination of capitalist control. In its stead I presented a framework that distinguishes three realms of the process of production.[154] I indicated how in combination these realms define the transformation of labour power into labour — the labour process — and how this shapes the form of struggles that in turn reshape (within limits) the nature of the labour process. In section 4, I suggested that Braverman's critique of capitalism, based on the ideal of craft autonomy, leads to a narrow vision of socialism. The transformation of relations in production and the transition to socialism, I argued, cannot be conceived outside the transformation of relations of production. In section 5, I suggested that Braverman's expressive totality fails to establish what that totality actually is or how it hangs together, and therefore succumbs to the illusion of appearances, of durability. As an alternative, I argued that it is first necessary to construct the totality by examining the conditions of existence of one part — the mode of production — and that only then can one examine the domination of the whole over the parts. That is, first one examines how the part determines the totality; then and only then can one study how the part dominates the totality.

But it is not enough to present an alternative. If a theory is to go beyond Braverman, it must explain Braverman. Following Marx's treatment of classical political economy, this involves two stages. First, the theory must be able to identify the limitations of *Labour and Monopoly Capital* as the product of a particular set of social and historical conditions — of a particular time and place. Second, it must be able to explain these conditions themselves.

Americanism and Fordism

The partiality of Braverman's study — that is, its concern with the destruction of the craft worker and the domination of capital as it is expressed throughout society — reflects the distinctiveness of capitalism in the United States. In 'Americanism and Fordism' Gramsci prefigures and places in a broader context the significance of work such as Braverman's.

> The American phenomenon . . . is . . . the biggest collective effort to date to create, with unprecedented speed, and with a consciousness of purpose unmatched in history, a new type of worker and of man. The expression 'consciousness of purpose' might appear humorous to say the least to anyone who recalls Taylor's phrase about the 'trained gorilla'. Taylor is in fact expressing with brutal cynicism the purpose of American society — developing in the worker to the highest degree automatic and mechanical attitudes, breaking up the old psycho-physical nexus of qualified professional work, which demands a certain active participation of intelligence, fantasy and initiative on the part of the worker, and reducing productive operations exclusively to the mechanical, physical aspects. But these things, in reality, are not original or novel; they represent simply the most recent phase of a long process which began with industrialism itself. This phase is more intense than preceding phases, and manifests itself in more brutal forms, but it is a phase which will itself be superseded by the creation of a psycho-physical nexus of a new type, both different from its predecessors and undoubtedly superior. A forced selection will ineluctably take place; a part of the old working class will be pitilessly eliminated from the world of labour, and perhaps from the world *tout court*. [155]

Here we have Braverman's thesis in a nutshell: the separation of conception and execution, the destruction of the craft worker, the effects of Taylorism and mechanization, the habituation of the worker — in short, the untrammelled domination of labour by capital.

There are other passages where Gramsci talks about the invasion of Taylorism into family and sexual life as well as community life — for example, with prohibition. In short, he discusses the reproduction of a new form of labour power. But Gramsci identifies this as a purely American phenomenon, and is ambivalent about its entering Europe. 'America does not have "great historical and cultural traditions"; but neither does it have this leaden burden to support. This is one of the main reasons (and certainly more important than its so-called natural wealth) for its formidable accumulation of capital which has taken place in spite of the superior living standard enjoyed by the popular classes compared with Europe. The non-existence of viscous parasitic sedimentations left behind by past phases of history has allowed industry, and commerce in particular, to develop on a sound basis.'[156]

So Gramsci is already laying out what is specific to the social formation of the United States — namely, the relative absence of precapitalist modes of production. But how is this linked to the domination by capital of labour and of society in general? 'Since these preliminary conditions existed, already rendered rational by historical evolution, it was relatively easy to rationalize production and labour by a skilful combination of force (destruction of working-class trade unionism on a territorial basis) and persuasion (high wages, various social benefits, extremely subtle ideological and political propaganda) and thus succeed in making the whole life of the nation revolve around production. Hegemony here is born in the factory and requires for its exercise only a minute quantity of professional political and ideological intermediaries. The phenomenon of the "masses" which so struck Romier is nothing but the form taken by this "rationalized" society in which the "structure" dominates the superstructures more immediately and in which the latter are also "rationalized" (simplified and reduced in number).'[157]

But how is hegemony born in the factory? How does the economic dominate the other realms of the social structure? What is the nature of the class domination that allows Braverman to de-emphasize struggle or resistance to Taylorism and mechanization while elevating the power of capital?

The Labour Process and International Capitalism

A number of well-known theories draw attention to the geographical specificity of what Braverman projects as the attributes of capitalism in general. There are the theories of corporate liberalism that dwell on the relationship of the dominant classes to the state. In the United States, it is argued, an enlightened 'hegemonic' fraction has emerged from the dominant classes to direct the operation of the state for the development of monopoly capital by presenting its interests as the interests of all. Then there are the theories of the open frontier and immigrant populations that explain the 'unmaking' of the American working class and its weakness in the face of capitalism's expansion.

While both types of theory obviously illuminate much about the specificity of the United States, I want to sketch an alternative account that might be of more immediate applicability to the understanding of the capitalist labour process in different places at different times. Briefly, my hypothesis is that the period in which capitalism begins to consolidate itself in a given social formation determines the relative timing of struggle, in particular of unionization and mechanization. This temporal sequence in turn governs the development of the labour process. I will illustrate the argument with the examples of Japan, the United States and Britain.[158]

Ronald Dore, in his study of similar corporations in Britain and Japan, has drawn out basic differences in the organization of production. To summarize his conclusions, we may say that whereas at English Electric workers were individualistic and class-conscious, at Hitachi they saw their own interests as coinciding to a greater extent with those of the enterprise. British workers also exercised greater control over the labour process than Japanese workers. Dore attributes many of the differences to Japan's late development. Here I want to isolate two elements of his theory as of particular importance in determining the rise of the enterprise: the effect of late development on class struggle and technology, and the temporal relationship between these. In Britain a powerful working class was forged in struggles against the excesses of the industrial revolution, and to some extent against capitalism itself, as well as in the struggles for political rights. These struggles laid the basis of a strong trade-union movement prior to the transition from competitive to monopoly capitalism — that is, prior to the rise of the large corporation and the scientific-technical revolution. From the rise of trade unionism to this day, British workers, through militant shopfloor organizations, have distinguished themselves in resisting, though by no means successfully, the expropriation of control over the labour process.

In Japan capitalism took root much later, with advanced techno-logy that had already been developed in other countries and when political and economic rights were understood as part and parcel of capitalism. Although there was considerable class struggle in Japan over the development of unionization, unions were effective organi-zations only after the emergence of and within large corporations. In other words, they consolidated themselves after the expropriation of skills. The labour process developed more through institutionalized patterns of collective bargaining than through militant shopfloor struggles. The political apparatuses of production, controlled from above rather than below, coordinated the interests of labour and capital. Moreover, given the capital intensiveness of the labour pro-cess, labour costs were relatively low and concessions were cor-respondingly easier to make without jeopardizing profits.

The United States appears on a continuum between Japan and Britain, owing to the consolidation of capitalism at an intermediary stage in the history of international capitalism. Because political rights rarely became the subject of militant protest, economic struggles, although violent and intense, did not produce a strong working class, as in England.

The timing of unionization shapes the development of the labour process not only in the monopoly sector but also in the competitive sector. Braverman depicts the penetration of capital throughout the economy, but has little to say about the specific sectoral forms of the labour process beyond noting that they are subject to the same expro-priation of skill. Where unionization is consolidated after the transi-tion from competitive to monopoly capitalism, it generally takes root most firmly in the monopoly sector, as in Japan and the United States. Concessions made to labour in that sector can be pushed onto the consumer — and onto the weaker competitive capitalists, who in turn seek to protect their profit margins by squeezing their workers. Rising wages, unionization and security of employment in one sector create their opposites in other sectors. The characteristic dualism of the United States and Japan can be attributed to the absence of a strong industrial unionism prior to the emergence of large corporations.

By contrast, in Britain and other European countries the dualism is less pronounced because of the strength of industrial unionism prior to the transition to monopoly capitalism. The competitive sector, because of effective resistance from unions, was less able to absorb costs externalized by the monopoly sector.[159]

In these extremely speculative remarks I am only trying to suggest, first, that there *are* variations in the labour process and particularly its political regime both within a given capitalist society and between capitalist societies; and, second, that these variations may be understood in terms of the historical constellation of struggles and competition as shaped by insertion into world capitalism. In reducing the first to lags in the development of the separation of conception and execution, Braverman misses the significance of the second. That is, by presenting capitalism as a monolith, Braverman denies the importance of variation and preempts the study of those forces which maintain or undermine existing forms of work organization. In concealing the preconditions of capital's dominance, Braverman's analysis expresses the United States experience. But where the power of capital is that much greater and the pockets of resistance are that much weaker, it becomes even more important to penetrate the ideology of domination to its presuppositions, if we are to avoid submission to appearances. It is not enough, as though in despair, to point to the widening gap between what is and what could be; we must also gain a sense of how that gap may be bridged. And this may be achieved in part through directly political practice, and in part through a broadening of our studies to encompass the conditions and limits of variation. This is what Gramsci sees in Machiavelli.

> Guicciardini represents a step backwards in political science with respect to Machiavelli. This is all that Guicciardini's greater 'pessimism' means. Guicciardini regressed to a purely Italian political thought, whereas Machiavelli had attained a European thought. It is impossible to understand Machiavelli without taking into account the fact that he subsumed Italian experience into European (in his day synonymous with international) experience: his 'will' would have been utopian, were it not for the European experience.[160]

But when all is said and done, and Machiavelli and Gramsci notwithstanding, does Braverman emerge unscathed? To be sure, he promotes pessimism, but perhaps not fatalism. To be sure, he does not bridge reality and potentiality, yet he does excite a refusal to be implicated. His is a tragic vision that represses what is possible rather than an ideological vision that represses what is impossible. There are no false promises. Braverman does not present a new revolutionary gospel, a new revolutionary strategy, a new revolutionary crisis, a new revolutionary contradiction, or even a new revolutionary subject. Capitalism is not an assemblage of interconnected parts in which the death of one implies the death of all. It is a totality, in which each part is implicated in every other. Rejection cannot be partial or strategic, but, like capitalism itself, must be total.

Notes

1. Harry Braverman, *Labour and Monopoly Capital: The Degradation of Work in the Twentieth Century*, New York 1974, p. 9.

2. Cambridge, Massachusetts 1971.

3. For a review of *Labour and Monopoly Capital* that picks up on the same tension but draws very different conclusions, see Russell Jacoby, 'Harry Braverman, *Labour and Monopoly Capital*', *Telos*, no. 29, Fall 1976, pp. 199-208.

4. Braverman, pp. 60, 120, 172.

5. Cited in David Montgomery, 'Workers' Control of Machine Production in the Nineteenth Century', *Labour History*, no. 17, Fall 1976, p. 485.

6. Braverman, p. 126.

7. Ibid., pp. 45-49, 113.

8. Ibid., pp. 229-33.

9. Ibid., p. 27.

10. Critical theorists such as Adorno, Horkheimer and Marcuse as well as Reich have tried to rescue the object–subject framework by using psychoanalysis to explain the destruction of subjectivity and the eclipse of the individual under capitalism. This 'negative psychoanalysis', as Jacoby calls it, is therefore a theory of the 'subjectless subject'. It is this psychological rather than philosophical dimension of subjectivity that is missing from the 'class in itself versus class for itself' problematic of both Lukács and Korsch. See Russell Jacoby, 'Negative Psychoanalysis and Marxism', *Telos*, no. 14, Winter 1972, pp. 1-22. However, the addition of such a psychological dimension to *Labour and Monopoly Capital* would not affect its argument or conclusions but merely reinforce them at another level of analysis.

11. Braverman, pp. 233, xiii (foreword by Paul Sweezy).

12. Ibid., pp. 27, 150.

13. The problem can be traced back to Durkheim and Weber. For Durkheim social control was activated more or less in response to pathologies and coordination. At the basis of social control was an *assumption* of consensus. We see the heritage in Parsons and the human relations school of industrial sociology. For Weber social control was ubiquitous — a mode of domination. But it is not clear why that domination is necessary. The typologies he constructs possess a transhistorical character even if they prevail in different historical periods. Their elaboration in organization theory has been more systematically carried out by Amitai Etzioni, in *A Comparative Analysis of Complex Organizations*, New York 1961.

14. Braverman, pp. 57-58.

15. Ibid., pp. 30, 57, 68, 86, 120, 125, 267, and passim.

16. Ibid., p. 57.

17. Marx makes the same argument in a number of other places. 'Economic conditions had first transformed the mass of the people of the country into workers. The combination of capital has created for this mass a common situation, common interests. This mass is thus already a class against capital, but not yet for itself. In the struggle, of which we have noted only a few phases, this mass becomes united, and constitutes itself as a class for itself. The interests it defends become class interests. But the struggle of class against class is a political struggle' (*The Poverty of Philosophy*, New York 1963, p. 173). In *The German Ideology* (Moscow 1968, p. 78), there is a footnote attributed to Marx: 'Competition separates individuals from one another, not only the bourgeois but still more the workers, in spite of the fact that it brings them together. Hence it is a long time before these individuals can unite, apart from the fact that for the purposes of this union — if it is not to be merely local — the necessary means, the great industrial cities and cheap and quick communications, have first to be produced by big industry. Hence every organized power standing over against these isolated individuals, who live in

relationships daily reproducing this isolation, can only be overcome after long struggles. To demand the opposite would be tantamount to demanding that competition should not exist in this definite epoch of history', or that the individuals should banish from their minds relationships over which in their isolation they have no control.'

18. As Marx and Engels write in *The Communist Manifesto* (in *The Revolutions of 1848*, Harmondsworth 1973, pp. 75, 79): 'But with the development of industry the proletariat not only increases in number; it becomes concentrated in greater masses, its strength grows, and it feels that strength more. The various interests and conditions of life within the ranks of the proletariat are more and more equalized, in proportion as machinery obliterates all distinctions of labour, and nearly everywhere reduces wages to the same low level. . . . The advance of industry, whose involuntary promoter is the bourgeoisie, replaces the isolation of the labourers, due to competition, by their revolutionary combination, due to association.'

19. From 'Wage Labour and Capital', in Robert Tucker, ed., *The Marx-Engels Reader*, New York 1972, p. 184. The non-zero-sum nature of working-class struggle must also be seen as a historically emergent feature of monopoly capitalism. Under early capitalism conflict between labour and capital was more usually zero-sum in terms of both use value and exchange value.

20. Braverman also recognizes the possibility of extending concessions to the working class when he talks about Ford and the five-dollar day (p. 149), but he misses its more widespread significance: that by increasing 'efficiency' of production, capitalism has been able continually to increase the standard of living of large sectors of the labour force without threatening its profitability.

21. Braverman in fact talks at one point about the linkage of short-term and long-term interests deep below the surface (pp. 29-30). But this isolated comment appears more as an act of faith than as a true bridge between two types of interests. As we shall see in the next section of this chapter, once we accept the possibility of the concrete coordination of the interests of capitalists and workers, the class-in-itself/class-for-itself model as well as its companion model of base–superstructure no longer retain their original plausibility or usefulness.

22. There is now an ever-burgeoning debate over the use of the concept 'mode of production'. Jairus Banaji's argument that one cannot reduce relations of production to a mode of expropriation is convincing ('Modes of Production in a Materialist Conception of History', *Capital and Class*, no. 3, Autumn 1977, pp. 1-44). Also convincing is Perry Anderson's insistence that 'pre-capitalist modes of production cannot be defined *except* via their political, legal and ideological superstructures, since these are what determine the type of extra-economic coercion that specifies them' (*Lineages of the Absolutist State*, NLB, London 1974, p. 404). See also Robert Brenner, 'The Origins of Capitalist Development: A Critique of Neo-Smithian Marxism', *New Left Review*, no. 104, July-August 1977, pp. 25-93; Barry Hindess and Paul Hirst, *Pre-Capitalist Modes of Production*, London 1975; Ernesto Laclau, 'Feudalism and Capitalism in Latin America', *New Left Review*, no. 67, 1971, pp. 19-38; and the classic set of essays in Rodney Hilton, ed., *The Transition from Feudalism to Capitalism*, NLB, London 1976. The concerns of these writers reflect the particular problems they are studying, and many of the debates would dissipate if this were made clearer. Since I am here not particularly concerned with feudalism as a concrete historical formation — with the feudal state, with the laws of motion of the feudal mode of production, or with the transition from feudalism to capitalism — what I have to say is not directly affected by the various debates.

23. 'The Basic Concepts of Historical Materialism', in Louis Althusser and Etienne

Balibar, eds., *Reading Capital*, New York 1970, pp. 209-24.

24. I deliberately use the term *relations in production* and not *forces of production* because I want to stress that I am talking about social relations and not an itemized set of 'things'. This has two major implications. First, the substitution of relations in production moves away from the optimistic teleology in Marx's notion of the development of the forces of production. Second, relations in production cannot be taken as given. To the contrary, just as relations of production must be reproduced so must relations in production. This crucial feature of any mode of production has been consistently overlooked through the use of the concept 'forces of production'.

25. Banaji remarks: 'If we now ask, which of these forms constituted the classical or fully developed structure of the feudal enterprise, the answer should not be difficult: the enterprise only "crystallized", that is, acquired its classical structure, when the ratio of the peasants necessary to surplus labour-time was directly reflected in the distribution of arable land between demesne and peasant holding. In other words, the form of organization of the labour-process specific to the feudal mode of production in its developed form would be one which permitted the lord to assert complete control over the labour-process itself — in which the peasant holdings assumed the form of, and functioned as, a sector of simple reproduction' (p. 19). Banaji goes on to argue that in fact this fully developed form appeared only when the feudal estate was a commodity-producing enterprise and became predominant only in the grain-exporting countries of Eastern Europe during the 'second serfdom' (pp. 19, 22-27).

26. As is widely recognized, this is very often not the case as when, for example, the water mill was introduced (Marc Bloch, *Land and Work in Medieval Europe*, Berkeley 1967, chapter 2). See also Hindess and Hirst, chapter 5.

27. See, e.g., Hilda Behrend, 'The Effort Bargain', *Industrial and Labour Relations Review*, no. 10, 1957, pp. 503-15; and William Baldamus, *Efficiency and Effort*, London 1961.

28. The assumption is that if the capitalist wanted to reveal the surplus by distinguishing it from necessary labour (and if this were possible!), then we would be back in feudalism where an extra-economic element would be necessary to guide the production cycle. I am also focusing here exclusively on the way capitalists cope with the problem in terms of the organization of work. Obviously they also try to seek solutions in the control of prices in the market; but that is another story.

29. The distinction being made here is one on which Marx also insists, the distinction between the production of things, or use value, and the production of surplus value, or exchange value. The distinction is embodied in the two aspects of the production process, the labour process and the valorization process. It is the labour process that workers experience under capitalism, while the valorization process is removed from the point of production and does not appear as such, but only in its effects. That is, workers look upon themselves as producing things rather than profit. The separation between labour process and valorization process parallels that between relations in production and relations of production. See Karl Marx, *Capital* Volume 1, Harmondsworth 1976, pp. 283-306, 949-1060.

30. Lukács, p. 90.

31. See, e.g., Stephen Marglin, 'What Do Bosses Do? The Origins and Functions of Hierarchy in Capitalist Production', *The Review of Radical Political Economics*, no. 6, Summer 1974, pp. 60-112; Katherine Stone, 'The Origins of Job Structures in the Steel Industry', *The Review of Radical Political Economics*, no. 6, Summer 1974, 113-73; David Brody, *Steelworkers in America: The Non-Union Era*, Cambridge, Massachusetts 1960; Stanley Aronowitz, *False Promises: The Shaping of American Working-Class Consciousness*, New York 1973; and André Gorz, ed., *The Division of Labour*, Atlantic

Highlands, New Jersey 1976.

32. See, e.g., Alvin Gouldner, *Patterns of Industrial Bureaucracy*, New York 1954; and Richard Edwards, 'The Social Relations of Production in the Firm and Labour Market Structure', *Politics and Society*, no. 5, 1975, pp. 83-108.

33. Braverman, pp. 124-25. Braverman also writes: 'Technical capacities are henceforth distributed on a strict "need to know" basis. The generalized distribution of knowledge of the productive process among all its participants becomes, from this point on, not merely "unnecessary", but a positive barrier to the functioning of the capitalist mode of production' (p. 82).

34. Lukács, pp. 24, 80.

35. 'What Is to Be Done?' in Lenin, *Selected Works*, 3 vols., Moscow 1963, vol. 1, p. 152.

36. Marx, for example, writes: 'The production of surplus value, or the making of profits, is the absolute law of this mode of production. Labour-power can only be sold to the extent that it preserves and maintains the means of production as capital, reproduces its own value as capital, and provides a source of additional capital in the shape of unpaid labour. The conditions of its sale, whether more or less favourable to the labourer, include therefore the necessity of its constant re-sale, and the constantly extended reproduction of wealth as capital. Wages, as we have seen, imply by their very nature, that the worker will always provide a certain quantity of unpaid labour. Even if we leave aside the case where a rise of wages is accompanied by a fall in the price of labour, it is clear that at the best of times an increase in wages means only a quantitative reduction in the amount of unpaid labour the worker has to supply. This reduction can never go so far as to threaten the system itself' (*Capital* Volume 1, pp. 618-19). But the question remains: how is the labour process organized so as to prevent that reduction which threatens the system? How is unpaid labour possible under advanced capitalism? It is a matter of the reproduction not merely of relations *of* production but also of relations *in* production. Again, Marx and Marxists have tended to take this for granted.

37. Braverman, p. 56.

38. Marx himself, in his analysis of the struggles over the working day, pointed to the role of 'force' in determining the amount of unpaid labour time the capitalist can command. 'There is here therefore an antinomy, of right against right, both equally bearing the seal of the law of exchange. Between equal rights, force decides. Hence, in the history of capitalist production, the establishment of a norm for the working-day presents itself as a struggle over the limits of that day, a struggle between collective capital, i.e., the class of capitalists, and collective labour, i.e., the working-class' (*Capital* Volume 1, p. 344). A key to the understanding of the development of capitalism lies in the transformation of such zero-sum conflicts into non-zero-sum conflicts, in which struggle comes to be organized around the distribution of marginal increments of use value.

39. Braverman, p. 97.

40. In this respect capitalism can be compared to slavery, in that the survival of the slave is intimately bound up with the survival of the slaveowner. And, as Eugene Genovese shows in *Roll, Jordan, Roll* (New York 1974), the paternalistic character of master-slave relations provides a mechanism through which slaves are able to turn privileges into rights, that is, to extract concessions.

41. Antonio Gramsci has laid the foundation for this view: 'Undoubtedly the fact of hegemony presupposes that account be taken of the interests and tendencies of the groups over which hegemony is to be exercised, and that a certain compromise equilibrium should be formed — in other words, that the leading groups should make sacrifices of an economic–corporate kind. But there is also no doubt that such sacrifices

and such a compromise cannot touch the essential; for though hegemony is ethical-political, it must also be economic, must necessarily be based on the decisive function exercised by the leading group in the decisive nucleus of economic activity *(Selections from the Prison Notebooks,* edited and translated by Quintin Hoare and Geoffrey Nowell-Smith, London 1971, p. 161). Adam Przeworski, in 'Material Bases of Consent: Economics and Politics in a Hegemonic System' *(Political Power and Social Theory,* no. 1, 1980, pp. 21-66), takes this and other ideas of Gramsci's as a point of departure for a theory of the durability of capitalist societies.

42. Braverman, pp. 180, 182, 171.

43. Ibid., p. 182.

44. Ibid., p. 27.

45. Ibid., p. 141.

46. Ibid., p. 29.

47. Braverman's relationship to industrial sociology warrants a study unto itself. But let me make a few comments. Undoubtedly, Braverman performs a crucial task in demystifying many widely held assumptions such as the historical tendency toward increasing skill involved in industrial occupations (chapter 20). Needless to say, his focus on control, expressed through the expropriation of skill and knowledge, is a major contribution. He puts to excellent use the works of manageriai practitioners (from industry or business schools) to substantiate his analysis, although, not surprisingly, his view of the labour process has a top-down bias. He extracts the rational kernel from 'business science', and in so doing recognizes that it both conceals and *expresses* a hidden reality.

Yet at the same time he adopts a very crude ideology–science distinction between industrial sociology and Marxism, or rather his own 'critical' Marxism. This, of course, may be attributable to his personal experiences as a worker, but his stance is unfortunate. By extracting from them their 'rational kernel', he could have put to good use the many celebrated works of industrial sociology such as the Harvard studies of human relations influenced by Elton Mayo, the Columbia studies of bureaucracy influenced by Robert Merton, the Chicago studies of occupations through participant observation influenced by Everett Hughes and William Foot Whyte, and even the Berkeley studies of industrialism influenced by Clark Kerr. Whatever their ideological bias, these are studies of lasting significance. They document in rich detail much of what Braverman asserts, and even if their conclusions tend to be complacent they contain a strong 'liberative potential'. For a statement of the liberative potential of academic sociology, see Alvin Gouldner, 'A Reply to Martin Shaw: Whose Crisis?' *New Left Review,* no. 71, January-February 1972, pp. 89-96. I have attempted to resituate the major industrial sociology studies within a Marxist framework in 'The Anthropology of Industrial Work', *Annual Review of Anthropology,* vol. 8, 1979, pp. 231-66.

48. Elton Mayo, *The Human Problems of an Industrial Civilization* (New York 1933) and *The Social Problems of an Industrial Civilization* (London 1940). Mayo was the guiding inspiration behind the birth of industrial sociology as the study of human relations on the shopfloor, directing attention away from the examination of objective working conditions. Whether in the form of reaction or of elaboration, the work of his team at Harvard has had a lasting impact on the study of organizations, both industrial and other. Within this school of thought, influenced by Durkheim and Pareto, the single most important empirical study is F J Roethlisberger and William Dickson, *Management and the Worker* (Cambridge, Massachusetts 1939), which summarizes the results of the Western Electric studies.

49. See also Norman Geras, 'Marx and the Critique of Political Economy', in Robin Blackburn, ed., *Ideology in Social Science* (New York 1973), pp. 284-305; and Lucio

Colletti, *From Rousseau to Lenin* (NLB, London 1972), chapter 2.

50. The literature on the Western Electric studies is extensive. Apart from Mayo and Roethlisberger and Dickson, there are a number of critical studies. See, e.g., Clark Kerr and L.H. Fisher, 'Plant Sociology: The Elite and the Aborigines', in M. Komarovsky, ed., *Common Frontiers of the Social Sciences* (Glencoe 1957), pp. 281-309; H.A. Landsberger, *Hawthorne Revisited* (Ithaca 1958); L. Baritz, *The Servants of Power: A History of the Use of Social Science in Industry* (New York 1965); A. Carey, 'The Hawthorne Studies: A Radical Criticism', *American Sociological Review*, no. 32, 1967, pp. 403-16.

51. Baldamus, p. 53. In writing about the attempts by Hawthorne counselors to manipulate dissatisfied workers' 'frames of reference', Daniel Bell recalls a folk tale that illustrates Baldamus's notion of relative satisfaction: 'A peasant complains to his priest that his little hut is horribly overcrowded. The priest advises him to move his cow into the house, the next week to take in his sheep, and the next week his horse. The peasant now complains even more bitterly about his lot. Then the priest advises him to let out the cow, the next week the sheep, and the next week the horse. At the end the peasant gratefully thanks the priest for lightening his burdensome life' *(The End of Ideology*, New York 1960, p. 423). Of course, workers see through such manipulations, just as they recognize that in seeking relative satisfactions they are adapting and accommodating to the coerciveness of industrial work. As Max Horkheimer and Theodor Adorno put it with reference to the culture industry: 'The triumph of advertising in the culture industry is that consumers feel compelled to buy and use its products even though they see through them' *(The Dialectic of Enlightenment*, New York 1972, p. 167). More generally, Herbert Marcuse refers to relative satisfactions as 'repressive satisfactions' or 'false needs'. 'Such needs have a societal content and function which are determined by external powers over which the individual has no control; the development and satisfaction of these needs are heteronomous. No matter how much such needs may have become the individual's own, reproduced and fortified by the conditions of his existence; no matter how much he identifies himself with them and finds himself in their satisfaction, they continue to be what they were from the beginning — the products of a society whose dominant interest demands repression' *(One-Dimensional Man*, Boston 1968, p. 5).

52. See, e.g., Huw Beynon, *Working for Ford*, London 1973; and Harvey Swados, *On the Line*, Boston 1957.

53. See, e.g., Peter Blau, *The Dynamics of Bureaucracy*, Chicago 1963; and Chester Barnard, *The Functions of the Executive*, Cambridge, Massachusetts 1938. Blau refers to work games as relieving status anxiety. Barnard talks about the informal group as an integral aspect of industrial organizations. Of course, the notion of informal group has come under much fire since then, as has its concomitant notion of informal organization. Nonetheless, it retains considerable tenacity since it is rooted in managerial ideology and expresses a presumed managerial prerogative of unilateral control over the labour process.

54. *Money and Motivation*, New York 1955, p. 38. Donald Roy probably made the first extensive foray into the study of work games, and his essays are now among the classics of industrial sociology. He has argued that games are an inevitable and ubiquitous form of adaptation to industrial work, offering a variety of social, psychological and physiological rewards as well as adversely affecting output. See Roy, ' "Banana Time": Job Satisfaction and Informal Interaction', *Human Organization*, no. 18, 1958, pp. 158-68; 'Work Satisfaction and Social Reward in Quota Achievement', *American Sociological Review*, no. 18, October 1953, pp. 507-14; and 'Quota Restriction and Goldbricking in a Machine Shop', *American Journal of Sociology*, no. 57, March 1952, pp. 427-42.

55. Michael Crozier, *The Bureaucratic Phenomenon*, Chicago 1964. On the other hand Jason Ditton argues that games that emerge from uncertainty or ill-defined norms *enhance* the power of management at the expense of workers. See Ditton, 'Perks, Pilferage, and the Fiddle', *Theory and Society*, no. 4, 1977, pp. 39-71; and 'Moral Horror versus Folk Terror: Output Restriction, Class and the Social Organization of Exploitation', *The Sociological Review*, no. 24, August 1976, pp. 519-44.

56. *The Human Group*, New York 1950. Elton Mayo takes a similar position when he writes of the emergence of a 'non-logical social code' or a 'social code at a lower level and in opposition to the economic logic' *(Human Problems*, p. 116). In a similar vein, although from a different theoretical perspective, James O'Connor regards games as an expression of class struggle over labour time. 'They are part of the process of dis-accumulation' ('Productive and Unproductive Labour', *Politics and Society*, no. 5, 1975, pp. 297-336).

57. A problem arises as to the origin of the preference orderings themselves. Are they inscribed in the game or imported from outside? What does one say about those people who play chess to 'lose'? It clearly becomes a different game! What happens when different players bring with them different utility curves? Or are utility curves fashioned at the point of production in a common system of values?

58. By emphasizing the coercive 'objective' features of work, Braverman misses the importance of these 'relative' freedoms, and the change in the character of freedom. As Max Horkheimer argues: 'For the average man self-preservation has become dependent upon the speed of his reflexes. Reason itself becomes identical with this adjustive facility. It may seem that present-day man has a much freer choice than his ancestors had, and in a certain sense he has. . . . The importance of this historical development must not be underestimated; but before interpreting the multiplication of choices as an increase in freedom, as is done by the enthusiasts of assembly-line production, we must take into account the pressure inseparable from this increase and the change in quality that is concomitant with this new kind of choice. The pressure consists in the continual coercion that modern social conditions put upon everyone; the change may be illus-trated by the difference between a craftsman of the old type, who selected the proper tool for a delicate piece of work, and the worker of today, who must decide quickly which of many levers or switches he should pull . . . the accretion of freedom has brought about a change in the character of freedom' *(Eclipse of Reason*, New York 1974, pp. 97-98).

Or as Marcuse puts it: 'The range of choice open to the individual is not the decisive factor in determining the degree of freedom, but *what* can be chosen and what *is* chosen by the individual' *(One-Dimensional Man*, p. 7). Although 'choice' may have diminish-ing relevance to the realization of human needs, critical theory emphasizes that it still remains. Indeed, we are forced to make choices. It is that act of 'choosing' that moulds participation within capitalist society and generates consent to its relations.

59. A fundamental distinction must be made between those who believe with Talcott Parsons that playing games, entering into exchange relations, and so forth rest on a prior *consensus*, and the position adopted here that it is the very participation in the game that generates *consent* to its rules.

60. Frequently games organized on the shopfloor have their own evolutionary dynamics that tend toward the undermining of managerial objectives. Thus, both Donald Roy ('Restriction of Output in a Piecework Machine Shop', Ph.D. dissertation, University of Chicago, 1952) and I have observed how the game of 'making out' enacted in a machine shop gradually causes the organization of work to drift in the direction of chaos. In the process of playing 'making out', mounting pressures lead to the relaxation of rules under the noncommittal and sometimes condoning eyes of the foreman, until higher management steps in to reimpose the original rules, when the cycle begins again.

Blau describes similar tendencies in the responses of workers in a state employment agency. He shows how the introduction of new rules generates competition among workers to increase individual output while the collective effect is to reduce efficiency. That is, the game itself produces conditions that make it more difficult to play the game. This contradiction is inscribed in the organization of work. Blau writes: 'This poses the interesting question, which cannot be answered here: What conditions determine whether this process ultimately levels off or reaches a climax in a revolutionary transformation of the competitive structure into a cooperative one?' p. 81). In other words, while games constructed on the shopfloor may produce consent to the rules and conditions that define them, at the same time they can sow the seeds of their own destruction through generating increased struggle with management. From my own experience and research, the existence and form of games on the shopfloor become the object of struggle not only between workers and management but also between different levels and fractions within management.

61. Throughout this section I have referred to the response of workers as 'adaptation' rather than 'resistance'. Both must be distinguished from Braverman's 'habituation', which implies no creative response but rather a mechanistic absorption into the environment, an extreme form of objectification that eliminates that crucial subjective moment implied by adaptation and resistance. In some respects my position is similar to Genovese's emphasis in *Roll, Jordan, Roll* on the way slaves shaped a world of their own through the manipulation of paternalism within the confines of slavery. But Genovese deliberately talks about resistance rather than adaptation, in order to provide a corrective to earlier studies of slavery. Like Braverman, these emphasized the destructive and degrading effects of slavery, conceived of as a 'total' or 'totalitarian' institution that permitted no outlets for creative subjectivity. Genovese further distinguishes between forms of resistance that constituted accommodation to slavery, as occurred in the ante-bellum South, and those that constituted a rejection of slavery through slave revolts, as occurred more frequently in Latin America and the Caribbean. According to Genovese, the type of religion slaves were able to create for themselves was a critical factor in the move from resistance to rebellion. An analogous exploration of resistance by workers under capitalism could be developed. Under what conditions does resistance lead to reconciliation with capitalism and under what conditions to struggles against it?

In this chapter, however, I have preferred to talk about worker responses in terms of adaptation, where Genovese, Edward Thompson and others might have used resistance. Words are not innocent. We have already noted the ambivalence of industrial sociology as to whether games are a form of adaptation or of resistance. From the point of view of the transformation of capitalism, I have argued that the worker responses I have been describing are ideological mechanisms through which workers are sucked into accepting what is as natural and inevitable. I find it difficult to talk of these as modes of resistance to capitalism, although they may be necessary for resistance. Rather, as Paul Piccone has pointed out, they are the arenas of subjectivity without which advanced capitalism cannot operate effectively ('From Tragedy to Farce: The Return of Critical Theory', *New German Critique*, no. 7, Winter 1976, pp. 91-104). Genovese's question then becomes, under what conditions do these fragmented arenas of subjectivity expand into collective struggle, or, more narrowly, under what conditions does adaptation turn into resistance? I will discuss resistance and struggle over the form of the labour process in the following sections.

62. Not only does the act of transforming raw materials into things (economic activities or practices) have ideological and political effects, but there exists at the point of production a set of political and ideological institutions or apparatuses of production.

The significance of the latter will become clearer in subsequent chapters of this book.

63. Braverman's very different view is expressed in the following passage: 'The variety of determinate forms of labour may affect the consciousness, cohesiveness, or economic and political activity of the working class, but they do not affect its existence as a class' (p. 410).

64. See Nicos Poulantzas, *Political Power and Social Classes*, NLB London 1973; Etienne Balibar, *On the Dictatorship of the Proletariat* NLB London 1977; and Adam Przeworski, 'The Process of Class Formation: From Karl Kautsky's Class Struggle to Recent Controversies', *Politics and Society*, vol. 7, no. 4, 1977, pp. 343-401.

65. 'The Peculiarities of the English', *Socialist Register*, 1965, p. 356. Of course, Thompson's *The Making of the English Working Class* (London 1963) is the classical elaboration of this view. It offers a very different perspective from that of Poulantzas and Przeworski in that it pays relatively little attention to the way the working class was shaped from above by pre-existing economic, political and ideological institutions. Rather, it is concerned with the process of and resistance to proletarianization — that is, the separation of labourers from the means of production, of labour from labour power — and not with the reformation, reorganization and restructuring that the *development* of capitalism forces upon the working class. Thompson's 'history from below' leads him to emphasize *resistance*, where Braverman, dealing with a different stage in the history of capitalism, emphasizes *habituation*. In this respect Poulantzas, Przeworski and I tend to steer a middle road. For a critical discussion of Thompson and his reliance on 'bottom up' history see Tom Nairn, 'The English Working Class', in Blackburn, pp. 187-206.

66. Braverman, pp. 85, 110, 171.

67. Ibid., p. 119.

68. One might note that it took Taylor two to three years to implement the changes at Midvale, even though he had complete management support and the advantage of having been a worker himself. Neither condition generally holds for the agents of scientific management. Furthermore, from the description of what happened it appears that the workers' resistance in this case was unusually spineless. And then, of course, we don't know what actually happened. Like so many of Taylor's descriptions it has a hollow ring to it.

69. Braverman, p. 139.

70. Blau describes the way this can happen and with what results in his study of the welfare agency, which is subject to rationalization and control. Donald Roy ('Efficiency and the Fix; Informal Intergroup Relations in a Piecework Machine Shop', *American Journal of Sociology*, no. 60, 1954, pp. 255-66) and Stanley Mathewson *(Restriction of Output among Unorganized Workers*, New York 1931) offer some graphic descriptions of workers' responses to Taylorism in industrial settings of the United States.

71. See Charles Maier, 'Between Taylorism and Technocracy: European Ideologies and the Vision of Industrial Productivity in the 1920s', *Journal of Contemporary History*, no. 5, 1970, pp. 27-61; Georges Friedmann, *Industrial Society*, New York 1955; Milton Nadworny, *Scientific Management and the Unions*, Cambridge, Massachusetts 1955; David Montgomery, 'Workers' Control of Machine Production in the Nineteenth Century', pp. 485-509; David Montgomery, 'The "New Unionism" and the Transformation of Workers' Consciousness 1909-1922', *Journal of Social History*, no. 7, 1974, pp. 509-29; Brian Maier, 'Class, Conception and Conflict: The Thrust for Efficiency, Managerial Views of Labour and Working-Class Rebellion 1903-1922', *The Review of Radical Political Economics*, no. 7, Summer 1975, pp. 31-49; and many more. Braverman himself states that 'Taylorism raised a storm of opposition among trade unions', but its significance was limited to underlining its success in 'the gathering up of all this

scattered craft knowledge, systematizing it and concentrating it in the hands of the employer and then doling it out again only in the form of minute instructions' (p. 136).

72. Eric Hobsbawm states unequivocally that initially the introduction of payment by results as part of scientific management had the effect of extracting more work from the labourer for the same wage. But he also maintains that labour savings were halted thereafter by the resistance of operatives. If there were gains from Taylorism they were short-lived. *(Labouring Men: Studies in the History of Labour*, London 1964, chapter 17.)

73. *Managers and Workers*, Madison, Wisconsin 1975, pp. 7-75.

74. Reinhard Bendix, *Work and Authority in Industry*, New York 1963, p. 281. David Noble also argues that Taylorism and scientific management were mobilized as the ideology of a specific group of school-trained industrial engineers in their struggles with the traditional 'rule of thumb' shopfloor management. See *America by Design: Technology and the Rise of Corporate Capitalism*, New York 1977.

75. Maier, 'Between Taylorism and Technocracy'. I am grateful to Jeff Haydu for pointing this out to me for the United States. See Haydu, 'The Opposition of Ideology: Socialist Thought in the Progressive Era', unpublished manuscript, University of California, Berkeley 1976.

76. Maier writes: 'Generally during the early post-war years technocratic or engineering models of social management appealed to the newer, more syncretic, and sometimes more extreme currents of European politics. ... Later in the decade, as the American vision of productivity was divested of its more utopian implications, it came to serve a useful function for business conservatives. Between the original enthusiasm for Taylorite teachings and the later *éclat* of Fordism lay an important evolution in the ideological thrust of Americanist doctrines. In general, however, all the variants enjoyed most appeal where representative government was deemed to be working badly. Ironically enough, American productivity contributed to the critical attitude towards parliamentary liberalism. What the Americanist vision seemed to promise through its brash teachings of productivity, expertise, and optimalization was an escape from having to accept class confrontation and social division. Albeit for very different reasons, all the enthusiasts for scientific management and technological overhaul were seeking to deny the necessary existence of the pre-war model of ideological conflict and to validate a new image of class relationships' (pp. 28-29).

77. It might be argued that where the transition was most rapid and far-reaching, the crises would be more severe and the strength of scientific management as part of a reactive ideology all the stronger. This might explain the greater ideological appeal of Taylorism in the United States, as compared with a country like Britain where the transition to monopoly capitalism was more drawn out.

78. Jürgen Habermas, 'Technology and Science as "Ideology" ', in *Toward a Rational Society*, Boston 1970, pp. 100-107; and Marcuse, *One-Dimensional Man*, chapters 1, 6.

79. This, of course, is the theme of Horkheimer *(Eclipse of Reason)* and of Horkheimer and Adorno *(The Dialectic of Enlightenment)*. It is also the basis of Marcuse's critique of Weber *(Negations*, Boston 1968, chapter 6).

80. Habermas, pp. 98-99.

81. The criticism that follows is similar to the one leveled by Brenner at the notion of labour control in Immanuel Wallerstein's *The Modern World-System: Capitalist Agriculture and the Origins of the European World-Economy in the Sixteenth Century*, New York 1974. Inasmuch as Wallerstein assumes that nations or their ruling classes are free to choose the system of labour control that is most efficient given their position in the world economy, his theory is neo-Smithian in that it ignores the constraints of class struggles. See also Brenner, pp. 58-60, 81-82.

82. Braverman, pp. 120-21.

83. Ibid., p. 92.

84. Ibid., p. 90.

85. Ibid., p. 85.

86. Ibid., p. 101. But note the examples of rationalization that took place before the middle of the nineteenth century. See, e.g., Erich Roll, *An Early Experiment in Industrial Organization: Being a History of the Firm of Boulton and Watt, 1775-1805*, London 1930. However, see Braverman's comment on the firm of Boulton and Watt, *Labour and Monopoly Capital*, p. 126.

87. Braverman does note that the *early* users of scientific management 'had to make their way against the fears of cost-conscious managers' (pp. 126-27).

88. Hobsbawm, 'Custom, Wage and Work Load', in *Labouring Men*, pp. 344-70.

89. David Montgomery, *Workers' Control in America*, New York 1979, chapter 2.

90. See, e.g., Braverman, p. 136.

91. Montgomery, *Workers' Control in America*, chapters 1, 4.

92. I cannot resist referring to the somewhat naive but significant comments of a 1904 government report devoted to labour productivity in the United States and Great Britain: 'Information relative to the subject of output is perhaps more difficult to obtain in Great Britain than in any other country. . . . It is virtually impossible among a people as individualistic and secretive as the British to arrive at any quantitative measure of the product turned out in a given time' (U.S. Bureau of Labor, Commissioner of Labor, *Regulation and Restriction of Output*, Eleventh Special Report, 1904, p. 721). Because they publicly defined levels of output in the form of rules, workers in the United States were more vulnerable to aggressive Taylorist practices than in England, where a heightened *class* consciousness expressed itself in secrecy.

93. See Nadworny.

94. Braverman, pp. 147, 170, 206, 236.

95. Ibid., pp. 79-82.

96. Ibid., p. 200 (see also fn.).

97. Bill Friedland and Amy Barton, *Destalking the Wily Tomato*, Department of Applied Behavioural Sciences, College of Agricultural and Environmental Sciences, University of California, Davis, 1975; Bob Thomas, 'Citizenship and Labour Supply: The Social Organization of Industrial Agriculture', Ph.D. dissertation, Northwestern University, 1981.

98. Braverman, p. 103.

99. A great deal of research could be profitably undertaken into the conjunctures when different industries or occupations undergo deskilling. Braverman himself acknowledges the uneven development of mechanization and Taylorism both through history and as they spread through the social structure (pp. 172, 208, 282). Much might be derived from an examination of those exceptional cases that have successfully resisted the expropriation of skill or mechanization. See, e.g., Gouldner, *Patterns of Industrial Bureaucracy*; E.L. Trist, G.W. Higgin, H. Murray and A.B. Pollock, *Organizational Choice*, London 1963; and Marglin, op.cit.; all these discuss the case of mining. See Arthur Stinchcombe, 'Bureaucratic and Craft Administration of Production: A Comparative Study', *Administrative Science Quarterly*, no. 4, 1959, pp. 168-87, for the construction industry; and Lupton, *On the Shop Floor*, and Sheila Cunnison, *Wages and Work Allocation*, London 1965, for the garment industry. Extending the ideas of Robert Blauner (in *Alienation and Freedom*, Chicago 1964) Arthur Stinchcombe has developed a theory of organizational persistence based on ideas of sunk costs, vesting of interests, and the prevention of change through competition by monopolization (Stinchcombe, 'Social Structure and Organization', in J.G. March, ed., *Handbook of Organizations*, New York 1965, pp. 142-69).

100. Braverman, p. 252.

101. There is possibly an alternative view in Braverman (pp. 169-71), but he is not clear. Part of the problem is that Braverman neither says much about the nature of the labour process under competitive capitalism nor makes clear the distinction between competitive and monopoly capitalism. See also section 5 of this chapter.

102. This is not to say that mechanization pushes itself forward without struggle. To the contrary. But once initial opposition is overcome, assuming it is, then the question becomes whether the effect of new machinery is to increase or diminish struggle. This will of course be linked to the ideological effects it promotes. It is very likely that new machinery, through its capacity to fragment, to increase 'freedom' of movement, to eliminate points of friction, to allow the introduction of rules, can lead to a diminution of solidarity among workers as against management. It can, of course, have the opposite effect.

103. Jean Monds criticizes Katherine Stone's 'The Origin of Job Structures in the Steel Industry' for presenting a similarly misleading portrait of nineteenth-century capitalism as 'the lost paradise of craft autonomy' ('Workers' Control and the Historians: A New Economism', *New Left Review*, no. 97, May-June 1976, p. 90). In writing of the destruction of crafts in the steel industry, Stone ignores the already created unskilled workers. The craft workers represented a small labour aristocracy that was not wholly of the working class but, to use Erik Olin Wright's terms, in a contradictory class location between workers and capitalists (Wright, 'Class Boundaries in Advanced Capitalist Societies', *New Left Review*, no. 98, July-August 1976, pp. 3-41).

104. Frederick Engels, *The Conditions of the Working Class in England*, St Albans 1969, pp. 163-239; but see also Chapter Two.

105. Alternative periodizations of the capitalist labour process can be found in Richard Edwards, *Contested Terrain*, New York 1979; Andrew Friedman, *Industry and Labour*, London 1977; and Craig Littler, *The Development of the Labour Process in Capitalist Societies*, London 1982. For my critique of these and a further alternative, see Chapter Three.

106. Braverman, p. 150. I am not suggesting that managerial attempts to increase meaning and participation will have the effect of augmenting class struggle, as is argued by Michel Bosquet ('The Prison Factory', *New Left Review*, no. 73, May-June 1972, pp. 23-24). A less optimistic view of the implications of recent trends in management practice and philosophy is to be found in Theo Nichols, 'The "Socialism" of Management: Some Comments on the New "Human Relations" ', *Sociological Review*, no. 23, May 1975, pp. 245-65. In an overview of the schemes for job enrichment, humanization, etc., James Reinhart argues that such changes frequently mask increased rationalization of the labour process; that managers are able to exercise greater control over the workforce in the name of work humanization (see 'Job Enrichment and the Labour Process', paper presented to New Directions in the Labour Process, a conference sponsored by the Department of Sociology, State University of New York, Binghamton, 5-7 May 1978).

107. See Habermas, 'Technology and Science as "Ideology" ', and Marcuse, *One-Dimensional Man*, chapter 6.

108. Braverman, p. 19.

109. Marx himself was, of course, optimistic about the development of the forces of production under capitalism. They contributed simultaneously to the necessity of the supersession of capitalism and to the possibility of the inauguration of socialism. 'Large-scale industry, through its very catastrophes, makes the recognition of variation of labour, and hence of the fitness of the worker for the maximum number of different

kinds of labour, into a question of life and death. . . . The partially developed individual, who is merely the bearer of one specialized social function, must be replaced by the totally developed individual, for whom the different social functions are different modes of activity he takes up in turn.' *Capital*, Vol. One, p. 618.

110. Braverman, p. 22.

111. For a discussion of these issues, see Ulysses Santamaria and Alain Manville, 'Lenin and the Problem of Transition', *Telos*, no. 27, Spring 1976, pp. 79-96.

112. As Erik Wright pointed out in conversation, the technical imperatives may take the negative form of ruling out rather than specifying certain features of the relations in production. Variations of fit between technology and productive relations have been explored by the school of 'socio-technical systems' associated with the Tavistock Institute. One of the most interesting and detailed of their studies was the one conducted in the British coal-mining industry, where they show how mechanization proves to be incompatible with the traditional form of work organization based on the self-regulating group, and leads to a decline in productivity. They conclude that mining can be organized in one of two ways, on the basis of either the self-regulating work group or an extremely punitive bureaucracy. See Trist, et al., *Organizational Choice*. Whereas in advanced capitalist nations miners have managed to resist the second alternative, the political circumstances of colonialism or apartheid in the nations of southern Africa facilitated the emergence of a coercive militaristic organization of work. It is interesting to study what happens to such a work organization when the relations of political power between black and white are transformed with the attainment of national 'independence'; see Chapter Five.

113. Braverman, p. 193.

114. Ibid., pp. 281-82, 229; see also pp. 194-95, 199, 227.

115. Ibid., p. 230.

116. Ibid., p. 232.

117. Note that Lenin said the same thing fifty years ago when Taylorism and the assembly line were the most advanced forms of capitalist technology. One wonders, then, what we will be saying fifty years hence. On what grounds can one claim that contemporary advanced technology is more viable than early machines under a prospective socialism, particularly if the machines themselves are neutral?

118. For a discussion of alternative notions of 'socialist socialization' see Santamaria and Manville; and Karl Korsch, 'What Is Socialization?' *New German Critique*, no. 6, Fall 1975, pp. 60-81.

119. Braverman, p. 230; see also p. 445.

120. The Frankfurt School is not altogether consistent on this matter. In Horkheimer and Adorno's *Dialectic of Enlightenment* and Marcuse's *One-Dimensional Man*, capitalist technology embodies and is irrevocably contaminated by the domination of people over people. Marcuse, in *Eros and Civilization* (New York 1972), and Horkheimer, in *Eclipse of Reason*, express a certain optimism in the emancipatory potential of the development of the forces of production.

121. Braverman, pp. 80, 118.

122. Inasmuch as the Babbage principle is reflected in the design of machines and the organization of work, it makes nonsense of the various attempts, such as those of Marglin and Stone, to separate efficiency from control.

123. Braverman, p. 206; see also pp. 193, 227.

124. Ibid., p. 170.

125. Yale Magrass suggested to me that a distinction be drawn between technology and machines. He also suggested that Braverman accepted the use of capitalist *technology* under socialism, but thought that this would give rise to socialist *machines*.

Thus, computer technology can be used alongside different types of machines that prepare and code data, some of which are conducive to the separation of conception and execution and some of which are not (see Braverman, pp. 331-32). In other words, while technology may be innocent, its embodiment in machines is tainted.

126. See Carter Goodrich, *The Frontier of Control*, New York 1920, pp. 3-50; and Monds. It may be useful to distinguish reunification of conception and execution at the individual level (job control or the restoration of the craft worker) from such reunification at the collective level, which might more closely approximate worker control. Moreover, collective reunification may prove to be compatible with individual reunification only under certain types of technology.

127. Lukács, p. 27.

128. Max Weber, *The Protestant Ethic and the Spirit of Capitalism*, New York 1958, p. 181.

129. Braverman, p. 233.

130. Horkheimer, 'Traditional and Critical Theory', in *Critical Theory*, New York 1972, p. 213. Unlike Weber, critical theorists, at least in principle, regard this form of domination not as inevitable but as the product of capitalism or more generally of the 'domination of nature'. Yet they, like Braverman, offer little in the way of hope for its supersession. Indeed, in an essay with remarkable parallels to *Labour and Monopoly Capital* ('The Authoritarian State', *Telos*, no. 15, Spring 1973, pp. 3-20) Horkheimer harks back to the council communists as a potentially emancipatory movement in much the same vein as that in which Braverman harks back to the craft tradition. Interestingly, the council communists were also frequently skilled workers.

131. As John Myles suggested to me, Braverman's individualism springs from his conception of human beings and human work: 'Human work is conscious and purposive, while the work of other animals is instinctual. . . . In human work . . . the directing mechanism is the *power of conceptual thought*. . . . Thus work as purposive action, guided by the intelligence, is the special product of humankind' (Braverman, pp. 30-31). From these premises Braverman is able to derive the central theme of his book: 'Thus, in humans, as distinguished from animals, the unity between the motive force of labour and labour itself is not inviolable. *The unity of conception and execution may be dissolved*. The conception must still precede and govern execution, but the idea as conceived by *one* may be executed by *another*' (pp. 41-49).

Thus, from the beginning, individualism is embodied in Braverman's notion of deskilling and the degradation of work. By contrast, my own point of departure regards the distinctive feature of human work as the *social relations* into which men and women enter as they transform nature. This draws on a different emphasis within Marx: 'Language, like consciousness, only arises from the need, the necessity, of intercourse with other men. Where there exists a relationship, it exists for me: the animal does not enter into *relations* with anything, it does not enter into any relations at all. For the animal, its relation to others does not exist as a relation. Consciousness is, therefore, from the very beginning a social product, and remains so as long as men exist at all' *(The German Ideology*, p. 42). Where Braverman focuses on domination and the destruction of the worker who simultaneously conceives and executes, I examine the reproduction of social relations that both obscure and secure surplus.

These differences parallel recent debates over critical theory's appropriation of psychoanalysis. As found in the work of Adorno, Horkheimer and Marcuse, critical theory embraces Freud's basic postulate concerning the innate aggressiveness and self-interest of the id, posing as central the relationship of the individual to society. Such a position on one hand leads to themes of the eclipse of the individual, and on the other hand harmonizes well with disillusionment over the possibility of socialism. Jessica Benjamin has exposed the link between the psychoanalytic presuppositions of orthodox critical theory and its overall pessimism. Drawing on object relations theory, she replaces the individualism of Freudian instinct theory with the postulate of the inherent sociability of men and women — their need for mutual recognition — and examines how this becomes distorted under capitalism. Naturally her position points to a more optimistic picture of any future socialism. See Jessica Benjamin, 'The End of Internalization: Adorno's Social Psychology', *Telos*, no. 32, Summer 1977, pp. 42-64.

132. Braverman, pp. 60, 120, 172.

133. Ibid., p. 280; see also chapter 13.

134. Ibid., p. 271.

135. 'The Working Class Has Two Sexes', *Monthly Review*, no. 28, July-August 1976, pp. 1-9.

136. Braverman, p. 275.

137. Ibid., pp. 377-90.

138. Ibid., p. 378.

139. By 'functionalism' I mean a form of causal analysis in which consequence determines cause. In its simplest form the mechanisms through which this occurs are unstated. More sophisticated forms specify the mechanisms and the conditions under which they are or are not effective in linking cause to consequence. See Arthur Stinchcome, *Constructing Social Theories*, New York 1968, chapter 3.

140. *Capital* Volume 1, Moscow 1954, p. 82.

141. There is some confusion here due to my use of politics, ideology and law in two different contexts: with regard to the reproduction of relations of production on one hand and of relations in production on the other. Unless otherwise stated, in this section I am referring to the first and larger context of politics, ideology and law, and when I talk of the mode of production or of the economic I am subsuming its own political and ideological realms.

142. Balibar, 'The Basic Concepts of Historical Materialism', pp. 226-33, and *On the Dictatorship of the Proletariat*, pp. 66-77; Poulantzas, 'L'Examen Marxiste du Droit et de l'Etat Actuels et la Question de l'Alternative', *Les Temps Modernes*, no. 20, 1964, pp. 274-302; and Poulantzas, *Political Power and Social Classes*.

143. The notion of a 'structured totality' comes from Louis Althusser, *For Marx*, London 1969, especially chapter 3; and Althusser and Balibar, *Reading Capital*. The defining features of a structured totality in contradistinction to an expressive totality are the 'relative autonomy' of its parts and their mutual determination through the conditions of each other's reproduction, producing what Althusser refers to as an 'overdetermination'.

144. *The Fiscal Crisis of the State*, New York 1973.

145. Braverman, pp. 284-89. Braverman does touch on the role of the state in the context of social coordination (p. 269). It might be argued that the theory of the state had already been dealt with adequately in the companion volume, *Monopoly Capital*, by Paul Baran and Paul Sweezy (New York 1966), and hence Braverman did not want to go over the same territory. Nevertheless, the absence of an analysis of the state or references to such an analysis conveys a certain picture of society that is not without political implications.

146. 'Theses on the Theory of the State', *New German Critique*, no. 6, Fall 1975, pp. 137-48.

147. *Legitimation Crisis*, Boston 1975.

148. *Late Capitalism*, NLB London 1975. The most important attempt to situate the analysis of the labour process within a logic of use value and exchange value is Michel Aglietta's *A Theory of Capitalist Regulation* — The U.S. Experience, NLB London 1979.

149. Gorz, 'Technology, Technicians and Class Struggle', in *The Division of Labour*,

pp. 159-89; Poulantzas, *Political Power and Social Classes*; and Gramsci, op. cit.

150. This is not entirely true. Braverman does refer at one point to the 'insoluble contradiction that exists between the development of the means of production and the social relations of production that characterize capitalism'. But even here he is referring more to capitalism's irrationalities than to a concrete analysis of its dynamics. At one point he asserts the tendency for productive labour to decline, but he does not draw any implications (pp. 280, 423; see also pp. 206, 282). Interestingly, however, he makes no reference to Baran and Sweezy's use in *Monopoly Capital* of productive and unproductive labour as a 'critical' concept.

151. Failure to examine the conditions of domination outside the very broad parameters of capitalist relations of production leads not only in the direction of unjustified pessimism but also, in conjunctures of social ferment, to equally unjustified optimism. Movement between these polarities signifies an inability to link ′ ¬pearances to their underlying forces or a tendency to mistake the former for the latter. ⎮hat other implications can be drawn from the adoption of one or the other totality? In a critical examination of Aronowitz's *False Promises*, which in many ways parallels my own treatment of Braverman, Jean Cohen suggests that the formulation of an expressive totality 'logically leads to conclusions that (Aronowitz) abhors — the necessity of a party' ('False Promises', *Telos*, no. 24, Summer 1975, p. 138). In this Cohen is, of course, drawing parallels with Lukács. Inasmuch as Braverman holds to the proletariat as the only revolutionary subject, Cohen's argument presumably applies to him as well. As regards the structured totality, it has been linked by some to the dangers of scientism and Stalinism. But again, by itself, without the importation of certain political premises, it has no unambiguous ideological implications.

152. Braverman, of course, does postulate the conditions of the dominance of capital in the continued existence of capitalist social relations (p. 22). To be sure, this is a definite advance over 'traditional theory', but it does not help us explore how that dominance might end.

153. Gramsci, p. 158.

154. The three realms of the production process are of course the economic, political and ideological, which include the political and ideological *aspects* of work as such, as well as the political and ideological apparatuses of production which regulate struggle.

155. Gramsci, pp. 302-3.

156. Ibid., p. 285. Gramsci unfortunately ignores the importance of slavery and the persistent heritage of racism it instigated — although it can be argued that racism has contributed to rather than retarded the accumulation of capital.

157. Ibid., pp. 285-86.

158. The following discussion draws on Ronald Dore's *British Factory–Japanese Factory*, Berkeley 1973, and on ideas thrown out by David Brody in a seminar he gave at Berkeley. See also Brody, 'The Rise and Decline of Welfare Capitalism', in J. Braeman, R. Bremner and David Brody, eds., *Change and Continuity in Twentieth-Century America: The 1920s*, Columbus, Ohio 1968.

159. This is not to say that there are no distinctions among the labour processes and conditions of work in the different sectors of the British economy, but that they are less pronounced. In his comparison of two British firms, a garment factory in the competitive sector and a transformer company in the monopoly sector, Tom Lupton suggests that the differences in the labour process may in part be attributed to the market contexts of the two firms.

160. Gramsci, p. 173.

2
Karl Marx and the Satanic Mills

This chapter seeks to resolve a historical anomaly by unravelling a theoretical paradox. The anomaly is the commonplace observation that in England, where Marx anticipated the outbreak of the first socialist revolution, the working class proved to be reformist in its political impulses, whereas in Russia, whose backwardness was supposed to delay the transcendence of capitalism, the working class proved to be the most revolutionary.[1] Although there have been many attempts to explain the anomaly within a Marxist framework, they have generally suffered from one of two shortcomings: either they have dwelt on the peculiarities of England or Russia, instead of providing a single framework which would explain both working-class reformism in the one and the spread of revolutionary momentum in the other; or they have lost sight of the centrality of the process of production in shaping the character of the working class. In this chapter I try to address both shortcomings by linking the historical anomaly to a theoretical paradox: that for Marx, capitalist production is both the spring of class struggle and an arena of undisputed domination of labour by capital.[2]

In *The Communist Manifesto* Marx and Engels write: 'The advance of industry, whose involuntary promoter is the bourgeoisie, replaces the isolation of the labourers, due to competition, by their revolutionary combination, due to association.' 'This organization of the proletarians into a class, and consequently into a political party, is continually being upset again by the competition between the workers themselves. But it ever rises up again, stronger, firmer, mightier.'[3] And in *Capital* Marx writes: 'Along with the constant decrease in the number of capitalist magnates, who usurp and monopolize all the advantages of this process of transformation, the mass of misery, oppression, slavery, degradation and exploitation grows; but with this there also grows the revolt of the working class, a class constantly increasing in numbers, and trained, united and organized by the very mechanism of the capitalist process of production.'[4]

But how does one get from one to the other — from competition, isolation, misery, oppression, slavery and exploitation to combination, association and struggle? This question cannot be passed over with a dialectical sleight of hand or dismissed as a Hegelian contamination.

There are four frequently encountered resolutions of this paradox. The first imputes to the working class a historic mission to overthrow capitalism, based on the degradation it experiences and the universal interests it carries. Here class struggle is ubiquitous, a primordial given and the prime mover of history. Whereas this resolution pushes aside the reality of domination and fragmentation as transient and superficial phenomena, a second resolution makes these factors central. Here the working class must wait for the inexorable laws of capitalism to precipitate the final catastrophe, at which point the transition to socialism is automatic. This is history without a subject. Neither of these is a serious solution, since both deny the paradox by suppressing one of its terms — in the first case the demobilizing effect of capitalist production, and in the second the appearance of the working class as a historical actor.

More sophisticated resolutions argue that neither is the working class inherently revolutionary nor is capitalism necessarily doomed by some immanent logic. Hence an external force must bring enlightenment to the working class. In its most orthodox version, this force is the unified and unifying vanguard party. Here the working class is prevented from becoming conscious of its revolutionary goal by the corrosive effects of the dominant ideology. The party intervenes to demystify that ideology, holding up a mirror to the working class so that it recognizes itself as a heroic actor. This presumes too much about the readiness of the working class to change its self-conception. Working-class consciousness does not drift with the prevailing ideological winds, but is firmly anchored in the process of production. This solution is also flawed as an interpretation of history. According to many Marxist and non-Marxist historians, the Russian revolution is the *locus classicus* of such an external agency. Recent social history sheds much doubt on this interpretation: the Bolshevik Party in 1917 was not the monolithic entity it was to become; instead, its success lay in its disunity, heterogeneity, and responsiveness to the indigenous impulses, militancy and grievances of a turbulent working class.[5]

Social historians have therefore turned to the sources of that turbulence in the totality of working-class experiences within and outside production. They offer a fourth bridge from domination to resistance, which distinguishes the capitalist mode of production from the capitalist system,[6] the logic of capital from capitalism.[7] Beyond the arena of production are institutions such as the family, the church, the neighbourhood, the pub, the friendly society and the political club, which provide the organizational resources for economic subordination to be turned into political struggle. Cultural, political and communal legacies from the pre-industrial era provide the clay out of which workers mould themselves into a class.[8]

As Calhoun[9] has argued with respect to Thompson's study (and as could be argued with respect to the others), the emergence of community and tradition as bastions of resistance was closely bound up with threats to production and to the control exercised by the direct producer. Bonnell has argued that where such craft or communal traditions are weak, as in Russia, the workshop itself becomes the citadel of resistance.[10] In each case we are thrown back to the workplace as a critical determinant of working-class struggle. This is, of course, explicitly recognized in many studies of factory production. Shorter and Tilly as well as Hanagan link the character of strikes and political mobilization in France to work organization and its transformation; Moore discovers the roots of rebellion in the violation of the contractual order between managers and workers; Foster ties the rise and fall of working-class radicalism in Oldham to the crises facing the cotton industry and to changes in the productive process; Montgomery unveils the workplace as a fund of resources with which American workers resisted managerial domination.[11]

While all these works recognize that production had ideological and political as well as economic consequences, this insight is too often buried in a search for the totality of working-class experiences. With some notable exceptions, social historians have sought to expand rather than contract the arenas shaping working-class struggles. In this chapter an attempt will be made to theorize the *centrality of production*, which underlies many of their studies. We shall distinguish the *labour process*, conceived as the coordinated set of activities and relations involved in the transformation of raw materials into useful products, from the *political apparatuses of production*, understood as the institutions that regulate and shape struggles in the workplace — struggles which I call the 'politics of production'. *Factory regime* refers to the overall political form of production, including both the political effects of the labour process and the political apparatuses of production. Marx himself was not unaware of these distinctions. But he failed to thematize the way that factory regimes shape interests and capacities, thereby linking domination to struggle, and the possibility that changes in the factory regime may occur independently of changes in the labour process. By returning to the scene of Marx's own analysis — the Lancashire cotton industry in the nineteenth century — we shall see that Marx's prototypical form of factory regime, market despotism, was not only rare but also inimical to the development of working-class struggles. Instead we discover different types of regime within the textile industry of early capitalism: the company state and patriarchal and paternalistic regimes in Lancashire; paternalism and market despotism in New England; and the company state in Russia.

Our first task, then, will be to examine the conditions of existence of different types of factory regimes, focusing on four main factors: the labour process, market competition among firms, the reproduction of labour power, and state intervention. The second and more difficult task will be to isolate the effect of factory regimes on struggles. It will be argued that variations in factory regime are *sufficient* to explain both working-class reformism in England and a revolutionary movement in Russia. Other factors enter the analysis only as determinants of factory regimes. This is not to say that the only effects of these other factors on struggles are indirect, mediated by production regimes, but rather that an account of their direct effects is not *necessary* to an understanding of the divergent trajectories of the two labour movements.

1. Marx's Prototype: Market Despotism

Marx and Engels had a definite notion of the emerging form of social regulation in modern industry. Marx describes the factory regime in the most advanced industry of his time, the textile industry, as follows:

> In the factory code, the capitalist formulates his autocratic power over his workers like a private legislator, and purely as an emanation of his own will, unaccompanied by either that division of responsibility otherwise so much approved of by the bourgeoisie, or the still more approved representative system. This code is merely the capitalist caricature of the social regulation of the labour process which becomes necessary in cooperation on a large scale and in the employment in common of instruments of labour, and especially of machinery. The overseer's book of penalties replaces the slave-driver's lash. All punishments naturally resolve themselves into fines and deductions from wages, and the law-giving talent of the factory Lycurgus so arranges matters that a violation of his laws is, if possible, more profitable to him than the keeping of them. [12]

This despotic regime of factory politics is considered the only one compatible with the exigencies of capitalist development. It is the counterpart within production of the market pressures which compel capitalists, on pain of extinction, to compete with one another through the introduction of new technology and the intensification of work. Anarchy in the market leads to despotism in production; the market is constitutive of the apparatuses of production, and we call this regime 'market despotism'.

Competition among firms is only the first of four conditions of existence of market despotism. The second condition is the real subordination of workers to capital, the separation of conception from execution. Marx recognized different forms of subordination in his delineation of three stages in the development of industrial production.[13] In the first, handicraft production, workers control and own the instruments of production but are subject to exploitation by merchants and to competition from ever more productive factories. In the second stage, the formal subsumption of labour to capital, workers are brought together under a single roof, retain control over the labour process, but no longer own the means of production, which are now the property of capital. This phase of wage labour gives way to the real subsumption of labour when workers lose control of the labour process. The worker is transformed from a subjective into an objective element of production.

> The lifelong speciality of handling the same tool now becomes the lifelong speciality of serving the same machine. Machinery is misused in order to transform the worker, from his very childhood, into a part of a specialized machine. In this way, not only are the expenses necessary for his reproduction considerably lessened, but at the same time his helpless dependence upon the factory as a whole, and therefore upon the capitalist, is rendered complete.[14]

Here is the third condition of market despotism: the worker's dependence on the employer, on the sale of labour power for a wage. This presupposes that workers are completely expropriated of the means of their subsistence. Dependence on a particular capitalist is consolidated by a reservoir of surplus labour. Marx examined this process of 'primitive accumulation' in some detail for England, but too easily assumed that complete expropriation would become the norm for all capitalist societies. Finally, Marx also took for granted — and this is the fourth condition of market despotism — that the state would preserve only the *external* conditions of production (conditions for the autonomous working of market forces); and, in particular, that it would not directly regulate either relations among capitalists or the process of production and its apparatuses. On examination, however, not only are these third and fourth conditions problematic, but their variation is crucial to the determination of factory regimes.

As Marx recognized, market despotism effectively undermined working-class resistance to managerial domination.'The organization of the capitalist process of production, once it is fully developed, breaks down all resistance. The constant generation of a relative surplus population keeps the law of the supply and demand of labour, and therefore wages, within narrow limits which correspond to capital's valorization requirements. The silent compulsion of economic relations sets the seal on the domination of the capitalist over the worker'.[15] How then can we explain the militant struggles of cotton operatives, particularly during the first half of the nineteenth century when textiles were the most advanced industry? The answer is simple: we find other factory regimes more conducive than market despotism to the development of struggles.

The four conditions of market despotism are rarely realized simultaneously. By treating them as four variables we can illuminate their independent effects on the form of factory regime via a succession of comparisons. The first comparison, that of throstle spinning and mule spinning in Lancashire, underlines the importance of the labour process for the factory regime. Real subsumption of labour in the former is associated with the company state, whereas formal subsumption in the latter is associated with patriarchal despotism. The second comparison, that of the power-driven mule and the self-acting mule, shows the importance of both the labour process and competition among firms for the transition from patriarchal to paternalistic regimes. The third comparison, between paternalism and market despotism in the New England mills, provides evidence of the importance of separation from the means of subsistence, whereas the fourth comparative study, dealing with Russia, adds the factor of state intervention to the model. Our independent variables can be arranged in a causal hierarchy (see figure 1), so that the first two (market forces and labour process) operate within limits defined by the second two (separation from the means of subsistence and state intervention). The model is obviously crude. It cannot explain all the variations in regimes, but it does highlight the critical factors determining the breakdown and transformation of factory politics.

Fig. 1 HIERARCHY OF DETERMINANTS OF FACTORY REGIMES
IN THE EARLY COTTON INDUSTRIES

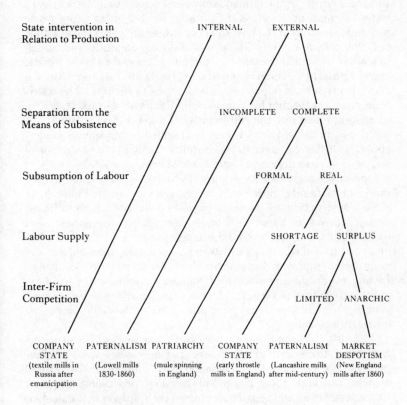

State intervention in Relation to Production		INTERNAL	EXTERNAL		
Separation from the Means of Subsistence			INCOMPLETE	COMPLETE	
Subsumption of Labour				FORMAL	REAL
Labour Supply					SHORTAGE SURPLUS
Inter-Firm Competition					LIMITED ANARCHIC

COMPANY STATE (textile mills in Russia after emanicipation

PATERNALISM (Lowell mills 1830-1860)

PATRIARCHY (mule spinning in England)

COMPANY STATE (early throstle mills in England)

PATERNALISM (Lancashire mills after mid-century)

MARKET DESPOTISM (New England mills after 1860)

2. Lancashire: From Company State to Patriarchy

At the heart of the industrial revolution lay the transformation of cotton textile manufacturing. After 1760 the flying shuttle was introduced into weaving, stimulating the demand for yarn. Until the middle of the eighteenth century spinning had been a slow and laborious process using spindle and distaff and sometimes the spinning wheel. The adoption of the jenny in the 1770s permitted a single operator to spin simultaneously on a number of spindles. These technological innovations did not transform the division of labour in domestic production. The jenny could be used in the home, although as the number of spindles increased it had to be harnessed to water power and a few jenny factories emerged. Although the jenny multiplied the power of human hands, 'the grip of the human hand and the drawing of the human arm were still essential.'[16] Arkwright's water frame, also known as the throstle, worked on an entirely new principle. Instead of the human hand, two sets of rollers would draw out the cotton roving, which was then continuously and simultaneously twisted and wound on a bobbin. It was the first automatic spinning machine, but it required more than human power to drive it and was often built in rural areas with access to streams. 'The water-frame was a substitute for human skill,' Chapman tells us. It, 'therefore, summoned into the cotton industry a lower class of labour . . . but it cannot be said to have displaced skilled cotton spinners in any appreciable degree, since it was confined chiefly to the production of warps which had previously been made of linen or wool.'[17]

Operatives were usually women or children: 'Masters often hired the head of family, however, for road-making, bridge-building, or plant construction while employing the wife and children in the mill.'[18] It was to these early mills that pauper apprentices were recruited, particularly around the turn of the century. They were less likely to be used where family labour was available, although they did not present employers with the problems associated with adult males. In any event the importance of the pauper apprentices has been exaggerated; they never formed more than a third of the labour force at any of the mills, and they were phased out in the early years of the nineteenth century.[19]

The real subsumption of labour in the factory, where managers controlled the speed of machinery and operatives were machine tenders, laid the basis for domination of the community by the mill owner. Through their control of housing, provisions, company stores, education and religion, masters were able to consolidate their rule in all spheres of life. Smelser distinguishes two types of early water-frame factory: 'those run by brutal, heartless capitalists who flogged their employees, especially the apprentices; and those run as "model" communities by humanitarian masters.'[20] The factory village became a state within a state, or what I call a 'company state', with its own coercive apparatuses. 'If we add to this economic and political power of the employer his power over education, housing and the like, it will be clear why management of a factory or mine might come to mean government of a whole community.'[21] The company state went beyond market despotism to intervene coercively in the reproduction of labour power, binding community to factory through non-market as well as market ties.

In England the water frame soon gave way to mule spinning, which was more efficient and provided the finer thread for weft.[22] The mule combined the principles of the jenny and the water frame — that is, roller drafting plus simultaneous stretching, twisting and winding which required the application of considerable skill and effort by the operator. The early mules, however, could be used in the home with human power. When the mule was brought into the factory and harnessed to non-human power, factory owners adapted the domestic organization of production to their own needs. They recruited adult male spinners who were paid by the piece and who in turn recruited their own helpers — women and children, often from their own families. Under this inside contracting arrangement, the master handed over responsibility for supervision and work organisation to the spinner. Thus, there were relatively few overseers in the mule factories compared with water-frame factories.[23] The system of payment was also different. In the mule factories, helpers (piecers and scavengers) were paid a fixed wage, while the contractor (spinner) was paid by the piece; the harder the latter drove the former, the greater were his dividends. Moreover, pressure from employers in the form of rate cutting could be passed on to helpers as the intensification of effort. In the throstle factory, because production was so completely controlled by management, operatives were paid an hourly rather then a piece wage.[24]

Whereas the real subsumption of labour in the throstle factory laid the basis of the company state, the formal subsumption of labour in the mule factory established the conditions for a patriarchal regime. Here production apparatuses were based on, or imitative of, the domination of the father over other members of the family. More specifically, the patriarchal regime involved a collaboration between subcontractor and employer, so that the former offered and organized the labour of the family or proto-family in exchange for wages and support of the autonomous domination of the patriarch over the women and children who assisted him. It is as if capital said to the patriarch: 'You will keep your people within the rules conforming to our requirements, in return for which you can use them as you see fit, and if they go against your injunctions, we will furnish you with support necessary to bring them back to order.'[25]

From the point of view of the cotton masters, patriarchal apparatuses of production had the advantage of containing struggles between the subcontractor and his helpers by relying on family bonds and by holding out to male helpers the possibility that they would one day become spinners. At the same time, there is no evidence to suggest that concern for his own or other children inhibited the spinner from sweating his piecers and scavengers.[26] Moreover, so long as this regime of production politics did not inhibit changes in the labour process, it was also in the interests of factory managers wishing to contract out the risk and responsibility for direct control over work. In England, at least, entrepreneurs in the beginning did not have the inclination and later did not have the resources (in cotton spinning) to impose a system of market despotism.[27]

There is a broad measure of agreement that during the period 1790–1820, cotton spinning and other trades frequently relied on the family for recruitment, division of labour, and supervision. Most of the early trade union regulations among spinners restricted the recruitment of assistants to a narrowly defined set of kinship relations.[28] But after 1820 technological changes — in particular, the rapid expansion of the number of spindles — increased the ratio of piecers to spinners, tending to break up the family as the organizing unit of production. According to Smelser, with partial confirmation from Thompson and Stedman-Jones, this disruption of the family was a major impulse behind the struggles of the factory operatives in the 1830s.[29]

Major strikes, part of whose aim was to defend the monopoly of the male spinners against displacement by women, broke out in 1818, 1824 and 1829.[30] John Doherty, leader of the Manchester spinners and architect of the Grand General Union and the National Association for the Protection of Labour, condemned the employment of women as spinners: 'In the first number of the *Journal,* on 6 March (1830), a letter was printed from "a poor man, a spinner with a wife and five children", who had lost his employment at 25 to 35s per week. Doherty commented that practice was harmful both to females, who must perform fatiguing labour in unwholesome conditions which made even male spinners old men by forty, and also to the workmen who were thereby supplanted. Thus, their natural roles were reversed, through the avarice of greedy employers, and "the miserable father has to take the place of the mother", looking after the children at home instead of providing for them at work.'[31] The defence of patriarchy —'natural roles' — is conducted as the defence of a family wage, the preservation of morals and the protection of women. What is good for patriarchy is good for all, and indeed there are definite material interests which may bind women to patriarchy.[32] Just as the spinners were successful in maintaining their monopoly against the encroachment of women, they were also able to restrict the work of piecers to avoid being usurped during turnouts.

The patriarchal regime not only directly shaped production

politics — that is, struggles confined to the sphere of production. It also stamped itself on the wider struggles in the realm of the state. The factory movement — the struggles for a shorter working day — showed how class interests came to be shaped by production politics. Although the ten-hours movement was presented as a drive for the protection of women and children, such protection was the most effective way of reducing the hours of men under a patriarchal regime. In a period of laissez-faire, men were held to be free and responsible agents who had no need of legislative protection, whereas women and children were dependants who did have such a need. The Factory Act of 1833 prohibited the work of children under the age of nine, while those aged between nine and thirteen were restricted to eight hours, plus two hours of education. The Short Time Committees of the operatives regarded the 1833 act as a major defeat, since children could now be worked in relays so that the hours of spinners remained the same or became even longer. Spinners and employers connived in the violation of the act, continuing to work children longer hours and falsifying their ages. In other words, when the male spinners were not successful in reducing their own hours, they did not take advantage of the legislation to reduce their children's hours. Indeed, in 1835 operatives began campaigning for a twelve-hour day, which would have *increased* the working hours of children and young adults, in order to place an upper limit on their own hours.[33] What was at stake in these struggles for the equalization of hours of men, women and children was the patriarch's control over production — more specifically, the protection of patriarchal apparatuses of production.

We therefore see, first, how operatives sought to defend rather than transform the existing patriarchal factory regime and, second, how that defence was carried into the wider political arena. This relatively unmediated relationship between production politics and state politics was facilitated by the rudimentary form of civil society, in particular the underdeveloped party system which excluded direct representation for the working classes.

3. Lancashire: From Patriarchy to Paternalism

In order to undercut the control exercised by spinners through the patriarchal regime, employers sought to perfect a fully automatic mule.[34] In 1832 Roberts overcame a number of technical problems to produce the first self-actor. Although some employers attempted to introduce direct control through the 'multi-pair' system, in which an overlooker managed six to eight pairs of mules tended by piecers, their attempts were unsuccessful.[35] Spinners, or, as they came to be known, minders of the self-acting mules, did not struggle so much against the new machinery, which brought in its train deskilling and lower wages, as against any attempt to undermine the system of inside contracting whereby they controlled the recruitment, payment and direction of their piecers.[36]

How was it that in England the system of inside contracting did not give way to direct managerial control, to market despotism, as it did in other countries? During the 1830s and 1840s, when the self-actor was first introduced, the minder-piecer system was left intact by virtue of the weakness of capital, divided by competition on one side and the strength of the spinners' organization on the other.[37] It was also in management's interest to maintain a patriarchal regime in order to minimize risks and maximize supervisory discipline, particularly as the self-actor was far from a perfected machine and was introduced only gradually. In 1842 minders and spinners consolidated themselves into the Association of Operative Spinners, Twiners and Self-Acting Minders. Although it lasted only a few years, this association led the way to subsequent powerful unionism and the successful defence of the privileged status of spinners and minders through restriction of the supply of labour.[38] In most Lancashire cotton towns, following the bitter confrontation during the Preston strike of 1853, the consolidation of wage lists laid the foundation of a relatively stable class compromise, distinguishing this new unionism from the radical movements which had sought to extend direct control over production.[39] This closed unionism of the spinners and minders was very different from the earlier open unionism of the power-loom weavers, who had fought for amelioration not on exclusivist but on inclusivist principles, through collective bargaining, strikes and legislation. It was the entrenchment of restrictive closed unionism that managed to stifle the growth of open unionism until it burst forth in the 1890s.[40]

The industrial unionism that emerged in the mill towns of Lancashire after the mid-century, dominated by the sectionalism of the spinners and minders, was part and parcel of a new paternalistic production politics. 'A conciliatory attitude professing the identification of the interests of employer and operative, was the mark of all cotton trade unionism in these years.'[41] The bedrock of the new production politics, according to Joyce, was the completion of the real subordination of labour to capital in virtually all the major processes of the cotton industry. The elevation of the minders of the self-acting mule to 'craft' status was not based on technical skills, and the retention of the system of inside contracting should not obscure the degree to which they had relinquished control over production, if not over their piecers and their recruitment. Cohen offers a complementary perspective in which the minder's real subordination in the factory labour process was compensated by a shift in his primary responsibility from that of an operative to that of a supervisor.[42] This elevation to a position of authority contributed to the minders' conciliatory attitude toward employers.

Centralization and concentration of the Lancashire cotton industry produced a number of large employers who had weathered the storms of earlier competition and crises and gained some control over anarchic markets.[43] Moreover, the prosperity of the third quarter of the nineteenth century permitted certain guarantees of material well-being for the operatives. In many cotton towns the masters had been established for many years and now became a symbol of their community. Their authority and influence permeated not only public life but also the day-to-day existence of their hands beyond as well as within the factory. Although factory owners rarely controlled more than a minority of operative housing, they exercised their influence by constructing a communal leisure life around the factory through the erection of swimming baths, day schools, Sunday schools, canteens, gymnasia, libraries and, above all, churches. There were local sports events, trips to the countryside and workers' dinners at the master's residence. There were public ceremonies and holidays to mark marriage, birth and death in the master's family as well as to celebrate his political victories.[44] In this way employees came to identify with the fortunes and interests of their employer. What industrial conflict there was, particularly strikes, had a ritual, pacific quality.[45]

The emerging paternalism was rooted in workers' dependence on a specific employer. This was reinforced by the employment of more than one member of the family in the same mill. According to Joyce, the family became a potent instrument of incorporation and deference in many of the mill communities.[46] Rather than exhibiting a linear differentiation, as claimed by Smelser, the family was now *reconstituted* within the context of paternalism. Even in power-loom weaving, which had long been the preserve of women operatives, a new patriarchy was organized and harnessed to a wider paternalism. 'Though operative employment of children in weaving existed before the 1840s it seems to have been limited in extent. The convergence of work and home roles was crucially facilitated by technological improvements, which meant that the number of looms that could be worked by the single operative increased in the 1840s. It was in that decade that the use of weavers' assistants, paid directly by the weaver as the piecer was by the spinner, increased enormously to meet the increased work load.'[47]

The family buttressed an overweening paternalism which reconstructed the mill community under the unitary authority of management, extending both rights and obligations to the hands. Contrasting paternalistic styles developed according to whether the master was Whig or Tory, Anglican or Non-Conformist.[48] In return for 'welfare' provisions, the hands were expected to render avid allegiance to the master's church and party. Finally, the rise of paternalism was accompanied by a new entrepreneurial ideology which replaced employers' earlier denial of responsibility for the poor with their leadership of a moral community shared by master and operative alike.[49]

There were important exceptions to the new paternalism. First, a distinction should be drawn between small and large employers. The former, being less able to afford the 'neo-feudal' paternalism of the local 'baron', tended to establish more arbitrary and personalistic factory regimes. In Oldham, the heartland of the limited company, we find both smaller mills and the absence of employer identification with the community. Paternalism never developed there as it did in Blackburn, Ashton, Preston and Bolton. In Burnley, a town of new cotton wealth, class domination was not softened by the legacy of a common historical identity binding employers and employees. In the big cities such as Manchester and Liverpool it was not possible to carve out a community insulated from the world outside. In the last instance paternalism always rested on labour's real subordination to capital in the labour process, so that in Yorkshire, where mechanization had proceeded more slowly and mills were smaller, paternalism was weaker and independent labour movements were correspondingly stronger.[50]

We can now summarize the importance of the transformation of the factory apparatuses for the rise and fall of working-class militancy among cotton operatives in Lancashire. Under the patriarchal regime the family secured considerable autonomy from employers, whereas under the paternalistic regime the family was shaped, regulated and subjected to close surveillance by employers. From government by the family we move to government through the family. Community also lost its autonomy, so that from a bastion of resistance it became a vehicle of domination. Under the patriarchal regime struggles burgeoned from the workplace into the wider political arena, whereas the paternalistic regime contained and regulated struggles within narrow limits. The militant defence of patriarchal production apparatuses was superseded by a distinctive working-class passivity in the Lancashire cotton areas in the second half of the nineteenth century. To be sure, other factors, such as the nature of the economic crisis facing the cotton industry and the form of state politics,[51] also contributed to the changing character of working-class struggles. But changes in the form of factory regime are sufficient to explain the essential shifts in the interests, capacities and, as a result, struggles of the leading sector of the labour force — the spinners.

4. New England: From Paternalism to Market Despotism

We have seen that market despotism was absent from precisely the process of production where Marx anticipated that its conditions would be most readily realized. In the transition from the throstle to the mule we found a correspondence between changes in the labour process (from real to formal subsumption of labour) and changes in factory regime (from company state to patriarchal despotism). The second transition, to the self-acting mule, highlighted the influence of market forces in shaping factory apparatuses. Thus, the change from formal to real subsumption of labour was accompanied by the concentration and centralization of capital, so that instead of market despotism we find a paternalistic regime replacing patriarchal despotism. The remainder of this chapter will try to demonstrate that, even together, the labour process and market factors do not wholly determine the form of factory regime; we must also consider the character of proletarianization and state intervention.

The combined and uneven character of capitalist development — that is, the timing of industrialization in relation to the history of world capitalism and the combination of the capitalist mode of production with pre-existing modes — sets the stage for the development of different factory regimes. We can see this already by crossing the Atlantic. Borrowing technology from England, the United States cotton industry skipped many of the drawn-out stages from the pre-industrial putting-out system and began its career with the adoption of Arkwright's water frame. Throstle spinning enjoyed a dominance in the United States that it never achieved in England: by 1811 the English industry already had twelve mule spindles for every throstle spindle, while in the United States mule and throstle spindles were approximately equal in number. The reasons for the difference have to do with England's position as an exporter of fine cotton cloth, which the throstle could not produce; the use in England of cheaper cotton, which required more sophisticated technology; the availability in England of skilled artisans who could operate the mule; and the mule's greater efficiency in the context of factory costs in England.[52] Moreover, it was only two decades after the common mule had been introduced into New England that it was replaced by the self-actor. The same transition took over forty years in England.[53] Boston capitalists and their mill agents could therefore adopt machinery developed abroad without facing the resistance encountered in Lancashire, rooted in entrenched legacies of past forms of work organization and production politics.[54]

The impetus to mechanization came from the conditions set by the surrounding economy. The New England factory system developed in symbiosis with a viable small-commodity production and subsistence farming, so that throughout the region skilled labour was scarce and expensive. This prompted the introduction of machinery that would be less reliant on skilled workers than in England, where skilled labour was more abundant,[55] and where the welding of pre-industrial and extra-industrial resources into collective organization presented a powerful obstacle to mechanization. In New England collective organization was both less urgent and more difficult, as workers could express their dissatisfaction by quitting. This in turn further encouraged deskilling, to reduce learning time.[56] In short, it was both more feasible and more profitable for New England mill owners to assume direct control over the organization of work.[57]

How they did this depended on the supply of capital and of *unskilled* labour. In southern New England and states to the south, what is known as the Rhode Island system emerged. There mill owners facing capital shortage managed to recruit the labour of poor farm families. This system was nearer the English pattern of fierce competition among small-scale firms, well suited to the production of a variety of fine and coarse cloths. Although the Rhode Island system began with a patriarchal regime, this soon dissolved into market despotism, with overlookers directing piecers.[58] In northern New England, however, the distinctive Waltham system developed to supply the power loom and a mass market for coarse but durable fabrics. Here capital abundance encouraged firms to expand and introduce economies of scale.[59] Rather than employ family labour, mill owners drew out single female operatives from the surrounding region, and a very different transition in factory regimes took place: from paternalism to market despotism. This Waltham system calls for close examination, because it underlines the influence of different patterns of proletarianization on the political apparatuses of production. The account will draw on Thomas Dublin's study of the Lowell mills,[60] which set the pattern for the region.

Financed by a small group of Boston capitalists, the Lowell mills opened their doors in the 1820s. They turned to the daughters of New England farmers for their labour. Wage labour and prospects of a new independence induced single women to leave their homesteads before marrying. Certainly their families did not require the extra income, and the women themselves decided how to dispose of their earnings. They lived in subsidized company boarding houses under the strict supervision of matrons responsible to mill management. The boarding houses tied workers to the mill and subjected them to 'moral policing'. Within the mills there was considerable opportunity for arbitrary tyranny to be exercised by male overseers. The employer's power of dismissal was absolute; if a woman left of her own accord, she was blacklisted and excluded from all the mills in the area.[61]

In the 1840s the Lowell mills began to lose their monopoly of the most advanced technology. Increased demand for cloth and competition from other firms led to falling prices. On the shopfloor the women experienced speed-ups and stretch-outs along with rate cutting. The labour process itself underwent changes as the self-acting mule replaced the throstle. According to one estimate, output per worker increased by almost forty-nine per cent between 1836 and 1850, while daily wages increased by only four per cent.[62] As conditions in the mills deteriorated, the 'freeborn' daughters left and management recruited its labour force from among the influx of immigrants, particularly Irish but also French Canadian, who arrived in New England in the late 1840s. There had always been immigrants in Lowell, but they were allowed to join the mills only when the owners, facing stiff competition, required a more tractable labour force. Whereas only 3.7 per cent of those employed at Hamilton Manufacturing Company in 1836 were foreign born, by 1860 the figure was 61.8 percent.[63]

Mill management adopted new strategies consonant with changing technology and the intensification of labour on one side and the changing labour force on the other. Originally, low wages had been based on the maintenance costs of the single female worker. Now they were based on the family labour system, in which children were expected to contribute substantial income. Thus, we find that the proportion of school-age children at Hamilton rose from 2.3 per cent of the labour force in 1836 to 6.5 per cent in 1860. Adult and school-age children together contributed an average of 65 per cent of family earnings in 1860, and among the many female-headed households the figure was 80 per cent.[64]

The transformation of the labour force, in particular its pattern of reproduction, invited the transformation of the factory regime. The single women were controlled through a paternalistic regime, reflecting their independence, which rested on their ability to return to their homesteads. This regime was very different from the Lancashire paternalism, which directly regulated the renewal as well as the maintenance of the labour force, governed through the family rather than without it, and arose in response to the organized strength of cotton workers (in particular the spinners), the declining competition among firms, and the real subsumption of labour to capital. However, the Irish and French Canadians, unlike the Yankee daughters but like the Lancashire operatives, were cut off from any subsistence economy. They were entirely dependent on wage labour for their survival. But unlike their fellow workers in Lancashire, they did not have a powerful collective organization with which to resist untrammelled domination at work. They were not mobilized around a system of inside contracting. Nor had they built up a system of wage lists as a guarantee against wage cutting. On the contrary, they were hired and fired at the whim of the overseer, and piece rates were set unilaterally by mill managers acting in concert. Here indeed we find an example of Marx's market despotism.

The political apparatuses of production also shaped patterns of struggle. The daughters of Yankee farmers built up a solidary community around their boarding houses, buttressed by republican traditions. They challenged wage cuts with strikes and actively participated in the ten-hours movement. When these failed, they left the mills. From the beginning the Irish and French Canadians faced a coercive regime which divided workers from one another. Lacking alternative sources of livelihood and often coming from even worse conditions, they accepted their lot in relative peace.

5. Russia: Migrant Labour and the Company State

Changes in nineteenth-century Lancashire cotton spinning suggested that market factors and the character of labour's subordination to capital in the labour process set limits on the form of apparatuses of production — limits indicated by the transition from the company state to patriarchal and then paternalistic regimes. The comparative case of New England drew attention to a casual factor held constant and therefore unidentified in the Lancashire studies: the effect of only partial separation of workers from the means of subsistence, reflected in the transition from paternalistic regime to market despotism. Similarly, the Russian factory regimes will highlight a factor which, because it was uniform, the studies of both Lancashire and New England took for granted: namely, the intervention of the state. Whereas in both Lancashire and New England the state intervened only 'externally', to uphold the self-regulation of capital accumulation, we shall see that in Russia the state not only regulated the reproduction of labour power but actually constituted the factory apparatuses. But first we must examine the impact of the labour process on factory regimes in Russia.

In Russia, to an even greater extent than in the United States, late development had the consequence of reorganizing stages of industrialization.[65] The cotton industry came particularly late to Russia, expanding most rapidly in the first half of the nineteenth century. Calico printing of imported cloth was the first process to take root, followed by the weaving of cheap imported yarn; last to arrive was spinning. Unlike the state enterprises in woollen and iron production which deployed serf labour, the cotton industry, developing under foreign sponsorship, hired wage labourers from the beginning, although in relation to the land these labourers remained serfs. Weaving began in large factories but moved into cottages as soon as workers had mastered the handloom. The putting-out system developed out of, and at the expense of, the factory so long as technology was relatively simple.[66] With the power loom, weaving re-entered the factory, but only slowly. Cotton spinning, on the other hand, only really began in the 1840s, when England lifted its prohibition on the export of the self-acting mule. Thus, spinning was factory-based from the beginning and never went through the putting-out phase.

The rhythm of late development also shaped the relative standing of occupations within the textile industry: 'The weaver's trade was considered to be a more skilled, prestigious, and (more problematic) highly paid profession than spinning.'[67] The Russian government even referred to weavers as a labour aristocracy, but Zelnik provides the necessary caution: 'Of course the Kränholm weavers never functioned as independent artisans, and the discretion content of their work was minimal, limited almost entirely to questions of pace. But combined with the difficulty of gaining access to their ranks and their higher level of education . . . the small degree of autonomy that the weavers could enjoy in the early years of the factory's existence elevated them in the eyes of their fellow-workers'.[68]

Although still weak, the artisan traditions were stronger in weaving than in spinning, and contributed to the relative standing of the two occupations in Russia. This hierarchy was the reverse of that found in England, where factory spinning emerged from an artisanal past and retained its craft status despite deskilling, while the greater discontinuity between handloom and power-loom removed the artisanal legacy and craft status of the English weaving operative. Whereas in England spinning continued to be dominated by men and weaving by women, by the end of the nineteenth century the opposite gender division of labour prevailed in Russia. [69]

Although differences in production apparatuses can in part explain the differential involvement of weavers and spinners in collective protest, their common situation is more striking. The adoption of advanced techniques, often under English or German management, established the real subsumption of labour to capital for both and the basis of a common despotic order. The character of that despotic regime was shaped by two forms of state intervention: the orchestration of the flow of labour between capitalist industry and feudal or peasant economies, and the direct constitution of a company state by the central state. We shall deal with each in turn.

Emancipation left the majority of peasants materially worse off than before. Not only did they have to pay heavy redemption payments for their allotments but, for the most part, these were inadequate to yield even a bare subsistence. [70] Overpopulation, poverty and tax arrears mounted during the last four decades of the nineteenth century, so that villagers were increasingly compelled to supplement subsistence production with independent, non-agricultural domestic production or by hiring-out their labour to industrial employers or former landlords. The emancipation legislation compounded the strangulation of the peasantry by continuing to make it extremely difficult to leave the village permanently for the city.

To achieve only limited urbanization, the state shored up the village commune (*obshchina*), extending its powers and responsibilities. It was responsible for the collection of state taxes and the annual redemption payments. The village council (*mir*) would sometimes impose forced labour on those in the community who did not discharge their financial obligations. It was impossible to sell one's land unless all tax arrears and over half the principle debt on the state redemption loan had been paid up. As if that were not enough, individuals could not permanently leave the village without the consent of the head of the household, and where the *mir* had powers to redistribute land in accordance with available family labour, parents were unwilling to release their children for fear of losing land. These 'repartitional communes' included the greater part of the peasant population and of the allotment area of the country.[71] The state also empowered the *mir* to control the issuing of internal passports, essential for any movement outside the village. The *mir* decided not only who should receive passports but also for how long, from six months to three years. A peasant found outside his or her village without a valid passport faced immediate deportation 'home'. As was understood at the time of the reform, 'the preservation of the *obshchina* meant substituting the bondage to the *mir* for the bondage to the *pomeshchik.'*[72]

The passport system was only one aspect of the commune's long reach into the city. Like migrants to other urban settings, Russian peasants were often introduced to the city through kin, and their lives were circumscribed by village or regional networks and associations — *zemliaki* — which offered security, acted as recruiting agencies for jobs, and above all reinforced ties to the village.[73] However, recent studies suggest that skilled workers and artisans had much weaker ties to rural life than did the unskilled, who were not only newer to the city but also more likely to rely on the village safety-net to make up for low wages and vulnerability to dismissal.[74]

What emerged, therefore, was a system of circulating labour migration in which the bulk of at least the unskilled workers retained a dual allegiance to land and industry, village and town. From the standpoint of capital, migrant labour made it possible to pay low wages that covered only the costs of maintaining single workers while they were employed. The costs of rearing new workers and supporting the old and infirm were borne in the *mir:* subsistence production subsidized capitalist profits. Yet the system of migrant labour was a two-edged sword. Workers' ability to return to their villages gave them a certain independence and posed the problem of retaining their allegiance to the factory. Workers were housed in 'dormitory cubicles' or 'common barracks' to facilitate constant surveillance and military discipline, and they were subjected to an elaborate system of factory police, company stores, piecework, fines, and discretionary renewal of contracts every six or twelve months. However, these could be used as instruments for the coercive extraction of effort only so long as workers could not 'exit'. The state worked hand in hand with the factory regime to regulate labour's mobility through the passport system. Workers could quit before the expiration of their contracts, but only at the risk of losing the passport which allowed them to move around and seek a new employer.[75]

A comparison of Moscow and St Petersburg illuminates the combined influence of the labour process and labour migration on the factory regime. Since the cotton mills began with an advanced technology and the real subsumption of labour, operatives had few resources with which to resist the depredations of the company state. Accordingly, the factory regimes of the cotton mills tended to be more coercive and more isolated from the world around them than were those of the metal fabrication industry, where mechanization was less advanced at the turn of the century. Although the industrial composition of both cities was mixed, the concentration of textiles in Moscow and of metal fabrication in St Petersburg is one factor explaining the predominance of the company state in the former rather than the latter. But another factor is also important: Moscow had a long history of symbiosis with the rural hinterland, so that circulating migration was more common there than in St Petersburg, where industrial development came later, was more abrupt, and drew on workers who were more skilled and from further afield. The looser relationship between community and work and between city and countryside — reflected in higher wages, more skilled workers, and less despotic regimes — contributed to the greater solidity of the St Petersburg protest movements after the turn of the century.

Yet a third factor led to the different factory regimes in the two cities: namely, the direct regulation of production apparatuses by state apparatuses. St Petersburg capitalists were more dependent on the central state (and foreign finance) than were Moscow capitalists, whose independence fostered autonomous company states. Thus St Petersburg capitalists, with their more capital-intensive technology, higher wages and shorter working hours, were keener supporters of factory legislation, hoping to eliminate competition from more labour-intensive firms that employed more women and children, for longer hours and at lower wages. The Moscow capitalists often fell into the latter category, and fought against state regulation of factory regimes.[76]

Throughout the second half of the nineteenth century, state regulation of factory administration was the subject of bitter and continual conflict not only outside but also within the state. Thus the turn of the century brought the climax of protracted struggles between the ministry of finance, which tended to defend the capitalists' 'right' to govern their workplaces without outside interference, and the ministry of the interior, which was commited to regulating factory despotism. The state interspersed repression with occasional concessions, but always increased its intervention. On the one side, strikes, for example, were never a private affair between capital and labour, but a question of public order. They became the occasion for ritual affirmation of the state, whose might would be mercilessly deployed against helpless workers.[77] On the other side, legislation, particularly the 1885 law, did attempt to establish a code of conduct for capital as well as a written contract and paybooks for workers. Factory inspectors were appointed to enforce the law; but since they had neither effective sanctions over employers nor the confidence of workers, they were largely unable to improve conditions.[78] More significantly, the 1886 legislation extended police surveillance of factory towns, bringing factory and state closer together.[79]

When direct repression and factory legislation failed, the state began to impose its own factory apparatuses. After, and partly because of, the textile strikes of 1896 and 1897, the ministry of the interior encouraged the development of what has been facetiously labelled 'police socialism'. State-sponsored factory apparatuses were designed to give workers the opportunity to pursue economic grievances, in the hope that this would divert them from the clutches of the Social Democrats. The most famous of these experiments was the Zubatov societies, named after their originator Sergei Zubatov, appointed chief of the Moscow Okhrana in 1896. But state sponsorship of the Zubatov societies was not without its contradictions, as the secret police found themselves defending their organizations against recalcitrant factory directors.[80] Although Zubatov societies did appear in St Petersburg, there it was the Gapon Assembly that captured most attention and support from workers. Father Gapon, a disciple of Zubatov, was the inspiration and leader of the Assembly of the Russian Factory and Mill Workers, formed in 1903. In order to gain legal recognition the Gapon Assembly was presented as a mutual benefit society, but its organizers intended it to go beyond self-help to demand basic economic and civil rights for workers.[81] From the beginning Gapon saw the assembly as a means of advancing its members' interests, rather than as a tool of state regulation. The Gapon Assembly had struck an uneasy relationship with the government when the dismissal of its members at the Putilov plant precipitated a confrontation with management. The conflict rapidly escalated from the specific grievance to demands for elementary economic and political rights, including an eight-hour day, a minimum wage, freedom of association, and legal protection for labour, which in turn led to the demonstration and massacre of Bloody Sunday and the ignition of the 1905 revolution.[82]

In the decade leading to 1905, production politics and state politics became increasingly interwoven. The Zubatov societies intensified the presence of the state in the factory, while the Gapon Assembly brought production politics into the public sphere. Instead of building confidence in the Czarist regime, the merger of the two forms of politics became a lightning rod for the massive uprising of 1905. Allowing workers to carve out a space for even such limited organizations could only fuel the momentum of struggles.

6. From the Satanic Mills to the Russian Revolution

How can we understand production as the site simultaneously of degradation and elevation, atomization and combination, isolation and association? That is the theoretical paradox with which this chapter began. The solution has been to distinguish the labour process from the political apparatuses of production. Whereas the former could account for domination and fragmentation, the latter could account for resistance and struggle. We have seen not only that the factory regime and labour process had independent effects on the formation of the interests and capacities of workers, but also that these two aspects of production varied independently of each other. In a series of historical and international comparisons we successively isolated four factors shaping factory regimes in the textile industry of early capitalism. They were, in ascending order of generality: market forces, the labour process, the reproduction of labour power, and the state. But how does this help us with our historical anomaly — that the militancy of English workers before 1860 was absorbed and turned in a reformist direction, whereas the Russian workers' struggles of 1905 grew into the revolutionary movement of 1917?

We have distinguished two modes of harnessing the family to accumulation under early capitalism. In the first, broadly English, pattern, the whole family is expropriated from access to the means of subsistence and becomes completely dependent on wage labour. The family wage is spread among a number of wage earners, and production relations are regulated by merging the family regime into the factory regime. In the second, which affected large segments of the Russian labour force, the family is split into two interdependent parts: the maintenance of the wage earner takes place at the site of production, while the renewal processes are organized by the rest of the family in the village. Subsistence production permits low wages, and production relations are regulated through the company state.

The different patterns of proletarianization are linked to different types of struggles. Thus, prior to 1850 in the leading sector of English industry male spinners sought to defend their patriarchal regime against the encroachment of capital. After 1850, in many parts of Lancashire, the partriarchal regime was replaced by a paternalistic regime — that is, government through the family rather than by the family. The new regime effectively contained struggles within the parameters of production. In Russia, however, the company state fostered struggles for its dismemberment, in 1905 by artisans and skilled workers and in 1917 increasingly by skilled and unskilled workers in large enterprises.[83]

The change in the centre of gravity over this period was due to the development of modern industry but also to the relationship between the state and factory regimes. In England the extension of political concessions to the working class during the second half of the nineteenth century — voting rights, trade union recognition, regulation of the working day, the repeal of the Masters and Servants Laws — tended to insulate production politics from state politics. In the same period, instead of extending concessions, the Czarist autocracy intensified repression and so furthered the fusion of state politics and production politics. In 1917, when the absolutist regime faced military and financial disaster and rising disaffection in both villages and towns, the crisis of the state was transmitted directly to the factory. There it established the destruction of the old and the creation of new political apparatuses. Management no longer had the crutch of the official and secret police, so workers could take into their own hands the regulation of production. Unwanted supervisors were carted out in the proverbial wheelbarrow, factory committees were established to oversee management and regulate the distribution of supplies, and workers' militias were formed as the coercive arm of the new factory regime. Not surprisingly, this transformation went furthest where the collapse of the state was felt most intensely: in the large state munitions factories.

At least in the beginning, direct workers' control of production was not inspired by anarcho-syndicalist visions but was often the only way to keep factories open. Although capital was initially prepared to make concessions, the escalation of the revolutionary movement in the middle of 1917 led it to counter with sabotage. Now the factory committees were forced to turn workers' control from a defensive measure into a more radical but still dimly perceived project of self-management. Moreover, as the economic crisis deepened, factory committees saw the necessity of central coordination; the fate of each depended on the fate of all. To the end the factory committees were ardent advocates of central planning. Indeed, in the first few months of the new regime they went further in this direction than Lenin himself, who was still optimistic about the potential of unfettered grassroots initiative.

The character of the factory committees was shaped by what they replaced and by the workers they represented. Unlike the metal-workers of the Clydeside, those of Petrograd were not steeped in conservative and sectional traditions. They were skilled workers without craft traditions. Their opposition to dilution and deskilling, for example, was much weaker than that of their brothers in England, whose organizations had grown up organically with capitalism. [84] Moreover, the coincident appearance of craft and industrial unions after 1905 meant that the sectionalism so stressed by Turner in his analysis of trade union growth in England[85] was much weaker. To be sure, there were divisions between skilled and unskilled, hereditary workers and *chernorabochie,* men and women, old and young. But the primary allegiance of workers — skilled and unskilled alike — was to their factory.[86] Indeed, according to Goodey the factory committee was the most powerful institution in Russia at the end of 1917.[87] Far from being obstacles to revolutionary mobilization, factory committees were its foundation, with unskilled workers continually pushing the more skilled toward more radical solutions. The latter in turn sought to curb and channel the militancy of the newer workers. [88] Recent social history, therefore, amply demonstrates that the Bolshevik Party's success lay in its ability to *respond* to a working-class radicalism that was decisively shaped by the factory regime.

The factory committees prefigured a new variant of the relationship between production politics and state politics: 'The remarkable fact about the Russian Revolution is that for a few months workers' organizations managed to combine democracy with centralization in a way which avoided bureaucracy on the one hand and anarchy on the other.'[89] However, the factory committees were soon subordinated to the state, the party, and particularly the trade unions, for reasons that are still hotly debated. Was it made necessary by the workers' sectionalism and parochialism?[90] Or were the factory committees crushed because they posed a threat to the centralizing imperatives of the Bolshevik Party?[91] Or did the more skilled workers who dominated the factory committees identify their own interests as the assimilation of those organs into a strong central state?[92] Or can we attribute the strangulation of the factory committees, at least in part, to Leninist prejudices which portrayed workers' control as an infantile disorder, which reduced all politics to state politics and presented the new state as the guardian of the proletarian interest?[93] Whatever the explanation for the suppression of the factory committees, the Russian experience suggests that the installation of workplace democracy requires a corresponding transformation of state politics. As Rosa Luxemburg put it, 'With the repression of political life in the land as a whole, life in the Soviets must also become more and more crippled'[94] — a view echoed a few years later in the Soviet Union by Alexandra Kollontai and the Workers' Opposition. But the inverse thesis may also hold — namely, that the successful transformation of the state can proceed only if there is also effective workplace democracy.

7. The Revolution Against 'Capital'

In December 1917, Antonio Gramsci described the Russian revolution as 'the revolution against *Capital*' — the repudiation of the canons of historical materialism, of the laws expounded by Marx that had anticipated the outbreak of socialist revolution in the most advanced rather than the most backward nations. Rather than reject *Capital*, I have attempted to reconcile it with the Bolshevik revolution by distinguishing between the labour process and its political regime. The factory regime shapes the struggles emerging from the point of production, resolving the theoretical paradox in *Capital* between an account of capital's unswerving dominance on the one side and of mounting resistance to that dominance on the other. Taking Marx's own example of the cotton industry, I have shown how its factory regime varies with both time and place according to the nature of the labour process, market forces, the reproduction of labour power, and the form of state. Furthermore, I have shown how the factory regimes that emerged in the most advanced industry in nineteenth-century England and in Russia in the early twentieth century were sufficiently different to explain the historical anomaly of English working-class reformism and the revolutionary spirit of Russian workers. In short, we do not have to abandon the point of production as the decisive arena for the formation of the working class.

But what does this theoretical innovation, the distinction between the labour process and production apparatuses, do for Marxism? First, and most obviously, the importance of political and ideological elements of production calls for at least a reconsideration of the classic distinction between 'base' and 'superstructure'. It is no longer possible to hold that the 'base' is the arena of objectivity, of ineluctable laws, while the 'superstructure' is the arena of subjectivity, of political action that translates inevitability into reality. Base *and* superstructure are both arenas of objectivity *and* subjectivity. Second, if we can no longer talk of laws of production, we must also rethink our conception of the state. Politics can no longer be reduced to state politics. Instead we find, for example, production politics, gender politics (in the family) and consumption politics (in the community). Politics is defined first by its *arena* and only secondly by its *goal* or *function*. The state is still the decisive centre of power which guarantees all other political apparatuses. What is distinctive about state politics is its 'global' character: it is the politics of politics. But this arena conception of politics implies that we cannot study the state apart from its relationship to production politics, gender politics, consumption politics, and so on.

Third, we must revise our understanding of socialism. It is no longer sufficient to concentrate on the transformation of the apparatuses of the state; we cannot avoid the distinct problem of destroying and reconstructing the apparatuses of production. The reconstruction of the state can lead only to a species of state socialism. Collective self-management which invokes collective participation at the level of production as well as at the level of the state requires the transformation of both sets of apparatuses along with their interrelations.

Finally, we no longer burden the working class with the mission of emancipating the whole of humanity. Nor, in despair, do we cry farewell to the working class, abandoning it for any social movement that catches the public eye. Avoiding the fallacies of philosophical imputation and fickle empiricism, we have undertaken a *sociological* analysis of how the sphere of production, in particular the apparatuses of production, determine actual working-class interventions in history.

This leaves open several questions. What are the consequences of the transformation of production and/or state politics for other forms of politics, in particular gender politics? To what extent are capitalist forces of production, more particularly the capitalist labour process, compatible with collective self-management? Does collective self-management require a new technology, a new labour process? Can a system of collective self-management, which involves collective guidance in central as well as production arenas, reproduce itself? Or does it possess an inherent tendency toward bureaucracy or anarchy? Does it tend to collapse into capitalism or state socialism? In short, the concepts of production politics and production apparatuses force us to consider collective self-management as one specific form of socialism. Moreover, it is a socialism which is certainly not inevitable, and which may not even be possible for more than short periods of time. Finally, who will lead the struggle for such a form of socialism? I have left open the precise relationship of the working class, however defined, to socialist projects. The foregoing agenda emerged from a comparative study of the Russian revolution, focusing on the transformation of factory apparatuses, the rise and fall of factory committees, the destruction of the Czarist state, and the subsequent trajectory of the Soviet state. But if the history of the Russian revolution raises these questions, it most certainly does not resolve them.

Notes

1. Three qualifications, one theoretical and two historical, are in order. First, I recognize that Marx, particularly in his later years, speculated on alternative routes to socialism. However, the only one he theorized — even if it was a flawed theorization — rested on the growing contradictions between private ownership of the means of production and socialized forces of production, which meant that the more mature capitalism became the more advanced was its contradiction. G.A. Cohen has recently clarified the premises and arguments of this position (in *Karl Marx's Theory of History: A Defence,* Oxford 1978). Second, I do not want to suggest that Russain workers made the revolution or were even its leading force. I am more interested in the fact that they became revolutionary in their deeds and their demands. Third, the contrast should not be overstated: English workers had their revolutionary junctures before 1850 and — among metalworkers, for example — after the First World War. Russian workers, on the other hand, are distinguished for their passivity before 1895 and after 1917. But the problem remains: how is it that English radicalism of the period before 1850 was subsequently absorbed, while the radicalism of Russian workers in 1905 deepened into a revolutionary movement in 1917? This third qualification makes nonsense of any simple essentialist or cultural explanation for the different trajectories of the two labour movements.

2. This is one of the paradoxes highlighted by Jean Cohen, *Class and Civil Society,* Amherst, Massachusetts 1982, especially chapters 2 and 6. Her critique of Marx leads toward a rejection of Marxism rather than its reconstruction.

3. In *The Revolutions of 1848,* pp. 79, 76.

4. *Capital* Volume 1, p. 929.

5. A. Rabinowitch, *The Bolsheviks Came to Power,* NLB,London 1976; R. Service, *The Bolshevik Party in Revolution: A Study in Organizational Change, 1917-1923,* New York 1979; and R.G. Suny, 'Toward a Social History of the October Revolution', *American Historical Review,* Vol. 88, no, 3, 1983, pp. 31-52.

6. W. Lazonick, 'The Subjugation of Labour to Capital: The Rise of the Capitalist System', *The Review of Radical Political Economics,* vol. 10, no. 1, 1978, pp. 1-31.

7. Edward Thompson, *'The Poverty of Theory' and Other Essays,* London 1978, pp. 247-62.

8. Thompson, *The Making of the English Working Class;* W. Sewell, *Work and Revolution in France,* Cambridge 1980; R. Aminzade, *Class, Politics and Early Industrial Capitalism,* Albany, New York 1981; A. Dawley, *Class and Community,* Cambridge, Massachusetts 1976; and H. Gutman, *Work, Culture and Society in Industrializing America,* New York 1977.

9. C. Calhoun, *The Question of Class Struggle,* Chicago 1982, especially chapter 4.

10. Victoria Bonnell, *Roots of Rebellion: Workers' Politics and Organizations in St Petersburg and Moscow, 1900-1914,* Berkeley 1984.

11. E. Shorter and C. Tilly, *Strikes in France 1830-1968,* Cambridge 1974; M.P. Hanagan, *The Logic of Solidarity: Artisans and Industrial Workers in Three French Towns, 1871-1914,* Urbana, Chicago and London 1980; B. Moore, *Injustice: The Social Bases of Obedience and Revolt,* White Plains, New York 1978; J. Foster, *Class Struggle and the*

Industrial Revolution, London 1974; and David Montgomery, *Workers' Control in America.*

12. *Capital* Volume 1, pp. 549-50.

13. Ibid., p. 645

14. Ibid., p. 547.

15. Ibid., p. 899.

16. S. Chapman, *The Lancashire Cotton Industry,* Manchester 1904, p. 53.

17. Ibid., pp. 53-54.

18. Neil Smelser, *Social Change in the Industrial Revolution,* Chicago 1959, p. 185.

19. M. Morris, 'The Recruitment of an Industrial Labour Force in India, with British and American Comparisons', *Comparative Studies in Society and History,* no. 2, 1960, pp. 305-28.

20. Smelser, p. 105

21. S. Pollard, *The Genesis of Modern Management,* Cambridge, Massachusetts 1965, p. 206.

22. Smelser, p. 121.

23. Isaac Cohen has culled the following figures, referring to 1833, from parliamentary papers. Males over eighteen constituted 35 per cent of employees in mule spinning and 10 percent in throstle spinning. Of working children under eighteen, 88 per cent were employed by operatives in mule spinning, whereas only 1 per cent were so employed in throstle spinning. The ratio of overseers to workers was 1 to 84 in mule spinning but as high as 1 to 14 in throstle spinning. 'Industrial Capitalism, Technology and Labour Relations', *Political Power and Social Theory,* no. 5, 1984.

24. The differences between the throstle and the mule parallel those between worsted and woollen production in the West Riding (P. Hudson, 'Proto-Industrialization: The Case of the West Riding Wool Textile Industry in the 18th and Early 19th Centuries', *History Workshop,* no. 12, 1981, pp. 34-61). Early worsted production was organized through a system of putting out. Domestic workers had access to only small and often infertile plots of land and so constituted for all intents and purposes a proletarianized labour force at the mercy of merchants. Here the early mills were run and financed by merchants, and a sizeable component of the labour force was made up of women and children with no connection to domestic production. In the woollen industry, by contrast, artisans themselves controlled production. They had much greater independence not only because they produced a complete product but also because they had access to considerable means of subsistence. Here the early mills were run by small manufacturers who often had been domestic workers themselves. The labour force was also dominated by such proto-industrial workers. As in throstle spinning, in worsted production there was a break between domestic and factory production, whereas in mule spinning and woollen production there was continuity. Although Hudson does not tell us, one would expect corresponding differences in the political apparatuses of production.

25. J. Donzelot, *The Policing of Families,* New York 1979, p. 50.

26. W. Lazonick, 'Industrial Relations and Technical Change: The Case of the Self-Acting Mule', *The Cambridge Journal of Economics,* no. 3, 1979, pp. 236, 247, 252. Marx had a great deal to say about child labour but little to say about the direct sweating of children and women by adult men. Instead he concentrated on the effects of displacement of men by women and children. 'Machinery, by this excessive addition of women and children to the working personnel, at last breaks the resistance which the male workers had continued to oppose to the despotism of capital throughout the period of manufacture' (*Capital* Volume 1, p. 526). Patriarchy in production is destroyed and all that the father can do is sell his wife and children. 'He has become a slave dealer'

(ibid., p. 526). Moreover, the destruction of patriarchy lays the basis for a 'higher form' of the family: 'The capitalist mode of exploitation, by sweeping away the economic foundation which corresponded to parental power, made the use of parental power into its misuse. However terrible and disgusting the dissolution of the old family ties within the capitalist system may appear, large-scale industry, by assigning an important part in socially organized processes of production, outside the sphere of the domestic economy, to women, young persons and children of both sexes, does nevertheless create a new economic foundation for a higher form of family life and of relations between the sexes' (ibid., pp. 620-21). Marx did not consider the possibility that capitalism could mobilize patriarchy in its own interest.

27. Lazonick, 'Industrial Relations and Technical Change'; Pollard, pp. 38-47; and Isaac Cohen, 'Workers' Control in the Cotton Industry: A Comparative Study of British and American Mule Spinning', *Labour History*, forthcoming. It would be worthwhile to look at the differences between small and large shops in cotton-spinning. There is substantial evidence that large manufacturers supported state-enforced factory legislation to undercut competition from smaller sweatshops, but I have not been able to discover much reliable information on corresponding variations in factory regimes, or the effect of such differences on the participation of workers in the factory movement. This is a topic for further research.

28. Smelser, chapter 9; M. Anderson, *Family Structure in Nineteenth-Century Lancashire*, Cambridge 1971, chapter 9; M. Edwards and R. Lloyd-Jones, 'N.J. Smelser and the Cotton Factory Family: A Reassessment', in N.B. Harte and K.G. Ponting, eds., *Textile History and Economic History*, Manchester 1973, pp. 304-19.

29. *The Making of the English Working Class*, pp. 222, 231, 373; G. Stedman-Jones, 'Class Struggle and the Industrial Revolution', *New Left Review*, no. 90, 1975, pp. 35-70. Because Smelser's analysis has been the focus of much controversy and because it intersects with the arguments of this chapter, a brief consideration of his critics is necessary. Building on the earlier essay by Edwards and Lloyd-Jones, Anderson offers the most detailed treatment (in 'Sociological History and the Working-Class Family: Smelser Revisited', *Social History*, no. 3, 1976, pp. 317-34). Anderson's claims are as follows. First, the changes from the family-based farmer-weaver system to family-based employment in the mills (absence of parents, father no longer wholly super-ordinate, father-son relationship shortened), looked at from the point of view of the spinner, were much greater than the changes of the 1820s and 1830s highlighted by Smelser. Second, spinners were in fact not usually drawn from the family-based farmer-weaver system, but were more likely to be former agricultural labourers and farm servants. Here the transition to the factory would have reunited the family, would have led to 'de-differentiation' rather than 'differentiation'. Accordingly, subsequent 'differentiation', to the extent that it occurred, would have been a return to the status quo ante. Third, again following on the work of Edwards and Lloyd-Jones, Anderson argues that even at the height of family-based employment it is unlikely that more than thirty per cent of piecers were co-resident kin of their spinners, so that any trend away from family employment over the period 1825-35 cannot have been as crucial as Smelser claims. Fourth, even if such a differentiation of the family was brought about by technological changes, it is not clear that this would lead *spinners* to struggle for reform, since their children would still be under their supervision, and thus their families would not be threatened with differentiation. Finally, Anderson claims that the struggles of the 1830s can be explained in terms of the attempt to maintain family incomes in the face of declining wages. Spinners wanted to employ their children for longer hours so as to maximize their earnings rather than to defend themselves against structural changes in the family. Kirby and Musson also claim that spinners' strikes in

this period are better understood as resistance to price cutting than as resistance to the 'differentiation' of the family (R.G. Kirby and A.E. Musson, *The Voice of the People: John Doherty 1798-1854*, Manchester 1975, pp. 147-48). These are important criticisms, underlining the fatal flaw in Smelser's analysis: his attempt to develop a *supra-historical* model — structural differentiation leads to protest which is ineffectual. In his concern for generality he fails (or, better, 'refuses') to specify the meaning of 'differentiation' and the particular interests at stake in the family. His model is so general, and therefore so vague, that it can always be shown to be both 'true' and 'false'. However, Anderson's criticisms could be met if Smelser were to delineate the significance of the family as a site of male domination (see Heidi Hartmann, 'Capitalism, Patriarchy, and Job Segregation by Sex', in M. Blaxall and B. Reagan, eds., *Women and the Workplace,* Chicago 1976, pp. 137-70) with a redistributive function (see J. Humphries, 'The Working-Class Family, Women's Liberation, and Class Struggle: The Case of Nineteenth-Century British History', *Review of Radical Political Economics,* vol. 9, no. 3, pp. 25-41). Of these two interests, male domination is the more fundamental, but its reproduction depends on certain material concessions to other members. Thus, Anderson is correct to point to the importance of maintaining the family income, but only as a means to patriarchy. We see that the transition to the factory under either of Anderson's models did not threaten patriarchy; but the increased number of piecers per spinner did pose such a threat by entailing that children would begin to earn more money than their fathers.

30. Smelser, p. 252; H.A. Turner, *Trade Union Growth, Structure and Policy,* London 1962, p. 142.

31. Kirby and Musson, p. 109.

32. See Humphries, op.cit.

33. Smelser, chapter 10; C. Driver, *Tory Radical: The Life of Richard Oastler,* New York 1946. William Reddy's account of the *linen* textile town of Armentières around the turn of the century ('Family and Factory: French Linen Weavers in the Belle Epoque', *Journal of Social History,* no. 8, 1975, pp. 102-12) also underlines the importance of the family as an integral unit of production. There it was the power-loom *weavers* who defended the patriarchal regime when technological changes threatened to *reduce* the number of apprentices. Through repeated strikes between 1899 and 1903, culminating in a general strike, the weavers managed to maintain the number of apprentices so that they could continue to hire members of their own families to assist them. Strikes by weavers effectively mobilized the community, but strikes by *spinners* had little support and petered out soon after they began. The explanation revolves around ties connecting community and work. In weaving, more than one member of the family was usually employed, so that technical changes threatened the family wage, whereas spinning was regarded as subsidiary employment and therefore less central to the family's stability. Reddy further notes that in the French *cotton* industry power looms were easier to run and female labour was employed from the beginning, just as it later displaced men in spinning. As I shall have cause to point out again, the labour process by no means uniquely determines the form of production apparatuses, but the latter are crucial in shaping class struggles. For a general sketch and periodization of French factory regimes (or 'forms of industrial discipline'), analysed as a response to rather than a determinant of struggles, see M. Perrot, 'The Three Ages of Industrial Discipline in Nineteenth-Century France', in J. Merriman, ed., *Consciousness and Class Experience in Nineteenth-Century Europe,* New York 1979, pp. 149-68.

34. H. Catling, *The Spinning Mule,* Newton Abbot 1970, p. 63.

35. Lazonick, 'Industrial Relations and Technical Change', p. 237.

36. Some of the most significant struggles toward the end of the nineteenth century

would be over the system of inside contracting rather than deskilling per se; see Craig Littler, 'Deskilling and Changing Structures of Control', in S. Wood, ed., *The Degradation of Work?* London 1982, pp. 122-45; and D. Clawson, *Bureaucracy and the Labour Process*, New York 1980. The debate between Hobsbawm and Pelling concerning the existence of a labour aristocracy in England revolves around the distinction between production apparatuses (stressed by Hobsbawm) and skill (stressed by Pelling).

37. Lazonick, 'Industrial Relations and Technical Change', p. 245; and Cohen, 'Workers' Control in the Cotton Industry'.

38. Lazonick, 'Industrial Relations and Technical Change', p. 246.

39. There had been numerous struggles over wage lists pre-dating the factory system, but wage lists in that era never achieved the widespread legitimacy, regional applicability and machinery for enforcement that they did in the third quarter of the nineteenth century.

40. Turner, pp. 139-232.

41. P. Joyce, *Work, Society and Politics*, New Brunswick, New Jersey 1980, p. 65.

42. Isaac Cohen, 'Craft Control, Immigrant Labour and Strikes: British Cotton Spinners in Industrial America 1800-1880', unpublished manuscript, 1983, p. 25.

43. G. Schulze-Gaevernitz, *The Cotton Trade in England and on the Continent*, London 1895, pp. 65-85.

44. Joyce, pp. 90-157.

45. Ibid., p. 68.

46. Ibid., pp. 111-16.

47. Ibid., p. 58.

48. Ibid., pp. 201-39.

49. Bendix, *Work and Authority in Industry*, pp. 99-116.

50. Joyce, pp. 76-79, 226. Joyce's rich account of factory politics follows in broad outline the classic work of Schulze-Gaevernitz who, like Marx before him, took the Lancashire cotton industry as capturing the features of the most advanced industries of the late nineteenth century. Unlike Marx, however, he saw centralization, concentration and mechanization leading to the incorporation of the working class. He shows that the more backward areas, such as Yorkshire and his native Germany, spawned a more radical politics than the peaceful and conservative industrial relations of the Lancashire cotton towns.

51. See Foster, *Class Struggle and the Industrial Revolution*.

52. See Cohen, 'Workers' Control in the Cotton Industry', and D.J. Jeremy, *Transatlantic Industrial Revolution: The Diffusion of Textile Technologies between Britain and America, 1790-1830s*, Cambridge, Massachusetts 1981, chapter 10.

53. See Cohen, 'Workers' Control in the Cotton Industry'.

54. The reasons for the more rapid mechanization of U.S. textile production and of U.S. industry generally have been the subject of a stimulating controversy sparked by Habakkuk's argument that labour scarcity led to the introduction of labour-saving machinery (H.J. Habakkuk, *American and British Technology in the Nineteenth Century*, Cambridge 1962). This has been disputed at a theoretical level by Temin, who argued that labour scarcity could not have had such an effect, and that the rate of interest on capital investments was more important (P. Temin, 'Labour Scarcity and the Problem of American Industrial Efficiency in the 1850s', *The Journal of Economic History*, vol. 26, no. 3, 1966, pp. 277-98). At a more empirical level, Earle and Hoffman have tried to unhinge Habakkuk's thesis by showing that there was an abundance of cheap unskilled labour in many parts of the country, even more so than in England (C. Earle and R. Hoffman, 'The Foundation of the Modern Economy: Agriculture and the Costs of

Labour in the United States and England, 1800-1860', *American Historical Review*, no. 85, 1981, pp. 1055-94). According to them, mechanization was the result of two processes: higher returns to capital (because of lower wages) led to higher rates of reinvestment, and the shortage of skilled labour led employers to introduce machinery operated by low-wage semi-skilled labourers. Finally, as Isaac Cohen has insisted, mechanization and direct control were also based on the collective weakness of the working class, skilled and unskilled alike (see 'Industrial Capitalism, Technology and Labour Relations').

55. R. Samuel, 'The Workshop of the World: Steam Power and Hand Technology in Mid-Victorian Britain', *History Workshop*, no. 3, 1977, pp. 6-72.

56. Jeremy, p. 214.

57. Lazonick, 'Production Relations, Labour Productivity, and Choice of Technique: British and U.S. Cotton Spinning', *Journal of Economic History*, no. 41, 1981, pp. 491-516.

58. See A. Wallace, *Rockdale: The Growth of an American Village in the Early Industrial Revolution*, New York 1978, pp. 177-80; Cohen, 'Workers' Control in the Cotton Industry'; C. Ware, *The Early New England Cotton Manufacture*, New York 1931, chapter 8; and Jeremy, pp. 210-12.

59. Jeremy, chapters 10, 11.

60. Thomas Dublin, *Women at Work*, New York 1979.

61. Ware, pp. 265-67; and C. Gersuny, ' "A Devil in Petticoats" and Just Cause: Patterns of Punishment in Two New England Textile Factories', *Business History Review*, no. 50, 1976, pp. 133-52.

62. Dublin, p. 137.

63. Ibid., p. 138.

64. Ibid., pp. 172-74.

65. A. Gerschenkron, *Economic Backwardness in Historical Perspective*, Cambridge, Massachusetts 1966, pp. 119-42.

66. M.I. Tugan-Baranovsky, *The Russian Factory in the Nineteenth Century*, Homewood, Illinois 1970, pp. 171-214.

67. R. Zelnik, 'Kränholm Revisited, 1872: Labour Unrest on the Narva River and the Life of Vasilii Gerasimov', paper presented at the Conference on the Social History of Russian Labour, Berkeley 1982, p. 11.

68. Ibid., p. 12.

69. R.E. Johnson, *Peasant and Proletarian*, New Brunswick, New Jersey 1979, pp. 17, 55. In *Labour and Scarcity in Tsarist Russia* (Stanford 1971, chapter 9) Zelnik offers an interesting account of the 1870 strike by cotton spinners at the modern Nevskii mill in St Petersburg. There we find a rudimentary system of inside contracting. Male spinners were supposed to deduct a fixed wage from their own piece-rate earnings to pay their helpers. The dispute arose from a long tradition in which helpers were paid for two or three holidays at Easter. The money came straight out of the spinners' own earnings. This particular April the spinners decided to buck tradition and to deduct a proportional amount from their helpers' wages for the time missed. However, always suspicious of the spinners' dealings with their assistants, the factory administration took it into its own hands to pay the helpers for their Easter holidays by deducting the whole amount from the spinners' earnings. Finding that their incomes were in any case low that month, the spinners demanded redress. Management refused and the spinners struck. Zelnik does not tell us how typical was this system of inside contracting, and, in a personal note, writes that the cotton industry has not been sufficiently researched for this question to be answered. One wonders whether it was imported with the English management. It is noteworthy that the spinners did not have the autonomy of their

English brothers. The foreman was continually interfering in their relations with their assistants and unilaterally deciding the distribution of tasks — something the English spinners would never have tolerated. Yet the spinners managed to prevent their helpers from entering the workshops during the strike — through force, persuasion, or sympathy? It also seems quite likely from the figures Zelnik cites that the wage differential between the helper and the spinner was less than in England, where, between 1823 and 1900, the self-acting mule-spinners' wages were never less than 221 per cent of their big piecers' (Hobsbawm, *Labouring Men*, p. 292).

70. Gerschenkron, 'Agrarian Policies and Industrialization: Russia 1861-1914', in H.J. Habakkuk and M. Postan, eds., *The Cambridge Economic History of Europe*, Cambridge 1965, vol. 6, part 2, pp. 741-42; T.H. Von Laue, 'Russian Labour between Field and Factory, 1892-1903', *California Slavic Studies*, no. 3, 1964, pp. 34-35.

71. G.T. Robinson, *Rural Russia under the Old Regime*, London and New York 1932, pp. 112-13.

72. Gerschenkron, 'Agrarian Policies and Industrialization', p. 753.

73. Zelnik's analysis of the memoirs of Semen Kanatchikov ('Russian Bebels: An Introduction to the Memoirs of the Russian Workers Semen Kanatchikov and Matvei Fisher, Part I', *The Russian Review*, vol. 35, no. 3, 1976, pp. 249-89) brings out the parental and communal pressures that might be brought to bear on migrant workers who attempted to turn their backs on the village. In 1897, 87 per cent of St Petersburg's textile workers with families maintained their wives and/or children in the countryside (Bonnell, p. 56). An 1899 survey of workers at the Emil Tsindel cotton mill reported that 94 per cent of the workforce of two thousand were peasants and over 90 per cent of male peasants possessed a land allotment (Johnson, p. 40). But one must be very cautious in inferring any continuing commitment to the village, as the average period spent in factory labour by these same workers was 10.4 years, and 56 per cent had fathers who had also been factory workers (D. Koenker, *Moscow Workers and the 1917 Revolution*, Princeton 1981, p. 50). Von Laue refers to another study, according to which '76 per cent of even the poorest peasants who had no land sent money home, 92 per cent of those with an allotment of up to three *desiatins*, only 62 per cent of those holding three to six *desiatins*, but again 91 per cent of those with plots of six *desiatins* and more' ('Russian Peasants in the Factory, 1892-1904', *Journal of Economic History*, vol. 21, no. 1, 1961, p. 65). Presumably such remittances indicate a continuing commitment to the village. Between 1904 and 1906 the government's agrarian policy underwent a volte-face. This was followed by the Stolypin reforms, enacted between 1906 and 1914, which encouraged peasant workers to consolidate their land, sell it, and leave permanently for the city. See Gerschenkron, 'Agrarian Policies and Industrialization', pp. 783-98; and Robinson, pp. 208-42.

74. Bonnell, pp. 52-57; Von Laue, 'Russian Peasants in the Factory', pp. 70-71; and S.A. Smith, *Red Petrograd*, Cambridge 1983, pp. 14-21.

75. It is interesting to compare the company state of the third quarter of the nineteenth century at Kränholm, then one of the biggest cotton mills in the world, with the company state of the copper mines of colonial Zambia before World War II. (See Zelnik, 'Kränholm Revisited'.) In both we find (1) 'colonial despotism', based on nationality in the one case and race in the other; (2) a regime with arbitrary powers to legislate and execute as well as to judge violations; (3) a juridico-police apparatus based on ethnic divisions among the workforce (nationality in the one case, tribal divisions in the other); (4) the election or appointment of worker representatives — elders — supervised by management and rejected and overturned by workers in times of conflict; (5) widespread use of fines and deductions, as well as the holding back of pay until completion of the contract; (6) physical punishment and arbitrary assaults on

workers by supervisors (although the Russian system of corporal punishment, beating and solitary confinement was absent in Zambia); (7) strict regulation of the movement of workers in and out of company premises; and (8) the company store, although this was less extortionate in Zambia. The colonial state and the absolutist state were actively involved in the regulation of the movement of labour but were reluctant to become entangled in industrial disputes unless they threatened law and order.

76. Tugan-Baranovsky, pp. 321-40; and Smith, *Red Petrograd*, p. 74.

77. G.V. Rimlinger, 'The Management of Labour Protest in Tsarist Russia: 1870-1905', *International Review of Social History*, no. 5, 1960, p. 245.

78. Rimlinger, 'Autocracy and the Factory Order in Early Russian Industrialization', *Journal of Economic History*, no. 20, 1960, pp. 82-87.

79. Rimlinger, 'The Management of Labour Protest in Tsarist Russia', pp. 231-37.

80. J. Schneiderman, *Sergei Zubatov and Revolutionary Marxism*, Ithaca 1976, pp. 145-55.

81. W. Sablinsky, *The Road to Bloody Sunday*, Princeton 1976, pp. 101-4.

82. Ibid., pp. 143-271.

83. See Bonnell; L. Engelstein, *Moscow 1905*, Stanford 1983; and Smith, *Red Petrograd*. This interpretation has recently been challenged by Hogan ('Industrial Rationalization and the Roots of Labour Militancy in the St Petersburg Metal-Working Industry, 1901–1914', *Russian Review*, vol. 42, no. 2, 1983, pp. 163–69; and 'Russian Metal Workers and Their Union: The organization, composition, and leadership of the St Petersburg metal workers' union, 1906–1914', paper presented to the American Historical Association, San Francisco, December 1983). She argues that between 1906 and 1914 the membership composition of the St Petersburg metalworkers' union shifted, from workers with varied levels of skill employed in large mixed-production factories toward a more homogeneous group of skilled workers in medium-sized factories facing work rationalization in the form of scientific management and job dilution. Unlike skilled workers in England, for example, the St Petersburg metalworkers did not have the organizational resources to resist rationalization from within the factory. They were therefore driven into the wider political arena to defend their position, shedding their loyalty to the Mensheviks and embracing the Bolsheviks. In other words, the centre of gravity within the leading section of the workers' movement was shifting toward rather than away from the artisans and skilled workers.

However, the evidence for this argument is less than convincing. First, it is not clear how much 'rationalization' was actually implemented and how much was simply policy statement, intentions or managerial ideology. Second, Hogan finds it difficult to give a precise account of when and where rationalization in its different manifestations was introduced. Third, she does not link the outbreak of collective mobilization among the metalworkers to those spheres of production most seriously affected by rationalization. Fourth, her data show that there was *some* continuity in union membership. Although a minority, the old-timers may still have been largely responsible for the new direction of metalworker protest. Finally, by stopping at 1914 Hogan leaves open the relevance of her analysis for the unfolding of the revolution in 1917. Hogan's work nicely complements Haimson's classic papers, which point to the mounting, but unsuccessful, strike wave of 1912-14 as evidence against any simple view that the destabilizing effect of the war was the essential precipitant of revolution (L. Haimson, 'The Problem of Social Stability in Urban Russia 1905–1917 (Part One)', *Slavic Review*, vol. 23, no. 4, 1964, pp. 619-42; and 'The Problem of Social Stability in Urban Russia 1905-1917 (Part Two)', *Slavic Review*, vol. 24, no. 1, 1965, pp. 1-22). Like Haimson, Hogan insists that however important rationalization may have been in propelling metalworkers into the political arena, such processes have to be situated in a much wider context when trying to explain the broader revolutionary momentum of 1917.

84. S.A. Smith, 'Craft Consciousness, Class Consciousness: Petrograd 1917', *History Workshop*, no. 11, 1981, pp. 42-45.

85. Turner, part 4.

86. Smith, 'Craft Consciousness, Class Consciousness'; but see also W. Rosenberg, 'Workers and Workers' Control in the Russian Revolution', *History Workshop*, no. 5, 1978, pp. 89-97.

87. C. Goodey, 'Factory Committees and the Dictatorship of the Proletariat (1918)', *Critique*, no. 3, 1974, pp. 27-48.

88. See Koenker, pp. 317-28; and Smith, *Red Petrograd*, chapter 8.

89. Smith, 'Craft Consciousness, Class Consciousness', p. 40.

90. Rosenberg, op. cit.

91. J. Keep, *The Russian Revolution*, New York 1976; O. Anweiler, *The Soviets: The Russian Workers, Peasants and Soldiers Councils, 1905-1921*, New York 1974; and M. Brinton, 'Factory Committees and the Dictatorship of the Proletariat', *Critique*, no. 4, 1975, pp. 78-86.

92. Goodey, op.cit.

93. C. Sirianni, *Workers' Control and Socialist Democracy: The Soviet Experience*, NLB, London 1983.

94. Rosa Luxemburg, *Rosa Luxemburg Speaks*, New York 1970, p. 319.

3
The Changing Face of Factory Regimes under Advanced Capitalism

This chapter has two targets and one arrow. The first target is the under-politicization of production: theories of production that ignore its political moments as well as its determination by the state. The second target is the over-politicization of the state: theories of the state that stress its autonomy, dislocating it from its economic foundations. The arrow is the notion of a politics of production which aims to undo the compartmentalization of production and politics by linking the organization of work to the state. The view elaborated here, as in the preceding chapter, is that the process of production contains political and ideological elements as well as a purely economic moment. That is, the process of production is not confined to the *labour process* — to the social relations into which men and women enter as they transform raw materials into useful products with instruments of production. It also includes *political apparatuses* which reproduce those relations of the labour process through the regulation of struggles. I call these struggles the *politics of production* or simply *production politics*.[1]

Although organization theory has recently begun to pay attention to micropolitics,[2] there has been a failure to theorize, first, the difference between the politics of production and the political apparatuses of production that shape that politics; second, how both are limited by the labour process on one side and market forces on the other; and third, how both politics and apparatuses at the level of production differ from and relate to state politics and state apparatuses.[3] The purpose of this chapter is to specify the form of politics at the levels of production and the state, and to examine their interrelationship through a comparison of an English and an American factory. The first part of the chapter develops the concept of production politics and the associated political apparatuses of production in the context of the dynamics of capitalism and its labour process. The second part uses the two case studies to highlight national variation in the form of production politics. The third part explains those variations in terms of the relationship between apparatuses of production and apparatuses of the state — a relationship decisively determined by the combined and uneven development of the capital–labour relationship. The final part considers the emergence of new forms of production politics in the latest phase of capitalist development.

1. From Despotic to Hegemonic Regimes

The Marxist tradition offers the most sustained attempt to understand the development of production within a systematic analysis of the dynamics and tendencies of capitalism, as well as the conditions of its reproduction. Production is at the core of both the perpetuation and the demise of capitalism. The act of production is simultaneously an act of reproduction. At the same time that they produce useful things, workers produce the basis of their own existence and that of capital. The exchange value added through cooperative labour is divided between the wage equivalent, which becomes the means of the reproduction of labour power, and surplus value, the source of profit which makes it possible for the capitalist to exist as such and thus to employ the labourer.

How is it that *labour power*, the capacity to work, is translated into sufficient *labour*, application of effort, so as to provide both wages and profit? Marx answers, through coercion. In his analysis, the extraction of effort occurs through a despotic regime of production politics.[4] Although Marx never conceptualizes the idea, he in fact describes a particular type of factory regime which I call market despotism. Here despotic regulation of the labour process is constituted by the economic whip of the market. Workers' dependence on cash earnings is inscribed in their subordination to the factory Lycurgus.

Marx does not recognize political apparatuses of production as analytically distinct from the labour process because he sees market despotism as the only mode of labour process regulation compatible with modern industry and the pressure for profits. In fact, as we have seen in Chapter Two, market despotism is a relatively rare form of factory regime whose existence is dependent on three historically specific conditions. First, workers have no means of livelihood other than the sale of their labour power for a wage. Second, the labour process is subject to fragmentation and mechanization, so that skill and specialized knowledge can no longer be a basis of power. The systematic separation of mental and manual labour and the reduction of workers to appendages of machines strip workers of the capacity to resist arbitrary coercion. Third, impelled by competition, capitalists continually transform production through the extension of the working day, intensification of work and the introduction of new machinery. Anarchy in the market leads to despotism in the factory.

If history has more or less upheld Marx's anticipation that competitive capitalism could not survive, it has not vindicated the identification of the demise of competitive capitalism with the demise of capitalism per se. What Marx perceived as the embryo of socialism — in particular the socialization of production through concentration, centralization and mechanization — in fact laid the basis for a new type of capitalism, monopoly capitalism. The distinguishing objective of twentieth-century Marxism has been to dissect the politics, economics and culture of this new form of capitalism. Curiously, it is only in the last decade that Marxists have begun to reconsider Marx's analysis of the labour process, in particular its transformation over time.

These studies have generally sought to locate historically the second and third conditions of market despotism: deskilling and perfect competition among firms. As we have seen, in *Labour and Monopoly Capital* Harry Braverman argues that deskilling really established itself only in the period of monopoly capitalism, when firms were sufficiently powerful to crush the craft workers' resistance. Andrew Friedman's analysis in *Industry and Labour* of changes in the labour process in England counters Braverman's unilinear degradation of work by underlining the importance of resistance in shaping two managerial strategies: direct control and responsible autonomy. Direct control corresponds to Braverman's process of deskilling, whereas responsible autonomy attaches workers to capital's interests by allowing them limited job control, a limited unity of conception and execution. In the early period of capitalism, responsible autonomy was a legacy of the past and took the form of craft control, whereas under monopoly capitalism it is a self-conscious managerial strategy to pre-empt workers' resistance.

In *Contested Terrain*, an even more far-reaching reconstruction of Braverman's analysis, Richard Edwards identifies the emergence of three historically successive forms of control: simple, technical and bureaucratic. In the nineteenth century, he argues, firms were generally small and markets competitive, so that management exercised arbitrary, personalistic domination over workers. With the twentieth-century growth of large-scale industry, simple control gave way to new forms. After a series of unsuccessful experiments, capital sought to regulate work through the drive system and the incorporation of control into technology, epitomized by the assembly line. This mode of control generated its own forms of struggle and, after the Second World War, gave way to bureaucratic regulation, in which rules are used to define and evaluate work tasks and to govern the application of sanctions. Although each period generates its own prototypical form of control, all nevertheless coexist within the contemporary US economy as reflections of various market relations. In a more recent formulation, Gordon, Edwards and Reich[5] have situated the development of the three forms of labour control in three social structures of accumulation corresponding to long swings in the US economy.

While all these accounts add a great deal to our understanding of work organization and its regulation, they are unsatisfactory as periodizations of capitalist production. We know that the period of early capitalism was neither the haven of the craft worker, as Braverman implies, nor confined to simple control, as Edwards maintains. Thus, Craig Littler and Daniel Clawson underline the importance of subcontracting, both inside and outside the firm, as an obstacle to direct control by the employer.[6] Nor can the period of advanced capitalism be reduced to the consolidation of deskilling. New skills are continually created and do not disappear as rapidly as Braverman suggests.[7] Finally, Edwards explicitly recognizes that each successive period contains and actively reproduces forms of control originating in previous periods. All these works point to, but do not actually enunciate, a distinction between the labour process conceived as a particular organization of tasks, and the political apparatuses of production conceived as its mode of regulation.[8] In contrast to Braverman, who ignores the political apparatuses of production, and Edwards, Friedman, Littler and Clawson, who collapse them into the labour process, I treat them as analytically distinct from and causally independent of the labour process. Moreover, these political apparatuses of production provide a basis for the periodization of capitalist production.

While not denying the importance of historically rooting Marx's second and third conditions of market despotism — competition among firms and the expropriation of skill — I want to dwell here on the first condition: workers' dependence on the sale of their labour power. In this connection we must examine two forms of *state* intervention which break the ties binding the reproduction of labour power to productive activity in the workplace.

First, social insurance legislation guarantees the reproduction of labour power at a certain minimal level independent of participation in production. Moreover, such insurance effectively establishes a minimum wage (although this may also be legislatively enforced), constraining the use of payment by results. Piece rates can no longer be arbitrarily cut to extract ever greater effort for the same wage.

Second, the state directly circumscribes the methods of managerial domination which exploit wage dependence. Compulsory trade union recognition, grievance machinery and collective bargaining protect workers from arbitrary firing, fining and wage reductions, and thus further enhance the autonomy of the reproduction of labour power. The repeal of Masters and Servants laws gave labour the right to quit, undermining employers' attempts to tie domestic to factory life.

Although many have pointed to the development of these social and political rights, few have explored their ramifications in the regulation of production. Now management can no longer rely entirely on the economic whip of the market. Nor can it impose an arbitrary despotism. Workers must be *persuaded* to cooperate with management. Their interests must be coordinated with those of capital. The *despotic regimes* of early capitalism, in which coercion prevails over consent, must be replaced with *hegemonic regimes*, in which consent prevails (although never to the exclusion of coercion). Not only is the application of coercion circumscribed and regularized, but the infliction of discipline and punishment itself becomes the object of consent. The *generic* character of the factory regime is therefore determined independently of the form of the labour process and competitive pressures among firms. It is determined by the dependence of the workers' livelihood on wage employment and the tying of the latter to performance in the workplace. State social insurance reduces the first dependence, while labour legislation reduces the second.

While despotic regimes are based on the unity of the reproduction of labour power and the process of production, and hegemonic regimes on a limited but definite separation of the two, the specific character of both types of regime varies with the forms of the labour process, competition among firms, and state intervention. Thus, the form of despotic regime varies among countries with the patterns of proletarianization: where workers retain ties to subsistence existence, various paternalistic regimes with a more or less coercive character emerge to create additional bases of workers' dependence on their employers (see Chapter Two). Hegemonic regimes also differ from country to country according to the extent of state-provided social insurance schemes and the character of state regulation of factory regimes. Furthermore, the factors highlighted by Braverman, Friedman and Edwards — skill, technology, competition among firms, and resistance — all give rise to regime variations within countries. Thus, variations in deskilling and competition among firms created the conditions for very different despotic regimes in nineteenth-century Lancashire cotton mills: the company state, patriarchal despotism, and paternalistic despotism (see Chapter Two). Under advanced capitalism the form of hegemonic regime also varies with the sector of the economy. In the competitive sector we find the balance between consent and coercion tilting further toward the latter than in the monopoly sector, although where workers retain considerable control over the labour process forms of craft administration make their appearance. Notwithstanding the important variations among despotic regimes and among hegemonic regimes, the decisive basis for periodization remains the unity/separation of the reproduction of labour power and capitalist production.

Exceptions to this demarcation further illuminate it. Thus, California agribusiness offers an example of monopoly industry with despotic control. There are two explanations for this anomaly. First, agriculture has been exempt from national labour legislation, so that farm workers are not protected from the arbitrary despotism of managers. Second, as workers are frequently not citizens, and are often illegal immigrants, they are unable to draw any social insurance and must constantly live in fear of apprehension. In effect, California agribusiness has successfully established a relationship to the state reminiscent of early capitalism in order to enforce despotic regimes.[9] Urban enterprise zones — selected areas in which lowered taxes and relaxed protective labour legislation encourage capital to invest — are similar attempts to restore nineteenth-century market despotism. However, they remain exceptional.

As others have argued,[10] attempts to dismantle what exists of the welfare state can achieve only limited success. More significant for the development of factory regimes in the contemporary period is collective labour's vulnerability to capitalism's national and international mobility, leading to a new despotism built on the foundations of the hegemonic regime. That is, workers face the loss of their jobs not as individuals but as a result of threats to the viability of the firm. This enables management to turn the hegemonic regime against workers, relying on its mechanisms of coordinating interests to command consent to sacrifice. Concession bargaining and quality of work-life programmes are two faces of this hegemonic despotism.

The periodization just sketched, from despotic to hegemonic regimes to hegemonic despotism, is rooted in the dynamics of capitalism. In the first period the search for profit led capital to intensify exploitation with the assistance of despotic regimes. This gave rise to crises of underconsumption and resistance from workers, and resolution of these conflicts could be achieved only at the level of collective capital — that is, through state intervention. This took two forms — the constitution of the social wage and the restriction of managerial discretion — which gave rise to the hegemonic regime. The *necessity* of such state intervention is given by the logic of capitalism's development. But the *mechanisms* through which the state comes to do what is 'necessary' vary over time and from country to country. Here we draw on an array of explanations that have figured prominently in recent debates about the nature of the capitalist state: the state as an instrument of an enlightened fraction of the dominant classes, the state as subject to the interests of 'state managers', the state as responsive to struggles both within and outside itself. There is, of course, nothing inevitable or inexorable about these state interventions; nothing guarantees the success or even the activation of the appropriate mechanisms. Thus, although we have theories of the conditions for the reproduction of capitalism in its various phases, and therefore of the corresponding *necessary* state interventions, we have only ad hoc accounts of the *actual*, specific and concrete interventions.

Nevertheless, the form and timing of capitalist development frame the nature of state interventions as well as shaping the factory regime. As will be discussed below, we can begin to locate the rapidity and unevenness of state interventions in the context of capitalism's combined and uneven development at an international level. Moreover, in the contemporary period the logic of capital accumulation on a world scale entails that state intervention is less relevant for the determination of changes and variations in the form of production politics. This is the argument of this chapter's final section. The very success of the hegemonic regime in constraining management and establishing a new consumption norm leads to a crisis of profitability. As a result, management attempts to bypass or undermine the strictures of the hegemonic regime while embracing those of its features which foster worker cooperation.

2. Factory Politics at Jay's and Allied

To highlight both the generic character and the various specific forms of the hegemonic regime, we will compare two workshops with similar labour processes and systems of remuneration situated in similar market contexts but different national conditions. The first company, Jay's, is a Manchester electrical engineering company with divisions overseas. In 1956, Tom Lupton was for six months a participant observer in a department which erected transformers for commercial use. Jay's was part of the monopoly sector of British industry, dominated by such giants as Vicker's. It was a member of an employers' association which barred competition from smaller firms and engaged in price fixing. The other enterprise, Allied, was the engine division of a multinational corporation whose primary sales ventures were in agricultural and construction equipment. For ten months, in 1974-75, I worked in the small parts department of this South Chicago plant as a miscellaneous machine operator. Donald Roy had studied the same plant thirty years earlier; at that time, before it was taken over by Allied, it was a large jobbing shop known as Geer.

The Labour Process

Allied's machine shop was much the same as any other, with its assortment of mills, drills and lathes, each operated by a single worker who depended on the services of a variety of auxiliary workers: set-up men, who might help set up the machines for each new 'job'; crib attendants, who controlled the distribution of fixtures and tools; the forklift 'trucker', who transported stock and unfinished pieces from place to place in large tubs; the time clerk, who would punch operators in on new jobs and out on completed ones; the scheduling man, who was responsible for the distribution of work and the chasing of materials around the department; and the inspectors, who would have to approve the first piece before operators could continue turning out work. Finally, the foreman, who would coordinate and facilitate production where necessary, signing the 'double red cards' which guaranteed a basic 'anticipated piece rate' when operators were prevented from getting ahead by circumstances beyond their control, and negotiate with auxiliary workers on behalf of the operators.

The labour process at Jay's was similar in that workers controlled their own instruments of production and were dependent on the services of auxiliaries. In the section in which Lupton worked, operators used hand tools such as soldering irons, wire-clippers and spanners. There was no mass production sequence: each electrical assembly was completed by an erector, or by two and sometimes even three 'working mates'.[11] There were fewer auxiliary workers than at Allied: the floor controller (scheduling man), the inspector, the charge hand (set-up man), the storekeeper (crib attendant) and the time clerk. There was less intra-section tension and conflict than at Geer and Allied, which sprang from the piece-rate operators' dependence on day-rate auxiliary workers. The basic lateral conflict at Jay's was between sections requiring delivery of the right parts at the right time and in the right quantity. Thus, the erectors at Jay's formed a relatively cohesive group based on antagonism toward and dependence on other sections and departments.

The System of Remuneration

The systems of remuneration were also organized on similar principles in the two shops. Operators at Allied were paid according to a piece-rate system, such that the methods department attached a rate to each job stipulating the number of pieces to be produced per hour — the '100 per cent' bench mark. Operators were expected to perform at 125 per cent of the 'anticipated rate', defined in the contract as production by a 'normal experienced operator working at incentive gait'. Producing at 125 per cent would earn the operator an extra 25 per cent on the *base* earnings established for the particular labour grade. In terms of *total* earnings, producing at 125 per cent brought in about 15 per cent more than did producing at 100 per cent. When operators failed to make out at the 100 per cent level, they nevertheless received earnings corresponding to 100 per cent. An operator's total earnings were thus composed of base earnings; an incentive bonus, based on percentage output; override, a fixed amount for each labour grade; a shift differential; and a cost-of-living allowance.

The weekly wage packet at Jay's was made up of three items. First, there was the hourly rate or guaranteed minimum — either a time rate, for day work, or a piecework rate. Second, there was a bonus, which was itself composed of three elements: a bonus of 45 per cent on the piece rate for time spent waiting for materials or inspection, or wasted on defective equipment; a negotiated percentage bonus for jobs that did not have a rate (known as 'covered jobs', as at Allied); and the piecework bonus itself. The third item of the wage packet was a group productivity bonus based on the entire section's output for the week.

The piecework bonus was derived as follows. Each job was given a rate in terms of 'allowed time'. A job completed in the allowed time obtained a bonus of 27½ per cent of the rate. Rate fixers were supposed to set the allowed times so that the erectors could, with little experience, earn an 80 per cent bonus. Workers were content when they could produce at 190 per cent. Thus, the anticipated rate of 125 per cent at Allied corresponded to the 180 per cent rate at Jay's. In monetary terms, then, the expected earnings from piecework relative to base rates were significantly higher at Jay's than at Allied, where the 140 per cent output was the collectively understood upper limit.

Making Out

The similarity in systems of remuneration and labour process at the two factories gave rise to similar operator strategies. At both Allied and Jay's, piecework was constituted as a game, called 'making out' in both plants, in which operators set themselves certain percentage output targets. Shopfloor activities were dominated by the concerns of making out, and shopfloor culture was couched in the successes and failures of playing the game. It was in these terms that operators evaluated each other. The activities of the rate fixer and the distribution of 'stinkers' (jobs with difficult or 'tight' rates) and 'gravy' (jobs with easy or 'loose' rates) were the subjects of eternal animation and dispute.

The rules of making out were similar in both shops. Workers engaged in the same forms of 'restriction of output'. That is, there was a jointly regulated upper limit on the amount of work to be 'handed in' (Allied — 140 per cent) or 'booked' (Jay's — 190 per cent). Higher percentages invited the rate fixer to cut the rates. Holding back work completed after these ceilings were reached was called 'banking' (Jay's) or 'building a kitty' (Allied). This practice enabled workers to make up for earnings lost on bad jobs by handing in pieces saved from easy ones. However, such 'cross-booking' ('fiddling' at Jay's, 'chiselling' at Allied) was easier and more legitimate at Jay's. Allied had clocks for punching on and off jobs — which made cross-booking more difficult — while there was no such constraint at Jay's. Moreover, cooperation from auxiliary workers in making out and fiddling by pieceworkers was more pronounced at Jay's.

This form of output or 'quota' restriction, in which workers collectively enforce an upper limit on the amount of work to be handed in, affects the second form of restriction. 'Goldbricking' occurs when operators find making the rate for a certain job impossible or not worth the effort. They take it easy, content to earn the guaranteed minimum. Goldbricking was more common at Allied than at Jay's, for two reasons. First, as already stated, it was much easier to cross-book at Jay's, so that a bad performance on a lousy job could often be made up with time saved on easier jobs. Second, the percentages earned on piecework were much higher at Jay's, and the achievement of 100 per cent was virtually automatic. Accordingly, the bimodal pattern in which output levels clustered around the upper and lower limits, observed by Roy at Geer and still discernible at Allied, could not be found at Jay's. These differences suggest that workers at Jay's had more control over the labour process, and therefore more bargaining power with management, than at Allied.

Rate Fixing

In broad outline, there are close resemblances in the patterns of conflict and cooperation as they are played out in the two shops. However, the continual bargaining and renegotiation at Jay's contrast with the broad adhesion to a common set of procedural rules at Allied. This is particularly clear in the relationship between rate fixers and operators. The Allied rate fixer was an 'industrial engineer' who retired to distant offices. Rather than stalking the aisles in pursuit of loose rates, as he had at Geer, he had become more concerned with changes in the organization of work, introducing new machines and computing rates on his pocket calculator. At Jay's, where piecework earnings were a more important element of the wage packet, the rate fixer was still the time-and-motion man with stopwatch in hand. His presence, as at Geer, created a 'spectacle' to which all workers in the section were drawn.

But the air of tyranny that pervaded Geer — the sly attempts of time-study men to clock jobs while they had their backs to the operators — was absent at Jay's. First, unlike at Geer and Allied, operators at Jay's had to agree to new rates before they were introduced. Second, the conflict which brought the rate fixer and the operator into opposition obeyed certain principles of fair play which both observed. The shop steward in particular maintained a constant vigilance to prevent any subterfuge by the rate fixer or hastiness by the operator. On those rare occasions when industrial engineers came down from their offices at Allied, shop stewards were usually far from the scene. They shrugged their shoulders, denying any responsibility for rate busters who would consistently turn in more than 140 per cent.

Bargaining over 'custom and practice'[12] rather than consent to bureaucratically administered rules shaped production politics at Jay's. Thus, jobs without rates became the subject of intense dispute between foreman and worker, whereas at Allied such jobs were automatically paid at the 'anticipated rate' of 125 per cent. In the allocation of work, operators in Jay's transformer section were in a much stronger position to bargain with the foreman than were the operators at Allied. Indeed, this was the basis of much of the factionalism in the section, intensified by the absence of well-defined procedures.

These differences exemplify a more general distinction between the two workshops. At Allied the balance of class forces was inscribed in rules which, though determined in three-year collective agreements between management and union, were essentially stable in form. For the duration of the contract, all parties agreed to abide by the constraints it set on the realization of interests. Strikes broke out when the contract under negotiation was unacceptable to the rank-and-file. At Jay's, in contrast, the balance of class forces was continually re-negotiated on the shop floor, and 'unofficial' short strikes were part and parcel of industrial life. In the one, the political apparatuses of production were severed from the labour process; in the other, the two were almost indistinguishable. The differences between the two patterns can be clearly discerned in the operation of the 'internal labour market'.

The Internal Labour Market

We speak of an internal labour market when the distribution of employees within the firm is administered through a set of rules defined independently of the external labour market. At Allied it worked as follows. When a vacancy occurred in a department, any worker from that department could 'bid' for the job. The bidder with the greatest seniority usually received the job, and his old position became vacant. If no one in the department was interested in the opening, or if management deemed the applicants unqualified, the job would be posted plant-wide. Only if there were still no acceptable bids would someone be hired from outside the plant. Generally, then, new employees entered on those jobs that no one else wanted, usually the speed drills. Similarly, workers facing redundancy could 'bump' others whose jobs they could perform and who had less seniority. An internal labour market presupposes not only some criteria for selecting among bids — in this case a heavy emphasis on seniority — but also some hierarchy of jobs based on basic earnings and looseness of piece rates. Otherwise workers would be in constant motion. Efficiency in the organization of the plant depends on a certain stability of job tenure, particularly where more sophisticated machines require a little more skill.

The internal labour market has a number of important consequences. First, the possessive individualism associated with the external labour market is imported into the factory. The system of bidding and bumping elevates the individual interest at the expense of the collective interest. Grievances related to the job can be resolved by the employee simply bidding on another job. Second, the possibility of bidding off a job gives the worker a certain autonomy vis-à-vis first-line supervision. If a foreman begins to give trouble, an operator can simply bid off the job into another section. The possibility and reality of voluntary transfer deter foremen from exercising arbitrary command, since turnover would lead to a fall in productivity and quality. The internal labour market is therefore much more effective than any human relations programme in producing supervisors sensitive to the personalities of their subordinates. Indeed, the rise of the human relations programme can be seen as a mere rationalization or reflection of the underlying changes in the apparatuses of production since the Second World War.

The third consequence of the internal labour market is the co-ordination of the interests of workers and management. Because seniority dictated the distribution of rewards — not only the best jobs but also vacation pay, supplementary unemployment benefits, medical care and pensions — the longer a person remained at Allied, the more costly it was to move to another firm and the more he or she identified with Allied's interests. From management's standpoint, this not only involved greater commitment to the generation of profit but also reduced uncertainties induced by changes in the external labour market. Thus, voluntary separations were necessarily reduced, particularly among the more senior and therefore more 'skilled' employees. And when layoffs occurred, the system of supplementary unemployment benefits retained hold of the same labour pool for sometimes as long as a year.

At Jay's the distinction between internal and external labour markets was harder to discern. There was no systematic job hierarchy, such a central feature of the organization of work at Allied. All piecework operators in the erecting section, except those undergoing training, were on the same piece or time wage. There was no system of bidding on new jobs and the issue of transfers never seemed to come up. Opposition to management could not be resolved by 'bidding off' the job. Grievances had to be lived with or fought out — or, as a last resort, workers could leave the firm. Thus, in contrast to Allied's organization of rights and obligations in accordance with seniority, a radical egalitarianism pervaded the relations among workers. Factional squabbles within the section frequently arose from the foreman's supposedly discriminatory distribution of work.[13] As others have argued,[14] English workers are acutely aware of differentials in pay and working conditions. Conflict on the shopfloor often arises from attempts by specific groups to maintain their position relative to other groups, rather than from an implacable hostility to management. Technological innovations that upset customary differentials are bitterly resisted by those whose positions are undermined. At Jay's, instead of a pursuit of individual interest through the manipulation of established bureaucratic rules, production politics revolved around notions of social justice and fairness. These differences are reflected more generally in the system of bargaining.

Systems of Bargaining

Formally, the internal labour market at Allied was an administrative device for distributing employees into jobs on the basis of seniority. By promoting individualism and enlarging the arena of worker autonomy within definite limits, it was also a mechanism for the regulation of relations between workers and management. It was similar in its effects to two other apparatuses of production, the grievance machinery and collective bargaining. Here, too, bureaucratic regulations dominated. Union contracts were renegotiated every three years by the local and the management of the engine division. Once the contract was signed, the union became its watchdog. The processing of grievances was regularized into a series of stages which brought in successively higher echelons of management and union. Grievances would always be referred to the contract. Workers would approach the shop steward as a guard rather than an incendiary. The shop steward would pull out the contract and pronounce on its interpretation. The contract was sacrosanct: it circumscribed the terrain of struggle.

Production politics at Jay's followed a very different course. There was no bureaucratic apparatus to confine struggles within definite limits. There the 'collective bargain' was a fluid agreement subject to spontaneous abrogation and continual renegotiation on the shopfloor. 'Custom and practice' provided the terrain of struggle, and diverse principles of legitimation were mobilized to pursue struggles. Rules lacked the stability, authority and specificity they had achieved at Allied. The engineering industry, of which Jay's was a member, did have a regularized machinery for handling grievances, but there was no clear demarcation between disputes over 'rights' and those over 'interests' — that is, between issues pursued as grievances and as part of collective bargaining. The results are clear. Whereas the grievance machinery at Allied dampened collective struggles by constituting workers as individuals with specific rights and obligations, grievances at Jay's were the precipitant of sectional struggles which brought management and workers into continual collision.[15]

We can *begin* to interpret the differences between the two firms in terms of the structure of relations between management and union in the two countries. At Allied (and more generally in the organized sectors of US industry) a single union (in this case, the United Steelworkers of America) had exclusive rights of representation at the level of the plant. It was a union shop, so that after fifty days' probation all employees covered by the contract had to join the union. Collective bargaining took place at plant level, although the issues were usually borrowed from negotiations between the union and the largest corporations, such as the United States Steel Corporation — a system known as pattern bargaining. Rank-and-file had to ratify the agreement struck between management and union, but once signed the collective bargain was legally binding on both sides of the industry.

At Jay's, and more generally in England, formal collective bargaining took place not at the level of the plant but at the national or regional level of the industry, and established only minimal conditions of employment. Shopfloor bargaining was therefore the adjustment of the industry-wide agreement to the local situation — which also explains why the wage system was much more complicated at Jay's than at Allied, despite the latter's graduated job hierarchy.[16] The adjustment to the conditions of the particular firm or workshop explains why it is necessary to amend national and regional agreements, but why are 'collective bargains' not struck first at plant level?

One set of explanations concerns the differences in union organization and representation in the two countries. Until recently, only a few British industries, such as coal mining, had exclusive representation at plant level. At Jay's, for example, two unions, the Electrical Trades Union and the National Union of General and Municipal Workers, competed for the allegiance of workers in the transformer section.[17] In the United States not only is there exclusive representation, guaranteed by a union shop, but disaffiliation of a local from its international is notoriously difficult.[18] Attempts by some Allied workers hostile to the United Steelworkers to change affiliation to the United Auto Workers were effectively smothered by union and management. Furthermore, the exclusive rights of representation, union dues check-off systems, and the greater number of paid officials enjoyed by unions in the United States contribute to a more complacent local. This complacency dovetails well with the union's role as night watchman over the collective agreement.

Not only do different British unions compete for the allegiance of the same workers, but a geographical region rather than the plant forms the basic organizational unit. These factors tend to foster shop-steward militancy, which is further encouraged by the branch's limited financial ability to pay union officials and by the union's need to collect its own dues. Finally, union rivalry and the legacy of a powerful craft unionism in Britain continue to lead to demarcation disputes and struggles to protect wage differentials, thereby threatening collective agreements. In the United States the struggles for union representation in a given plant — jurisdictional disputes — are no longer as important as they were when industrial unionism was in its expansionary phase.

A second set of reasons for the contrasting status of 'collective bargains' in the two countries revolves around the relationship between apparatuses of production and apparatuses of the state. Thus, in England the collective bargain is not legally binding: it is a voluntary agreement of no fixed duration which either side can break. Strikes may be 'unconstitutional' (in violation of the collective agreement) or 'unofficial' (in opposition to union leadership) but only under exceptional circumstances are they illegal. In the United States, on the other hand, collective bargains are legally binding, and no-strike clauses can lead to legal action against a striking union. Unlike its British counterpart, the US trade union is a legal entity subject to legal provisions: it is legally responsible for the actions of its members. The law is one mode through which the state can shape factory politics, one expression of the state regulation of factory regimes.

3. Production Apparatuses and State Apparatuses

We have now dealt with our first target by showing that factory regimes both vary independently of the labour process and affect shopfloor struggles. But how do we explain the differences between the hegemonic regime at Jay's based on fractional bargaining and the one at Allied based on bureaucratic rules? As we have controlled for labour process and market competition, these cannot be the source of the differences. A more promising variable is the form and content of state intervention. Confirmation that some such national variable is at work comes from the industrial relations literature dealing with the post-war period, which suggests that fractional bargaining has been typical of the manufacturing industry in England[19] just as bureaucratic procedures have been typical of the corporate sector of the United States.[20]

What is it about state interventions that creates distinctive apparatuses? The same two interventions that served to differentiate early capitalism from advanced capitalism also serve to distinguish among advanced capitalist societies. The first type of state intervention separates the reproduction of labour power from the process of production by establishing minimal levels of welfare irrespective of work performance. In the United States workers are more dependent on the firm for social benefits (although these may be negligible in the unorganized sectors) than they are in England, where state social insurance is more extensive. The second type of state intervention directly regulates production apparatuses. As we intimated at the end of the last section, in England the state abstains from the regulation of production apparatuses, whereas in the United States the state sets limits on the form of those apparatuses, at least in the corporate sector.

Our two case studies demonstrate the existence of different hegemonic regimes and point to the state as a key explanatory variable, but they present a static view in which, moreover, the relevant contexts appear only indirectly. We must now move away from Allied and Jay's themselves to examine state interventions in their own right — both their form and their origins. We must develop a dynamic perspective, situating the two factories in their respective political and economic contexts through a broader historical and comparative analysis. To do this we must first complete the picture of state interventions by adding two more national configurations of state regulation of factory regimes and state support for the reproduction of labour power. Our third combination is represented by Sweden, where extensive safeguards against unemployment — an active manpower policy and a well-developed welfare system — coexist with substantial regulation of factory regimes. In Japan, our fourth combination, the state offers little by way of social insurance, this being left to the firm, and is only weakly involved in the direct regulation of production apparatuses. The following table sums up the different patterns.

		State Support for the Reproduction of Labour Power	
		HIGH	LOW
Direct State Regulation	HIGH	Sweden	United States
of Factory Regime	LOW	England	Japan

These, of course, represent only broad national patterns. Within each country, there may be wide variations in the relationship of production apparatuses to the state.[21] State interventions give rise to only the generic form of factory regime: its specific forms are also determined by the labour process and market forces.

But what determines the form of state intervention? We must now withdraw our arrow from the first target and point it in the opposite direction, at the second target: theories of the state that explain its interventions in terms of its own structure, divorced from the economic context in which it operates. Nor is it sufficient to recognize the importance of external economic forces by examining their 'presence' in the state, as in corporatist bargaining structures or the struggles of parties, trade unions, employers' associations, and so forth, at the national level. As Leo Panitch has argued, the effects of class forces cannot be reduced to their mode of 'internalization' in state apparatuses.[22] State politics does not hang from the clouds; it rises from the ground, and when the ground trembles, so does it. In short, while production politics may not have a directly observable presence in the state, it nevertheless sets limits on and precipitates interventions by the state. Thus, the strike waves in the United States during the 1930s and in Sweden, France, Italy and England in the late 1960s and early 1970s all led to attempts by the state to reconstruct factory apparatuses.

Accordingly, just as the state sets limits on factory apparatuses, so do they on the form of state interventions. Examined statically, there is no way of giving primacy to one direction of determination over the other. Considered dynamically, however, as I will suggest below, the direction of determination springs from the substratum of relations of production. Capitalism's combined and uneven development — that is, the timing and character of the juxtaposition of advanced forms of capitalism and pre-capitalist societies — shapes the balance of class forces in production, setting limits on subsequent forms of the factory regime and its relationship to the state.

England

We can begin with England and its distinctive pattern of proletarianization. In the early stages of industrialization, workers either were expelled from the rural areas or migrated to the towns of their own accord. By the end of the nineteenth century all new reserves of labour had been exhausted. Although lack of access to means of subsistence weakened workers as individuals, it also impelled them to develop collective organization. In countries which industrialized later, wage labourers often had access to alternative modes of existence, in particular subsistence production and petty-commodity production, which tended to undermine working-class organization.

Britain's second phase of industrialization (1840-95) was dominated by the search for outlets for its accumulated capital, which turned to exports based on the development of heavy industry at home. In addition, Britain's imperial expansion laid the basis of class compromise between labour and capital.[23] As the erosion of the British Empire was gradual, so was the changing balance of class forces. As a result, British labour history offers no parallel to the powerful wave of strikes that swept the United States in the 1930s. Even the general strike of 1926 soon fizzled out and marked a definite weakening of labour through the containment of factory politics.[24]

If the patterns of proletarianization and colonialism provided the impetus and conditions for labour to erect defences against the encroachment of capital, it was the development of capitalist production that provided the means. Located in the pioneer industrial nation, English capital traversed all the stages of development, from handicrafts through manufacture to modern industry. From the earliest beginnings capital and labour advanced together, strengthening each other through struggle. Capital was dependent on the skills of pre-industrial craft workers, as was apparent in the prevalence of systems of subcontracting.[25] Competition among firms weakened capital and increased its dependence on labour. Thus, relative to other countries, English workers were often better organized to resist capital. We can see this in the early development of craft unions, although as Turner has persuasively argued,[26] the sectionalism of craft unions would eventually retard the development of a cohesive labour movement, postponing the development of general unions until late in the nineteenth century.

In the manufacturing sector, in particular engineering industries, the strength of craft unions retarded mechanization and provided the basis of continuing shopfloor control,[27] as we saw at Jay's. Only in the last decade has there been a shift from informal, fragmented workplace bargaining to plant-wide agreements.[28] Particularly in the new industries with automated production, factory regimes more closely approximate the United States pattern (although comparisons with France suggest that this change should not be exaggerated).[29]

In England the transition from despotic to hegemonic regimes has been gradual. Craft traditions led the labour movement to advance its position through the control of production and the labour market rather than through state-imposed regulations. Trade unions and the

Labour Party aimed to keep the state out of production.[30] Employers, concerned to protect their autonomy to bargain directly with labour, were equally mistrustful of state intervention. As the post-war consensus unravelled in the 1960s, Labour and Conservative governments tried to impose incomes policies, but with little success. As the Donovan Commission of 1968 underlined, workplace bargaining outside the control of trade union leadership undermined any centralized wages policy. Therefore, from the late 1960s governments sought to regulate production politics through legislative measures. Most famous of these was the Industrial Relations Act of 1971, which attempted a comprehensive restructuring of production politics by restricting the autonomy of trade unions. For three years the unions mounted a unified assault on the act, until the Conservative government was forced out of office. The new Labour government repealed the law in 1974 and, as part of the 'social contract', a spate of new laws was introduced. The Trade Union and Labour Relations Act of 1974 (amended in 1976), the Employment Protection Act of 1975, the Health and Safety at Work Act of 1974, and the Sex Discrimination and Race Relations Acts of 1976 all protected the rights of employees and trade unions, but within narrower limits. However, these statutory reforms did not of themselves have much impact on production politics.[31] The really determinative forces at this level must be sought in the changing relations of capital and labour and in the broader economic changes of which they formed part. We shall return to this in the last section of this chapter.

The United States

Compared with England, in the United States capital moved through its stages of development more rapidly while proletarianization proceeded more slowly. The development of enclaves of black and immigrant labour combined with mobile white workers to balkanize and atomize the labour force, militating against strong unions. With the notable exception of the IWW, those unions that did form were usually craft unions. During the First World War unions enjoyed a short reprieve from the open-shop drive. Arbitrary employment practices such as blacklisting, imposition of 'yellow dog' contracts, and discrimination against union members were prohibited, and labour was protected from arbitrary layoff through the enforcement of the seniority principle.[32] Employers renewed their offensive against independent unions in the 1920s, and company unions were created in their stead. This was the era of welfare capitalism, when despotic factory regimes were combined with material concessions in the form of social benefits. Company paternalism collapsed with the Depression, however, as unemployment increased and wages and benefits were cut.[33] Massive strike waves assaulted production apparatuses as the source of economic insecurity. Despite rising unemployment, workers were able to exploit the inter-connectedness of the labour process and the interdependence of branches to bring mass production to a standstill. At the same time, the exhaustion of new supplies of non-proletarianized labour limited capital's ability to counter the strikes.[34]

Only an independent initiative from the state in opposition to capital could pacify labour — an eventuality made possible by the fragmentation of the dominant classes in this period. The Norris–La Guardia Act of 1932 and the National Industrial Recovery Act of 1933 inspired union organizing efforts, even though both had uncertain constitutional validity and ineffective enforcement mechanisms. Nevertheless, the newly created National Labour Board pursued its mission with bureaucratic enthusiasm. Denounced by industry and ignored by the Roosevelt administration and the courts, but supported by the American Federation of Labour (AFL) and aided by a series of fortuitous circumstances, Robert Wagner manoeuvred the National Labour Relations Act through Congress in 1935.[35] The National Labour Relations Board (NLRB) set about replacing despotic production politics with new forms of 'industrial government' based on collective bargaining, due process, compromise and independent unions.

In the immediate aftermath, unions developed through the momentum of self-organization, but in the face of a renewed employer offensive in 1937-39, the NLRB helped to defend workers' gains. In 1939 the Board itself came under heavy attack for being too partisan and was forced to moderate its policies. Subsequently, the National War Labour Board (1942-46) guided the development of unions — establishing their security but curtailing their autonomy. Collective bargaining was confined to wages, hours, and a narrow conception of working conditions; grievance machinery defined the unions' role as reactive; and an army of labour experts was created to administer the law.[36] Taft–Hartley was only the culmination of a decade-long process in which the pressure of class forces constrained factory politics within ever narrower limits. Over time the NLRB was moulded to the needs of capital: industrial peace and stability.

Nevertheless, the emergent labour legislation that governed the post-war period still bore the marks of the time in which it was created, reflecting in particular the response to despotic factory regimes and workers' dependence on capricious market forces. On the one hand, social and labour legislation offered, albeit in a limited way, the one thing workers strove for above all else: security. Welfare legislation, particularly unemployment compensation, although slight compared with other countries, meant that labour did not have to put up with arbitrary employment practices. As we saw at Allied, rights attached to seniority and union recognition did offer certain protections within the plant. On the other hand, dismayed with the initial legislation, capital has managed to reshape it to suit its own needs, containing conflict within narrow limits through restrictive collective bargaining and grievance machinery. Internal labour markets may have offered security to labour but, by the same token, they introduced a predictability to the labour market that corporate capital had already achieved in supply and product markets. Even the social legislation which boosted the purchasing power of the working class, reconstituting the consumption norm around the house and the automobile, steered capital out of its crisis of overproduction.[37]

If, in the course of time, corporate capital would stamp its interests on the new labour legislation, small-scale competitive capital could not afford concessions to labour, and unionization in this sector faced greater obstacles. A distinctive dualism developed in which the gains of the corporate sector came at the expense of the competitive sector. In England, where unionization had developed before the consolidation of large corporations and across most sectors of industry, such dualism had been weaker.

In summary, the very success of United States capital in maintaining its dominance over labour through factory despotism simultaneously created crises of overproduction and unleashed massive resistance from labour, demanding state intervention and the installation of a new political order in the factory. The hegemonic regimes which established themselves after the Second World War, such as the one at Allied, undermined labour's strength on the shop-floor and led to its present vulnerability.

Japan

It is difficult to penetrate the mythologies of harmony and integration associated with the Japanese hegemonic regime, but for that very reason the task is all the more necessary. It is easy to miss the coercive face of paternalism.[38] Of our four cases, the Japanese most closely approximates the despotic order of early capitalism in which the state offers little or no social insurance and abstains from the regulation of factory apparatuses. In the aftermath of the Second World War, Japan adopted labour laws similar to those of the United States, but these have not led to the same extensive state regulation of production apparatuses. In the early years of US occupation, trade unions expanded their membership from under a million in 1946 to over 6.5 million in 1949. However, the consequences of the top-down formation of unions through legislative acts were very different from those of the plant-by-plant conquests that shaped production politics in the basic industries of the United States. Where militant enterprise unions did develop, they were often replaced by management-sponsored 'second unions'.[39] Labour legislation has not held back the development of an authoritarian political order within the Japanese enterprise.

The basic organizational unit of the trade union in Japan is the enterprise. Its leadership is often dominated by managerial personnel and provides little resistance to the unilateral direction of work. At best it is a bargaining agency for wage and benefit increases — and even then it is usually a matter of average increases, internal distribution being left largely to management's discretion.[40] In the bargaining itself unions generally accept the parameters defined by management without reference to the rank-and-file.[41] Moreover, the few concessions unionized (permanent) employees may obtain within large enterprises come, at least in part, at the expense of the temporary employees (up to fifty per cent of the total), of which a large proportion are women. There are few avenues for workers to process grievances. They must rely on personal appeals to their immediate supervisor, who is often their union representative as well.[42] Moreover, in the absence of regularized procedures for moving between jobs, such as a bidding system, workers can exercise little autonomy in relation to their supervisors.[43] The result is intense rivalry among workers.[44] Undoubtedly Japanese 'paternalism' has its despotic side.

The unusually low level of state-provided social insurance compounds employees' subordination, making them dependent on the enterprise welfare system for housing, pensions, sickness benefits, and so on. Dore, for example, has calculated that receipts other than direct payment for labour were divided in the ratio of 4 to 1 in favour of enterprise as opposed to state benefits in Japan, whereas in Britain the division was roughly equal.[45] In the corporate sector of the Japanese economy, where the *nenko* system of 'lifetime employment' has been most fully developed, the importance of enterprise benefits is correspondingly greater. Since benefits and wages are linked to length of service, the longer workers remain with a company the more costly it is to move to another, the more they identify with the company's interests, and the greater is their stake in company profits. This dependence on the enterprise, without the countervailing feature of the US system of internal labour markets and grievance machinery, leaves labour with fewer opportunities to carve out arenas of resistance.

One can begin to explain the Japanese system of production politics in terms of the timing of industrialization and the availability of reserves of cheap labour. Late development entailed that the early stages of industry — handicrafts and manufacture — were skipped, with direct entry into modern industry and large-scale enterprises. Recruitment from the rural reserves of labour compounded labour's defencelessness against capital. Japanese labour never developed job rights and job consciousness, so central in the United States, because industry never passed through an intensive phase of scientific management and detailed division of labour resting on careful job specification. The very concept of job is amorphous, and job boundaries are more permeable than in the nations that industrialized earlier. Instead of a system of rights and obligations there developed a more flexible system of work-group relations and job rotation which permits a limited collective initiative, carefully monitored from above.[46] As in the United States, the corporate sector with its welfare regimes has advanced at the expense of the subordinate competitive sector. Dualism is, if anything, more marked in Japan than in the United States by virtue of the weakness of both labour and capital in sectors dependent on large corporations.

Just as welfare capitalism in the United States broke down with the Depression, so the Japanese 'permanent employment system' is also vulnerable to down-turns in the economy. Cutbacks in production can be absorbed by transferring workers or expelling transient workers, but at the expense of increasing the proportion of permanent employees. The more general problem afflicting the *nenko* system, that of an aging labour force, is exacerbated in times of economic contraction, so that older workers are demoted, displaced into peripheral jobs, or encouraged to retire.[47] None of the solutions to these problems is satisfactory, as all would increase the costs of production.

Sweden

Our fourth case, Sweden, is the polar opposite of Japan. Here we find state regulation of production politics combined with one of the most highly developed welfare systems. Underpinning this pattern is the 'Swedish model' of class compromise, developed during the forty-four years of social democratic rule (1932-76) and revolving around the centrally negotiated 'frame agreement' between the employers' federation (SAF), the federation of industrial unions (LO) and the largest white-collar federation (TCO). Sweden is unique among the advanced capitalist countries in that 87 per cent of its paid labour force is unionized. LO organizes 95 per cent of all blue-collar workers, while TCO represents 75 per cent of salaried employees. SAF covers the entire private sector. Both LO and SAF exercise power, including significant economic sanctions, over their member organizations.[48]

The central frame agreement provides the basis for both industry bargaining and plant-level collective bargaining. Two principles inform the central process. The first is an incomes policy which seeks to limit wage increases so as to guarantee Swedish industry's international competitiveness. The second is a 'solidaristic wages policy' which attempts to equalize wage differentials across sectors. Apart from the goal of social equity, the principle of equal pay for equal work irrespective of the employer's ability to pay is designed to encourage technological change and to force uncompetitive enterprises out of business. At the same time, the Swedish welfare system offers compensation for those laid off, and an active manpower policy redistributes workers in accordance with capital's needs. In short, while capital accepts the centralized wages policy, trade unions are expected to cooperate in the pursuit of efficiency.

Swedish central wage agreements are not determinate at the level of the firm, although they are more closely adhered to than in England. Wage drift — local deviation from central stipulations — has accounted for about half of recent increases in actual earnings.[49] Sectors of the labour force in stronger bargaining positions have been able to extract higher wage increases, binding workers more effectively to individual firms. The extensive use of locally negotiated piece rates has facilitated disproportionate increases in actual earnings while basic wages conform more closely to central agreements. Unofficial strikes, although not as frequent as in England, have nevertheless been another major force behind wage drift, indicating the independence of production politics from centrally imposed agreements.[50]

Despite the centralized pattern of wage negotiations, production apparatuses assume a form quite similar to the hegemonic regime at Allied.[51] Hugh Clegg writes:

The work of Swedish and American workplace representatives, however, is determined less by union rules than by the procedure agreements under which they operate. In other countries the substantive collective agreements are tightly drawn to provide standards intended to be strictly followed within the plan. ... Consequently in both countries, but especially in the United States, the first and overriding job of the workplace organization is to supervise the application of standards set by the agreements and to raise 'grievances' where the shop stewards discover any kind of infringement. In both countries the procedure agreements prohibit the use of strikes and other sanctions so long as a grievance is in procedure, and since collective bargaining is binding in law in both countries, such strikes are unlawful. ... Consequently the agreements which give workplace representatives their authority also place limitations on their power.[52]

Although plant-level policing of the collective agreement assumes similar forms in the two countries, there is a lower level of coordination of the interests of labour and capital in Sweden. On the one hand the extensive rewards to seniority are absent, while on the other hand social insurance and the active manpower policy offer workers greater independence from capital.

How are we to explain the distinctive combination of state regulation of production apparatuses and an extensive welfare state? Are Weir and Skocpol correct when they argue that the centralized character of the Swedish state accounts for the development of 'social Keynesianism'?[53] Certainly the form of the state shapes the solutions devised to meet specific economic problems, but this does not imply that the problems themselves are unimportant in determining public policy. Precisely because, for example, the Swedish and American states encountered different balances of class forces inscribed in different factory regimes, their responses to the Depression were bound to be different regardless of their state structure.

Industrialization came late and fast to Sweden. It occurred when labour movements on the continent were already influenced by socialism and linked to social democratic parties. Early craft unions sponsored the Swedish Social Democratic Party in 1889, which was soon active in promoting further unionization. The LO was formed in 1898, and a nationwide strike in 1902, demanding general suffrage, prompted employers to form the SAF. Late industrialization had led to highly concentrated industry dominated by the export-oriented engineering sector.[54] It was relatively easy for employers to form a powerful association. Following a major lockout, the first industry-wide agreement was signed in 1905. And in 1906 came the 'December

Compromise', according to which employers recognized unions and, in return, the LO accepted management's right to hire and fire and to direct work.[55] Again, because of late development and the resulting mechanization of the labour process, craft unions were never strong and were soon subordinated to the industrial unions favoured by the SAF. These retained considerable power on the shopfloor while, in line with the customary strategy of industrial unionism, they pursued their interests through state politics — that is, through public regulation of conditions rather than exclusive controls over work and labour markets.[56]

In 1928 legislation made collective bargaining legally binding, and strikes over issues covered in existing contracts became illegal. When the Depression came, labour was widely organized into industrial unions and supported a relatively strong social democratic party. The major struggles during the Depression would therefore centre not on the reconstruction of factory regimes but on the extension of social insurance. Again we see how the form of factory regime is shaped by capitalism's combined and uneven development, in particular by the concentrated and centralized character of capital resulting from late development and the legacy of weak craft traditions, as well as by capital's relationship to the state.

4. The Rise of a New Despotism?

So far we have argued that the different forms of state intervention are conditioned by class interests and class capacities defined primarily at the level of production. The autonomous dynamic comes from the relations and forces of production which shape both the character of the factory regime and its relationship to the state. We periodized capitalism in terms of the transition from despotic to hegemonic regimes. Thus, we characterized early capitalism not in terms of competition among capitalists, not in terms of deskilling, but in terms of workers' dependence on the class of employers, the binding of the reproduction of labour power to the production process through economic and extra-economic ties. This provided the basis for the autocratic despotism of the overseer or subcontractor.

Despotism was not a viable system from the point of view of either capital or labour. On the one side, workers had no security and therefore sought protection from the tyranny of capital through collective representation within production and social insurance without. An external body, the state, would have to impose these conditions on capital. On the other side, as capital expanded through concentration and centralization, it required the regulation of class relations in accordance with the stabilization of competition and interdependence among firms. At the same time, the success of despotic regimes had so reduced workers' purchasing power that capital faced worsening crises of overproduction — it could not realize the value it produced. Individual capitalists therefore had an interest in boosting the wages of workers employed by all other capitalists, but not by themselves. Again only an external body, the state, could enforce for all capitalists mechanisms for the regulation of conflict and a minimal social wage. In short, both capital and labour had an interest in state interventions that would establish the conditions for a hegemonic production politics; the specific form of those interventions was influenced by the character of the state itself.

However, if the separation of the reproduction of labour power from the production process helped to resolve the crisis of overproduction and to regulate conflict, it also laid the basis for a new crisis of profitability. Thus, in the United States hegemonic regimes established in the leading sectors of industry placed such constraints on accumulation that international competition became a growing threat. First, in some countries, such as Japan, the hegemonic regime gave capital greater room to manoeuvre. Second, in semi-peripheral countries such as South Africa, Brazil and Iran, manufacturing industry did not install hegemonic regimes but relied on a combination of economic and extra-economic means of coercion. Third, in yet other countries with export-processing zones, women workers were subjected to an autocratic despotism fostered by the state.

Advanced capitalist states have responded by carving out arenas in which labour is stripped of the powers embodied in hegemonic regimes. The urban enterprise zone is one such attempt to return restricted areas to the nineteenth century through the withdrawal of labour protection and the abrogation of minimum wage laws, health and safety regulations, and national labour relations legislation. In other countries, such as Italy and, to a lesser extent, the United States, one finds the re-emergence of artisanal workshops and sweated domestic work subcontracted out by large firms.[57] Portes and Walton refer to this phenomenon as the peripheralization of the core.[58] Sassen-Koob describes a more complex picture of peripheralization and recomposition. The exodus of basic manufacturing from some of the largest cities, such as New York, has been followed by the creation of small-scale manufacturing based on low-paid immigrant labour servicing the expanding service industry and the 'gentrified' life styles of its employees.[59]

Peripheralization at the core, although growing, is still a marginal phenomenon, subordinate to the (albeit declining) manufacturing core. In the old manufacturing industries such as auto, steel, rubber and electrical, a changing balance of class forces is giving rise to a new despotism. Two sets of conditions, in particular, are responsible for this new political order in the workplace. First, it is now much easier to move capital from one place to another, as a result of three phenomena: the generation of pools of cheap labour power in both peripheral countries and peripheral regions of advanced capitalist societies; the fragmentation of the labour process, so that different components can be produced and assembled in different places (sometimes at the flick of a switch); and the metamorphoses of the transportation and communications industries.[60] All these changes are connected to the process of capital accumulation on an international scale; a second set of changes is located within the advanced capitalist countries themselves. The rise of hegemonic regimes, tying the interests of workers to the fortunes of their employers, embodying working-class power in factory rather than state apparatuses, and the reinforcement of individualism have left workers defenceless against the recent challenges of capital. Even industrial workers in England, the acme of shopfloor control, find themselves helpless before job loss through rationalization, technological change and, particularly, the intensification of work.[61]

The new despotism is founded on the basis of the hegemonic regime it is replacing. It is in fact a *hegemonic despotism*. The interests of capital and labour continue to be concretely coordinated, but where labour used to be *granted* concessions on the basis of the expansion of profits, it now *makes* concessions on the basis of the relative profitability of one capitalist vis-à-vis another — that is, the opportunity costs of capital. The primary point of reference is no longer the firm's success from one year to the next; instead it is the rate of profit that might be earned elsewhere. At companies losing profits, workers are forced to choose between wage cuts — even zero-pay plans have been introduced — and job loss. The new despotism is not the resurrection of the old; it is not the arbitrary tyranny of the overseer over *individual* workers (although this happens too). The new despotism is the 'rational' tyranny of capital mobility over the *collective* worker. The reproduction of labour power is bound anew to the production process, but, rather than via the individual, the binding occurs at the level of the firm, region or even nation-state. The fear of being fired is replaced by the fear of capital flight, plant closure, transfer of operations, and plant disinvestment.

The pre-existing hegemonic regime established the ground for concession bargaining. Alternatively, management may bypass the hegemonic regime. Recent fads such as Quality of Work Life and Quality Circles signify management's attempt to invade the spaces created by workers under the previous regime and to mobilize consent to increased productivity. There have been concerted attempts to decertify unions and fire workers for union activities. At the same time, states and communities are pitted against one another in their attempts to attract and retain capital. They outbid each other in granting tax shelters and relaxing both labour legislation and welfare provisions.[62]

Labour's response has been conditioned by pre-existing hegemonic regimes and their relationship to the state. Thus, in the United States debates in the labour movement have revolved around whether or not to make concessions, symptomatic of the confinement of production politics to the level of the plant. Occasionally, plant closures have been followed by worker buy-outs, but it is hard to see these as more than attempts to contain the level of community devastation. In England, there were attempts to extend the sphere of production politics from the regulation of the labour process to the regulation of investment, with workers either taking over plants or producing alternative plans.[63] This was a short-lived movement during the last Labour government, which dissolved before the unleashing of market forces when the Conservative Party took office.

More ambitious and potentially more effective strategies aim at state control of the flow of capital, involving a range of measures from plant closure legislation to nationalization and indicative planning. The state's ability to do this varies from country to country. Thus, in both the United States and Britain, but particularly in the former, labour has supported the export of capital as part of the post-war economic expansion. In both countries the state is unaccustomed and ill-equipped to regulate flows of domestic capital. These two hegemonic powers have maintained their dominance through the free movement of financial and industrial capital. In other countries one finds an inverse relation between the constraints imposed by production politics on state politics and the capacity of the state to regulate investment.[64] In Sweden, where the welfare state reflects the constraints of production politics, the state has not had much success in controlling investment, whereas in Japan production politics poses weaker constraints and the state has been more effective in regulating the movement of capital. In Sweden the working class has supported attempts to collectivize the investment process through the establishment of 'wage earner funds' from the taxation of company profits. But in a country so dependent on the export sector such gradual attempts to expropriate capital are bound to meet with powerful resistance, even when the Social Democrats are in office.

Irrespective of state interventions there are signs that in all advanced capitalist societies hegemonic regimes are developing a despotic face. Responses may reflect the different relations between production apparatuses and state apparatuses, but the underlying dynamics, the changing international division of labour and capital mobility, are leading toward a third period: hegemonic despotism. One can anticipate that the working classes will begin to feel their collective impotence and the irreconcilability of their interests with the development of capitalism, understood as an international phenomenon. The forces leading to working-class demobilization may also stimulate a broader recognition that the material interests of the working class can be vouchsafed only beyond capitalism, beyond the anarchy of the market and beyond despotism in production.

Notes

1. Definitions are not innocent. I have defined each politics by its characteristic *arena*, so that state politics involves struggles in the arena of the state, production politics struggles in the arena of the workplace, and gender politics struggles in the family. For others, such as John Stephens, politics is always state politics and what distinguishes one form from another is the *goal* (*The Transition from Capitalism to Socialism*, London 1979, pp. 53-54). Thus, production politics aims to redistribute control over the means of production, consumption politics focuses on the redistribution of the means of consumption, and mobility politics involves struggles to increase social mobility. These differences in the conception of politics are not merely terminological; they reflect alternative understandings of the transition from capitalism to socialism. Whereas Stephens sees the transition as a gradual shift in state politics from consumption and mobility issues to production issues, I see it in terms of the transformation of production politics and state politics through the reconstruction of production apparatuses and state apparatuses. What Stephens regards as the driving force behind the transition to socialism — the 'changing balance of power in civil society', in effect the organization of labour into trade unions — I regard as the consolidation of factory regimes which reproduce the capital–labour relationship more efficiently.

2. Tom Burns, L.E. Karlsson and V. Rus, eds., *Work and Power*, Beverly Hills 1979; Stewart Clegg and David Dunkerley, *Organization, Class and Control*, London 1980; and M. Zey-Ferrell and Michael Aiken, eds., *Complex Organizations: Critical Perspectives*, Glenview, Illinois 1981.

3. A notable exception is the recent work of Paul Edwards, who also tries to link workplace relations and state activities through a comparative study of Britain and the United States. In explaining the differences between the two countries' industrial relations systems, Edwards underlines the critical role of employers ('The Political Economy of Industrial Conflict: Britain and the United States', *Economic and Industrial*

Democracy, vol. 1, 1983, pp. 461-500).

4. *Capital* Volume 1, pp. 549-50.

5. David Gordon, Richard Edwards and Michael Reich, *Segmented Work, Divided Workers*, Cambridge 1982.

6. Littler, *The Development of the Labour Process*; Clawson, *Bureaucracy and the Labour Process*.

7. Erik Olin Wright and Joachim Singlemann, 'Proletarianization in the Changing American Class Structure', in Michael Burawoy and Theda Skocpol, eds., *Marxist Inquiries*, Chicago 1983, pp. 176-209. See also Larry Hirschhorn (*Beyond Mechanization*, Cambridge, Massachusetts 1984), who argues that technological developments in the 'post-industrial' era require a new type of skilled work and a new reunification of conception and execution. Wright and Singlemann argue that while deskilling may be occurring within sectors, there is an overall shift of the labouring population to less proletarianized sectors. Mike Davis, however, offers the bleak prognosis of an increasing polarization of conception and execution ('The Political Economy of Late Imperial America', *New Left Review*, no. 143, 1984, pp. 6-38).

8. A similar conclusion is drawn by Paul Thompson in his comprehensive discussion of contemporary theories of the labour process (*The Nature of Work: An Introduction to Debates on the Labour Process*, London 1983).

9. Robert Thomas, 'Citizenship and Gender in Work Organization: Some Considerations for Theories of the Labour Process', in Burawoy and Skocpol, pp. 86-112; and M. Wells, 'Sharecropping in Capitalist Commodity Production: Historical Anomaly or Political Strategy?' *American Journal of Sociology*, forthcoming.

10. Frances Piven and Richard Cloward, *The New Class War*, New York 1982, and Theda Skocpol and John Ikenberry, 'The Political Formation of the American Welfare State in Historical and Comparative Perspective', unpublished manuscript, 1982.

11. Tom Lupton, *On the Shop Floor*, pp. 104-5.

12. W. Brown, 'A Consideration of "Custom and Practice" ', *British Journal of Industrial Relations*, no. 10, 1972, pp. 42-61.

13. Lupton, pp. 142-63.

14. Richard Hyman and I. Brough, *Social Values and Industrial Relations*, Oxford 1975; I. Maitland, *The Causes of Industrial Disorder*, London 1983.

15. Maitland, op.cit.

16. Lupton, pp. 137-38.

17. Ibid., p. 115.

18. R. Herding, *Job Control and Union Structure*, Rotterdam 1972, pp. 267-70.

19. Richard Hyman, *Industrial Relations: A Marxist Introduction*, London 1975; O. Kahn-Freund, *Labour and the Law*, London 1977; Hugh Clegg, *The Changing System of Industrial Relations in Great Britain*, Oxford 1979; and Maitland, op.cit.

20. G. Strauss, 'The Shifting Power Balance in the Plant', *Industrial Relations*, vol. 1, no. 3, 1962, pp. 65-96; M. Derber, W. Chalmers and M. Edelman, *Plant Union-Management Relations: From Practice to Theory*, Champaign, Illinois 1965; Herding, op.cit. and David Brody, *Workers in Industrial America*, New York 1979, chapter 5.

21. Although the focus here is on differences between societies, the existence of variations within societies cannot be overemphasized. Thus, in the United States the marked difference in factory regimes between sectors is a product not merely of market factors but of different relations to the state defined by Taft–Hartley provisions, exclusion of up to half of the labour force from the NLRB, state right-to-work rules which outlaw union shops, free speech amendments favouring employer interference in organizing campaigns, disenfranchisement of strikers in union elections, and so on.

22. Leo Panitch, 'Trade Unions and the State', *New Left Review*, no. 125, 1981, pp. 21-44.

23. Eric Hobsbawm, *Industry and Empire*, Harmondsworth 1969, chapters 6-8.

24. R. Currie, *Industrial Politics*, Oxford 1979, chapter 4.

25. Littler, *The Development of the Labour Process*, chapter 6.

26. H.A. Turner, *Trade Union Growth, Structure and Policy*, part 4.

27. Hugh Clegg, *The Changing System of Industrial Relations in Great Britain*, chapter 2.

28. W. Brown, ed., *The Changing Contours of British Industrial Relations*, Oxford 1981.

29. Theo Nichols and Huw Beynon, *Living with Capitalism*, London 1977; Duncan Gallie, *In Search of the New Working Class*, Cambridge 1978.

30. Currie, op.cit.

31. Clegg, *The Changing System of Industrial Relations*, chapter 10.

32. H.J. Harris, 'Responsible Unionism and the Road to Taft–Hartley', unpublished manuscript, 1982.

33. Brody, *Workers in Industrial America*, chapter 2.

34. G. Arrighi and B. Silver, 'Labour Movements and Capital Migration: The United States and Western Europe in World Historical Perspective', in Charles Bergquist, ed., *Labour in the Capitalist World-Economy*, Beverly Hills, California 1984.

35. Theda Skocpol, 'Political Response to Capitalist Crisis: Neo-Marxist Theories of the State and the New Deal', *Politics and Society*, no. 10, 1980, pp. 155-202.

36. Harris, op.cit.

37. Aglietta, *A Theory of Capitalist Regulation*.

38. Because few ethnographic studies of work in Japanese factories have been available in English, the translation of Satoshi Kamata's account of his experiences as a seasonal worker at Toyota is particularly welcome (*Japan in the Passing Lane*, New York 1983). Kamata presents a rich and detailed description of the factory regime: the company union is inaccessible and unresponsive to the membership; outside work, life in the dormitories is subject to police-type surveillance; on the shopfloor workers face the arbitrary domination of management, whether in the form of compulsory transfers between jobs, speed-ups, overtime or the company's carefree attitude toward industrial accidents. Regular employees face equally oppressive conditions but have more to lose (in terms of fringe benefits) by quitting than do the seasonal workers. As one of Kamata's co-workers put it, life-time employment becomes a life-time prison sentence. In his introduction, Ronald Dore tries to explain away the coercive features at Toyota in the early 1970s as atypical, but the fact that they exist at all in such a large corporation says a great deal about hegemonic regimes in Japan.

39. J. Halliday, *A Political History of Japanese Capitalism*, New York 1975, chapter 6; I. Kishimoto, 'Labour–Management Relations and the Trade Unions in Postwar Japan (1)', *Kyoto University Economic Review*, no. 38, 1968, pp. 1-35; S. Levine, 'Labour Markets and Collective Bargaining in Japan', in W. Lockwood, ed., *The State and Economic Enterprise in Japan*, Princeton 1965, pp. 651-60; and Robert Cole, *Japanese Blue Collar*, Berkeley and Los Angeles 1971, chapter 7.

40. R. Evans, *The Labour Economics of Japan and the United States*, New York 1971, p. 132.

41. Ronald Dore, *British Factory -- Japanese Factory*, chapters 4, 6; Cole, *Japanese Blue Collar*, chapter 7.

42. Ibid., p. 230.

43. Cole, *Work, Mobility and Participation: A Comparative Study of American and Japanese Industry*, Berkeley and Los Angeles 1979, pp. 111-4.

44. Cole, *Japanese Blue Collar*, chapter 6.

45. Dore, p. 323.

46. Cole, *Work, Mobility and Participation*, chapter 7.

47. Robert Thomas, 'Quality and Quantity? Worker Participation in the United States and Japanese Automobile Industries', unpublished manuscript, 1982.

48. Walter Korpi, *The Working Class in Welfare Capitalism*, London 1978, chapter 8; J. Fulcher, 'Class Conflict in Sweden', *Sociology*, no. 7, 1973, p. 50.

49. Andrew Martin, 'Distributive Conflict, Inflation and Investment: The Swedish Case', paper prepared for the Brookings Project on the Politics and Sociology of Global Inflation, 1980.

50. Fulcher, op.cit.

51. G. Palm, *The Flight from Work*, Cambridge 1977, pp. 9-65; Korpi, chapters 7, 8.

52. Hugh Clegg, *Trade Unionism under Collective Bargaining*, Oxford 1976, p. 61.

53. M. Weir and Theda Skocpol, 'State Structures and Social Keynesianism: Response to the Great Depression in Sweden and the United States', unpublished manuscript, 1983.

54. Geoffery Ingham, *Strikes and Industrial Conflict*, London 1974, pp. 45-8.

55. Korpi, p. 62.

56. Göran Therborn, 'Why Some Classes Are More Successful than Others', *New Left Review*, no. 138, 1983, pp. 52-3.

57. C. Sabel, *Work and Politics*, Cambridge 1982, chapter 5.

58. Alejandro Portes and John Walton, *Labour, Class and the International System*, New York 1981.

59. S. Sassen-Koob, 'Recomposition and Peripheralization at the Core', *Contemporary Marxism*, no. 5, 1982, pp. 88-100.

60. F. Fröbel, J. Heinrichs and O. Kreye, *The New International Division of Labour*, Cambridge 1980.

61. D. Massey and R. Meegan, *The Anatomy of Job Loss*, London 1982.

62. Barry Bluestone and Bennett Harrison, *The Deindustrialization of America*, New York 1982.

63. Ken Coates, ed., *The Right to Useful Work*, Nottingham 1978; H. Wainwright and D. Elliott, *The Lucas Plan: A New Trade Unionism in the Making?* London 1982.

64. J. Pontusson, 'Comparative Political Economy of Advanced Capitalist States: Sweden and France', *Kapitalistate*, No. 10/11, 1983, pp. 43-74.

4
Workers in Workers' States

In Chapter One, I specified the essential character of capitalism through a comparison with feudalism. This comparison has two advantages: first, feudalism was an actually existing social formation; and second, its existence was untainted by the capitalism that followed it. In Chapters Two and Three we undertook a series of comparisons within the framework of capitalism outlined in Chapter One. We now come to a third, often unarticulated, comparison which is always presumed in Marxist expositions of capitalism. Whether it be the capitalist state, the capitalist family, the capitalist city or any other capitalist institution, there is an implicit contrast with a real or imagined socialism which gives the analysis its critical moment and political significance. It is all too easy to shy away from the problems this presents, to bury assumptions in a cavalier 'obviousness' and to retreat into the misleading comparison of the realities of capitalism with some idealized version of socialism obtained through repudiation of all we find repellent about capitalism. Critique becomes sufficient unto itself, a substitute for analysis of the limits of the possible, of what is feasible in the best of all worlds, and of the possibilities within limits, of what is feasible within the parameters of the existing order. [1]

This refusal to address the meaning of socialism is particularly apparent in the study of the labour process. Whatever is taken to be the defining feature of the capitalist labour process is mechanically inverted to yield a productivist vision of socialism. [2] Work becomes the arena of emancipation to the exclusion of all else. Thus, if the capitalist labour process is defined by the separation of conception and execution, then the socialist labour process must be the obverse — the reunification of conception and execution; if the capitalist labour process is defined by deskilling, then socialism must herald the restoration of the craft worker — a romantic resurrection of the past; if the capitalist labour process is defined by hierarchy, then the socialist labour process is defined by the abolition of hierarchy; control by capital gives way to control by workers. And if capitalist technology makes it impossible to realize workers' control, the abolition of hierarchy, or the reunification of conception and execution, then a new technology will be required to inaugurate socialism. In each instance the realities of capitalism are juxtaposed with some utopian construction of socialism obtained through the miraculous abolition of, for example, alienation, atomization, subordination.

All too often there is a systematic failure to examine the technical, political and psychological conditions of such unarticulated utopias, and whether it is at all feasible to combine all that is deemed 'good' or to eliminate all that is 'bad'. In other words, there is an aversion to looking upon socialism as a system, as an organic whole with its own contradictions and its own distinctive combination of positive and negative. This aversion is powerfully present in Marx and Engel's contempt for the study of utopias, which has had at least two unfortunate consequences. First, apologists for the Soviet Union can claim it as *the* incarnation of socialism or even communism. Second, critics of the Soviet Union can dismiss it for not living up to some ideal. It becomes instead a perversion of capitalism (state capitalism, state monopoly capitalism, bureaucratic state capitalism) or'a corruption of socialism (degenerated workers' state). Failing to confront the nature of the socialist project, theorists withdraw into the explanation of deviations from some putative ideal type. We hear a great deal about historical legacies, conjunctures, personality cults, leadership errors and so on, but very little about the actual nature of actually existing socialism. Whether Soviet-type societies harbour the possibility of dreams or the realization of nightmares, their history and their future cannot be ignored. Moreover, the assessment of capitalism is fundamentally incomplete without an assessment of what Nuti has called socialism on earth.

What then shall we mean by socialism? Two distinct periodizations of history can be found in Marx's writings. At certain places, the fundamental break is between capitalist and pre-capitalist societies. Here capitalism's decisive feature is the separation of state and civil society. Socialism is organically linked to capitalism: it is born in capitalism's bowels. Elsewhere, however, the fundamental break is marked by the rise of an emancipated society in which people make their own history — that is, collectively participate in determining their own destiny. All previous history, or 'pre-history', is made against its subjects, despite them, behind their backs. A necessary but insufficient condition for such a collectively directed society is the reunification of state and civil society. Thus, in the terminology of this book, all socialisms have the characteristic feature of fusing production politics and state politics. The fusion may be from below, in which case the guiding force comes from organs of producers in a system I call *collective self-management*. Or it may come from above, with central organs providing the directing force in a system that I call *state socialism*.

To define socialism in a way that does not necessarily involve working-class direction of society or some form of workers' control is controversial, so let me offer some preliminary justifications. First, such a framework permits the examination of actually existing socialisms, and does so, moreover, in a way that does not embrace any theory of convergence. Indeed, the next section of this chapter highlights the differences between an economy based on centralized redistribution of goods and services and one based on private production for profit in a market. In subsequent sections I show the implications of central planning for the development of different factory regimes. While it is true that capitalism and state socialism have both supplemented their own system with features dominant in the other, the consequences of such 'transplants' are decisively different in the two new homes. On the other hand, the repudiation of convergence theory does not imply acceptance of the alternative 'divergence' theory — namely, the distinction between a command economy and a market economy. Nor does it mean that I subscribe to the now fashionable focus on informal relations and bargaining structures which permeate state socialism.[3] Although this switch of emphasis is an important corrective to the totalitarian stereotypes, I argue in sections 3 and 4 that neither bargaining nor despotic institutions can alone capture the dynamics of state socialism. Rather, bargaining and despotism are inextricably interwoven, producing and reproducing each other in accordance with the dynamics of state socialism.

A second advantage of our framework is that it permits analysis not only of actually existing socialisms but also of alternative socialisms that have not existed in stable forms for any length of time. Thus, we are able to examine state socialism and collective self-management as well as the relationship between the two. Indeed, I shall claim that each generates social forces leading in the direction of the other. Finally, the characterization of state socialism as one but only one species of socialism serves to break down the unilinear view of history in which the only post-capitalist future is a definitive socialism and all that lies between is in transition from one to the other. Just as capitalism can take different routes into the future, the same is true of state socialism.

1. Capitalism and State Socialism

Our first task must be to outline the relations of production which define capitalism and state socialism — that is, the distinctive mechanisms through which surplus is pumped out of direct producers.[4] Only in this context will we be able to comprehend the different forms of production politics described in the following sections. At this point, therefore, we are not concerned with the differences between and within state socialist societies, nor will we attend to the combination of state-socialist, capitalist, petty-commodity and domestic modes of production found in East European countries. These will be the subjects of subsequent sections, where we spell out some of the features of one particular East European society. For now, we are concerned to develop two ideal-typical models which do not necessarily correspond to any given reality but represent the essence of capitalism and state socialism, from which we can understand their concrete manifestations.

Relations of Production

A mode of production is a way of appropriating surplus from direct producers. Under capitalism surplus is appropriated *privately*. It takes the form of unpaid labour time — that is, labour expended beyond that which is necessary for the reproduction of labour power. Under state socialism surplus is appropriated *centrally*, by the state. Surplus is the difference between what is appropriated and what is distributed back to the direct producers in the form of wages, benefits and subsidies. Whereas under capitalism the unit of production (the firm) coincides with the unit of appropriation, under state socialism the two no longer coincide.

Under capitalism surplus labour is realized as *profit*. Without profit a firm cannot survive. *Markets* serve as mechanisms for the allocation of inputs and the distribution of outputs. Markets provide the basis for the *competition* among firms that determines which shall be profitable and which shall not. Using Kornai's terminology, capitalist firms face *hard budget* constraints. Under state socialism the *plan* guides the flow of inputs and outputs of production. The planners represent a class of teleological — that is, purposeful — redistributors whose interest it is to maximize the appropriation of surplus from the direct producers via the firm.[5] A system of *plan bargaining* between the central redistributors and the enterprise directors determines the plan *targets* and therefore the eventual success or failure of enterprise production. The enterprise, however, does not have to meet stringent financial criteria of efficiency. Instead it faces *soft budget* constraints. Its performance is assessed by redistributors who are in *paternalistic* relationship to the firm.[6]

Profit levels are the product of the activities of all competing capitalists and are thus beyond the control of any individual capitalist. Market forces lead capitalists continually to innovate, to intensify labour or reduce wages in order to keep up with competitors. The price of a product emerges independently of the activity of a single capitalist. Under state socialism central planners set the parameters for the evaluation of performance. Because of soft budget constraints and the notorious and inevitable ambiguity of plan indices (production value, cost reduction, physical quantity, value added, and so on), enterprise management may have considerable room to manoeuvre. Hence, just as the *profit motive* leads to the production of waste, so *plan fetishism* too dissociates what is produced from what is needed. The enterprise produces long nails when the criterion is length, fat nails when the criterion is weight, according to labour-intensive production processes when the criterion is value added, and so on. Except where there is no product differentiation (gas, oil, coal), a physical plan can never be centrally specified in the detail necessary to avoid distortion.

Capitalist competition finds its analogue in state socialism's plan bargaining. Enterprise directors bargain with the central planning agency for a loose plan that can be easily fulfilled. Thus, enterprise directors conceal information, underestimate their plant's capacity, hold back the reporting of production achievements. If a director manages to negotiate a loose plan he will limit levels of overfulfilment; a taut plan encourages considerable underfulfilment in the hope of achieving a looser plan in the next period. Such 'restriction of output', analogous to shopfloor goldbricking and quota restriction, also serves to accumulate 'kitty', or unrevealed production, for the next period.

Under capitalism firms attempt to contain the pressure of competition through the formation of trusts, cartels and the like. Competition itself deals a death blow to many smaller enterprises, leading to *concentration and centralization* (although at the same time small competitive enterprises, often based on labour-intensive production, are continually produced even in the era of monopoly capital). Equivalently, socialist enterprises seek to increase their power vis-à-vis central planners through *expansion*. The bigger they are and the more important their product, the greater their bargaining strength. There are tendencies toward concentration through the appropriation of investment resources and centralization through backward integration to control supplies.

The capitalist firm makes investment decisions on the basis of profitability, leading to cycles of over-production, surplus capacity and reluctance to undertake new investments. Under state socialism, soft budget constraints and pressures to expand lead to an insatiable investment hunger. *Over*-investment predominates. Nuti and Kalecki see over-accumulation in state socialist societies as the result of deliberate and autonomous decisions by planners, by the class of teleological redistributors.[7] Bauer and Kornai provide a more convincing institutional picture of plan bargaining as the source of over-investment. Whereas resources necessary for reproduction at existing levels can be stipulated by central planners, the resources for new investment projects are more difficult to assess. Therefore, despite the common interest in expansion shared by central planners and enterprise directors, the allocation of investment resources is subject to fierce bargaining rather than unilateral determination.

Bauer provides a theory of investment cycles which shape the rhythm of economic development in state socialist societies. In seeking state approval for their investment projects, enterprises draw up low outlays for the first year. Once they are 'hooked on to the plan' — once the state has granted initial support — investment outlays climb rapidly in subsequent years. The result is an investment cycle of four phases: 'run-up', when investment projects are begun and investment outlays are within the bounds of the plan; 'rush', when the financing of these projects and the starting of new ones generate considerable investment tension; 'halt', when the rate of approval of new projects falls to zero. At this point the intensification of shortage is felt throughout the economy. The expansion of investment resources is achieved at the expense of consumption and/or worsening of the balance of trade. In the final phase, 'slow-down', existing projects may be suspended until the growth rate of completed projects exceeds the growth of investment outlays. Investment tension begins to fall, consumption and balance of trade move toward their earlier levels, and pressure builds up to allocate resources to suspended or postponed projects. The cycle begins anew with 'run-up'.

The escalation of investment demand becomes the driving mechanism behind shortages in all goods and services needed for production. This is as true for labour as it is for raw materials and capital equipment. The growth of state socialist societies intensifies the demand for labour, so that reserves become exhausted and labour shortage prevails. Full employment is not so much a policy decision as it is the outcome of the drive for expansion through investment bargaining under soft budget constraints. Capitalist investment is based on profitability, and hard budget constraints are upheld through market competition. Here there is a tendency toward the unemployment of resources, not least that of labour. In other words, there is not a single equilibrium position where supply equals demand; as Kornai argues, there are two positions: the socialist economy, in which supply acts as a constraint, and the capitalist economy, in which demand acts as a constraint. At the same time, each system adopts features of the other to soften its constraints. Thus, the capitalist *state* provides unemployment compensation, protects workers against arbitrary depredations of capital, and creates new jobs, all of which boost *demand*; while under state socialism the promotion of domestic production, petty commodity production and small private enterprises operating through *markets* alleviate *shortages*.

We can now explore the effect of the relations of production on the dynamics of the labour process. Under capitalism there are strong pressures to increase relative surplus value through marginal increases in productivity, work intensity, technological innovation and lower wages. We can discern long-term changes in the organization of work within a given industry. In the short term, competitive pressures and demand constraints lead to cycles of expansion and contraction in production and also in levels of employment. Are there corresponding pressures under state socialism? Pressures for secular change stem from the hierarchical relationship between firm and enterprise as well as between enterprise and state. Central enterprises or ministries, because they can never be sure of the actual capacity of a given firm, operate on a ratchet principle in which yearly norm cuts are normal. Over the long run, if firms are to avoid being squeezed they must either garner new investment resources for new machinery, attempt to organize production more efficiently, or change their product (since a new product means new and hopefully looser norms). Once the annual norm cuts are regarded as a fact of life, manager and workers share an interest in increasing productivity.

In the short term, however, supply constraints and dictates from central planners generate uncertainty in the labour process itself rather than in levels of employment. In a shortage economy enterprise directors, when they are not bargaining with their bosses, are competing for supplies — materials, equipment and services as well as labour. Enterprises search and queue for scarce resources. They hoard when possible, thus exacerbating shortage. If they are not successful in any of these strategies, they may be forced to substitute one input for another or even to alter the output profile to match the available inputs. All such manipulations involve uncertainty in the labour process: first, the irregular arrival of supplies leads to the continual reallocation of the temporal sequences of production processes; and second, spasmodic changes in the form and quality of supplies require continual reorganization of work and resetting of machines. These temporal and compositional uncertainties due to supply shortages are often compounded by changing dictates from the central planning agency, continually updating the plan in the light of unanticipated bottlenecks. Product mixes change suddenly and arbitrarily. Finally, the attempt to meet plan targets leads to the phenomenon of rushing or storming, in which the bulk of production is crammed into the last quarter of the plan period. The pace of work may be relatively slow for the greater part of the year but pick up a wild tempo in the last few months to fulfil output norms.[8]

The anarchy of the capitalist market finds its analogue in the anarchy of the socialist plan. Under capitalism demand constraints make themselves felt through the absorption and expulsion of *labour power*. Under state socialism supply constraints generate continual reorganization of the *labour process*. The fluidity of task structure and the continual need to redistribute workers among machines makes it very difficult to deskill production — to separate conception and execution. Where this does occur it often requires an army of auxiliary workers to orchestrate improvisation. The need to respond frequently and rapidly to changing requirements gives a great deal of power to the skilled and experienced workers, who over time develop a monopoly of knowledge essential to the running of the enterprise. From the management side the penetration of external uncertainties onto the shopfloor elicits two strategies. On the one hand management can seek to reward cooperation, particularly of the core workers; on the other it can intensify surveillance and control, particularly over the more peripheral workers. The Stakhanovites used a combination of these strategies — rewarding the super-worker while driving those whom he or she led.

As with our study of the capitalist labour process, the guiding question turns from why workers under state socialism restrict output and operate at a low tempo to why they cooperate in production at all. We observed how, under capitalism, the despotic regimes gave way to hegemonic regimes as the economic whip of the market was softened by unemployment compensation outside the factory and the arbitrary dictatorship of the overseer was contained by grievance machinery and bargaining rights inside the factory. Has there been any corresponding change in production politics under state socialism? Has the anarchy of the plan been tamed in a way analogous to the taming of the anarchic market?

The Hungarian Reforms

The development of the planned economies of the Soviet Union and Eastern Europe is conventionally divided into two periods. In the first, *extensive* period, primitive accumulation was completed and workers were separated from the means of production through collectivization of agriculture and absorbed into the socialist sector as wage labourers. During this period, in the Soviet Union — the picture is less clear in post-war Eastern Europe — draconian labour legislation penalized quitting and absenteeism, work books were introduced to regulate the flow of labour, and performance at work was linked to survival outside work through piece rates and the distribution of housing and food rations.[9] The second, *intensive* period began with the emergence of labour shortages. At least in certain countries of Eastern Europe, the distribution of basic subsistence goods, particularly housing and food, independently of the enterprise and of the worker's performance within it, brings increased autonomy for labour. Coercive forms of control are no longer so widespread; but how then do the new factory apparatuses elicit cooperation on the part of the workers?

The transition from extensive to intensive patterns of accumulation has implications not only for labour but also for the direction of the economy as a whole. Shortage of labour exerts pressure toward labour-saving production techniques. More generally, scarcity leads to more efficient utilization of existing resources rather than the excavation of new ones. Thus, the transition has often been linked to the economic reforms of the 1960s, which attempted to decentralize decision-making by granting autonomy to enterprises and introducing market-type incentives. However, as Nuti has been at pains to emphasize, there is no necessary linkage between the two since the reforms depended on a certain liberalization of the public sphere.[10] Where such liberalization was autonomously forthcoming it established the conditions for reforms but, as in Czechoslovakia, was then repressed with military force. More usually, economic pressures (often related to the investment cycle) built up for decentralization, but the corresponding institutional change would have required at least a limited opening up of civil society. Since this was not forthcoming, the planned decentralization led to increased anarchy and inflation, prompting recentralization, and the cycle would begin anew. This was very much the character of reforms in the Soviet Union and Poland in the 1960s. Only in Hungary did they have some staying power.

The principal features of the New Economic Mechanism, introduced by the Hungarian reforms of 1968, were as follows. Central specification of enterprise production and sales plans was abandoned, and enterprises were permitted to determine their production profiles on the basis of contracts with customers. With a few exceptions, central allocation of material inputs ended. One-year operational plans disaggregated to the enterprise level were discontinued, and the five-year plan was to provide overall guidance for the economy. Central allocation of investment resources was changed to a system in which self-financing from profit was supposed to play an important role, although central supervision of investments remained strong. The chief objective of the enterprise was to be the pursuit of profit. The reforms introduced greater flexibility of prices, and administrative changes encouraged the export of products to socialist and capitalist markets. Finally, central direction of labour was to be lifted and centrally fixed wages ended, but average wage levels were to be severely constrained through taxation.[11]

Does this add up to a transition to state capitalism? Are enterprises endowed with the autonomy to accumulate from their own resources? Has profit become the criterion of investment? This is indeed Bettelheim's claim in his analysis of Soviet-type societies in the contemporary period.[12] Yet such a conclusion exaggerates the effects of the reforms and fails to examine their operational context. The party still plays a leading role in facilitating and shaping inter-enterprise relations, while ministries continue to have a significant say in the allocation of investment and the determination of product mixes — decisions which only weakly respond to profits.

Plan bargaining continues, although its content has been modified. Profit is incorporated as a criterion of enterprise success. Yet the survival of 'state paternalism' entails that budget constraints remain soft. Profit is not a measure of efficiency but reflects price adjustments and bargaining among enterprises and between enterprises and the state. In other words, the introduction of profit has been used not to eliminate the hierarchical relations between planners and enterprises but to change the content of bargaining within those relations. The language of bargaining has also shifted from physical quantities to cash flows, yet it is the former that ultimately govern transactions. Budget constraints, while harder than before, are still soft. Physical and human resources, not financial solvency, remain the real constraints. The distinctive features of a shortage economy are still present: sellers continue to dictate to buyers, who queue, search, hoard and enter into forced substitution of inputs and outputs. The same patterns of rushing and vertical integration are observed, even though enterprises are more independent and not so completely absorbed by plan fetishism.[13] To the extent that the reforms have led to decentralization and greater enterprise autonomy, horizontal relations have assumed greater, and vertical relations less, importance. That is, greater enterprise independence from central planners has been accompanied by greater dependence on regional party apparatuses, particularly the regional secretary, whose assistance is essential for coordinating inter-enterprise relations.

The reforms therefore appear not to have significantly affected those problems of labour control in the workplace which stem from the penetration of external uncertainties. But did they increase management's capacity to deploy labour to meet the variability of work organization? Szelényi has argued that the reforms were designed to increase the supply of labour from the rural to the urban areas through the concentration and rationalization of regional management, so that inequalities within regions grew.[14] Infrastructure developed, albeit slowly, in the urban centres, while the outlying villages suffered increasing impoverishment. They became the home of the old and the unemployable, the marginal and the unqualified, while in the towns material standards of living increased. The result was an increase in labour mobility, legitimated by the relaxation of restrictions on quitting. Moreover, as we shall see, the rise of the second economy also gave more leverage to some workers since wages did not keep up with increases in productivity and gross domestic product. Indeed, so mobile was labour as a result of the liberalization of restrictions on movement that already in 1970 the government began taking back some of the reforms by introducing nation-wide starting wages and centralized norms. More significant, however, was the government's attempt to curtail labour mobility by instituting a compulsory job placement system for those who left their jobs without notice or who changed employment more than twice a year.[15]

In order to encourage workers as well as management to increase production, the reforms introduced a system of bonuses based on profitability. But these bonuses were restricted to 15 per cent of their earnings in the case of workers, 50 per cent in the case of middle managers, and 85 per cent in the case of top management. When they became known, these blatantly unequal rewards for increased productivity and production created a storm of protest. Officially the figures were revised, but management still received a disproportionate share of bonuses. Moreover, to the extent that they were awarded according to criteria of profitability and cost-cutting, the opposition of interests between managers and workers was only intensified.[16]

In short, although attempts were made to coordinate the interests of workers and management, these do not appear to have been very successful, and the question remains: how is it that workers cooperate with management to fulfil targets, turning out products to the extent that they do? With access to a second economy, with full employment and labour shortage, with the right to quit, how is it that workers expend any effort at all on the shopfloor? For answers we must turn to a case study.

2. Red Star Tractor Factory

Between 1971 and 1972 Miklós Haraszti, a Hungarian poet and sociologist, worked in Red Star Tractor Factory in the outskirts of Budapest. He relates his experiences there in *Piece Rates*, which appears in English as *A Worker in a Worker's State*.[17] Haraszti was brought to trial by the Hungarian government, accused of writing a book likely to stimulate hatred of the state, falsifying the facts, and generalizing on the basis of a deceptive picture. There is no doubt that Red Star Tractor Factory was at that time in crisis and as a result management-worker relations had been deteriorating. During the fifties Red Star had benefited from the subsidies which it attracted as a result of agricultural mechanization. In the sixties, however, it had lost those subsidies, and in 1971, under pressures from the New Economic Mechanism, it was struggling for survival. 'The gravity of the situation required severe remedies.'[18] Indeed, to anyone familiar with machine shops in the United States or Britain, the remedies were unthinkable. Although Haraszti has little to say about the circumstances of Red Star, I will reconstruct its particular situation to illuminate the general forces at work in a state socialist economy.

Haraszti's experiences at Red Star fly in the face of the conventional wisdom that labour intensity is much lower in state socialist societies than in advanced capitalist societies. On the basis of Haraszti's account, I would estimate that he did twice as much work as similar operators in the very similar machine shop in which I worked in South Chicago. In an interview with *Labour Focus on Eastern Europe*, Haraszti recognizes but does not resolve the paradox:

> I didn't intend it as a comparison with any other factory. For me it was a high tempo. But I'm now sure that in socialist countries, the tempo is generally slower than in the West, and that is not just because of under-development. It is a feature of a totally state monopolistic system: workers are deprived of their rights but have a certain job security. Very crudely put, the lack of unemployment is a basic factor causing a slower tempo of work, whatever economic analysis one might make of hidden unemployment. The technocracy has paid a big price, in terms of slower work tempo, for integrating the working class into the super-monopolistic factory system. My factory was run on the piece-rate system ... and such workers face one of the highest tempos of work. Semi-automated workers perhaps face an even higher tempo, but in general piece-workers have a higher tempo than time-workers. The piece-rate system was very prevalent in the Stalin period, and it is once again being reintroduced.[19]

Given all we know about the employment conditions in Eastern Europe, how was such an intense work tempo, which involved running two machines at once, possible? Second, how typical were Haraszti's experiences?[20] In this section I try to answer the first question using my experiences at Allied as a point of comparison, and in the next section we shall attempt to answer the second question.

Labour Process and the Dictatorship of the Norm

The piecework machine shop at Red Star was in many ways very similar to the one at Allied. The same machines were to be found — mills, drills, lathes and so forth, operated by single male workers on piece rates. These were helped or hindered by various auxiliary workers (more numerous at Red Star) — the set-up man, inspector, crib attendant, time clerk, truck driver and foreman. The auxiliary workers were on time rates in both shops.

In terms of sheer effort, however, the norms described by Haraszti seem unbelievable. After his period of probation Haraszti was introduced to the 'two-machine system'. The rate fixers had decided that operators should run two machines at once whenever this was at all possible. Haraszti initially thought this a means to earn more money, until he discovered that for such jobs (in the case of his machine, the mill, this was most jobs), the piece time had been cut in half, with the possibility of earning an additional fifth as compensation:

Working on two machines at once is very difficult: it is dangerous and exhausting; you have to use all the brains you've got. When I work on one machine, it is boring and tiring, certainly, but the moments during which it functions automatically do lead to some satisfaction. It seems that I dominate the machine: I have fed it, my hands rest upon its casing, and now it works. It's true that I only feel these almost tender sentiments when I switch from two machines to one; even then, they vanish after a little while. But when I am working on two machines, such feelings are utterly impossible. You can't dominate two machines: they dominate you. ... I change into a senseless, mindless machine.[21]

It is true that I often ran two machines at Allied. But the conditions and consequences were very different. One of the machines was an automatic saw which did not require continuous attention, so that I could devote my energies to working on another job. Not only did this mean that I was always building up a store of pieces which I could turn in any time, but I could also refuse to run two machines unless I was guaranteed an acceptable output on the saw. In other words, running two jobs at once was all gravy, just as Haraszti had originally thought it would be.

But how was Haraszti compelled to work like a madman? Part of the answer must lie in the nature of the piece-rate system. At Red Star the system operated in very much the same way as described by Marx. There was a basic wage, but it was 'a pure formality'[22] and did not constitute a guaranteed minimum. However, this hourly wage was important in other ways. First, it might determine the wage a worker would receive were he or she to move to another enterprise. In keeping the hourly wage as low as possible, the foreman was not so much saving the factory money but, more significantly, deterring workers from quitting.[23] Second, the hourly wage determined the mid-month advance workers received, as well as holiday and sick leave pay — 'Not that you can afford to be ill with an hourly wage that low.'[24] Third, the hourly wage or corresponding worker category was used by the foreman in distributing work to operators. Jobs with the easier piece rates generally went to workers in higher categories — that is, on higher hourly wages.[25] Fourth, for the first three months foremen were entitled to guarantee the workers' hourly wage even if their output did not warrant it. Thereafter operators were on their own. When piece rates were impossible, there was nothing workers could do to bring their earnings up to the hourly wage. The only recourse was first fury, then frenzy. At Allied and at Geer the situation was very different. Workers were guaranteed a minimum wage, so that if the rate was impossible to make they would take it easy and 'goldbrick', even hoping that the rate might be loosened.

Since Red Star had no minimum wage, earnings were directly proportional to the number of pieces produced. Each piece had a price, supposedly fixed at a rate that would allow operators to make their hourly wage, which was pegged at an output of a hundred per cent. By following the directions of the blueprint, the stipulated speed, feed and cutting depth, Haraszti found that it was impossible to produce the pieces at a rate which would earn him his hourly wage. Moreover, the piece-rate system did not allow any time for setting up (as it did at Allied), getting pieces checked, or other contingencies.[26] To make the hourly wage, let alone a living wage, operators had to break the rules and safety regulations by increasing speeds and feeds, and taking dangerous short-cuts.[27] Only in this way could an operator produce over a hundred per cent. This 'cheating of the norm', known as looting, dominated the entire shopfloor experience of the operator. It consumed his concentration and, when successful, offered some sense of accomplishment. The unity of conception and execution was thus partially restored, but in the interest of the bosses.

> 'Nerves' brought about by the necessity of looting cannot be calmed by anything except loot itself. We have to stake all our inventiveness, knowledge, imagination, initiative and courage on getting it. And when this comes off, it brings a certain feeling of triumph. This is why workers on piece-rates often feel that they have beaten the system, as if they'd got the better of someone.[28]

Although foremen, inspectors and rate-fixers are 'there to see that the rules are observed', they 'turn a blind eye ... so long as you do not force your looting to their attention.'[29] Indeed, the foreman's bonuses and prestige rest on operators risking life and limb in the pursuit of loot.

But in going beyond the norm to make a living wage, operators provided the rate-fixer with ammunition for speed-ups. The pursuit of maximum economic gain forced down the price per piece.

> To make our living, we are forced to provide the rate-fixers with irrefutable arguments for the revision of norms, and so for the reduction to an ever more unreal level of the time per piece and consequently the pay per piece. This incites us to speed up the rate still more to try and reach a greater level of production. Therefore we prepare the ground, slowly but surely, for another increase of the norms.[30]

Revisions of the norm were not only made job by job but also, and more significantly, on a collective basis. Workers were exhorted to increase their output in the common interest and were 'rewarded' with a general 'readjustment' of the norms which hit everyone.[31]

It is significant that what Red Star operators called 'looting', Allied operators called 'making out'. At Allied they expected and were expected, by management and fellow-workers alike, to exceed the 100 per cent level. Indeed, the 'anticipated rate' was 125 per cent, and each operator set his own target (between 125 and 140 per cent) for 'making out'. So long as operators did not exceed 140 per cent they were assured that their rates would not be cut by the methods department. It was in their interest to hold back production so as not to turn in more than 140 per cent. There was little point in operators at Red Star engaging in such 'quota restriction'. So long as they were cheating the norm they could expect arbitrary rate-cutting; norms would be revised irrespective of the actual levels of output.

We can already begin to appreciate reasons for the differences in labour intensity in the two machine shops. At Red Star *employment security* was combined with *wage insecurity*, whereas at Allied *employment insecurity* (although workers were rarely fired, redundancy was always a possibility) was combined with *wage security*. Workers at Red Star were guaranteed a job but not a living wage — this had to be earned through intensification of effort. Thus, in 1971 average hourly earnings in the engineering sector of industry were 11.2 forints. Based on the type of work Haraszti normally received, this involved an average production level of 147 per cent.[32] But we must ask why the workers at Red Star failed to challenge the dictatorship of the norm or to bargain for a more favourable relationship between reward and effort. This requires an examination, first, of the political and ideological effects of the labour process and, second, of the political apparatuses of the factory.

Ideological Effects of the Labour Process

How was it that workers cooperated in their own barbaric subordination? The need to survive and the power this gave to management were obviously critical. Yet there was something about the labour process that generated a certain complicity of the workers in their own subordination. The mechanism through which workers were drawn into their own dehumanization was the uncertainty of outcomes. 'Insecurity is the main driving force in all payment by results. . . . The manifest coercion and dependence which characterize payment by the hour change into a semblance of independence with piece-rates. . . . Uncertainty is the great magician of piece-work.'[33] At the same time, too much uncertainty would make workers indifferent to the outcomes. If rate-fixers pushed their luck too far, or if a general revision of norms was too drastic, the operators would leave.[34]

Thus, the ideological effects of the labour process and the piece-rate system were very similar at Allied and at Red Star. Once workers thought it was possible to survive under a piece-rate system, they took up the challenge to their ingenuity, will and endurance, and blamed themselves for failure.[35] In this way they were sucked into participating in their own brutalization.

> Of course, (the worker) knows perfectly well that he is being cheated. But his active participation in this trick against himself makes it impossible for him to see the deception; or to identify it with his conditions of life, as can the worker on hourly wages.
>
> Instead, he has a sharp eye for petty discrimination, injustice or manipulation, and fights against such things in the belief that such victories can be set against the defeats. He tends to judge everything in terms of pay, and when he has a good month, he believes, from the bottom of his heart, that he is not the dupe but the victor.[36]

Once compelled to engage in this preoccupation for loot, the conditions which made it necessary receded into the background as unalterably given: 'not only the two-machine system, but also the nature of work itself, seemed unchangeable.'[37]

> The system of norms is far more effective at shackling the imagination than at stimulating production: the most daring dream of piece-rate workers is to achieve a fair and sufficient hourly wage: in other words, to be delivered from the norm. If a utopia of productive relations where they could determine their goals together threatens to break to the surface, they immediately force it back.[38]

Rather than conceiving of alternative ways of organizing production, workers were absorbed by the variations they faced from day to day: good jobs rather than bad jobs, one machine instead of two, the possibility of supplementary wages and bonuses, and so forth. Such apparently insignificant differences came to overwhelm all other experiences on the shop floor.

> We are like natives who, in the early days of colonialism, handed over everything, their treasures, their land, and themselves, for worthless trinkets and who became aware that they had been robbed only when they failed to get the usual junk in return.[39]

And the very relativity of the gains had the effect of only further mystifying the basis of wage labour.

> One might think that the two-machine system itself is so outrageous that it would shatter the illusion that we are really being paid, and with it the illusion of paid work in general. But the truth is that it enhances the power of the illusion. When it emerges that the two-machine system does not improve our pay in comparison with the old system, or with hourly wages, this does not appear to us as a brutal manifestation of the famous relations of production, we feel fucked: well and truly fucked.[40]

Again, I found the same at Allied, where we became angry with management when it failed to provide the necessary conditions — acceptable piece rates, adequate tooling and fixtures, prompt service from auxiliary workers, and so on — for making out.

No matter how much knowledge one brought to the shopfloor, no matter how many times one had read *Capital*, the experience was the same. A monomania set in which concentrated all energies and ingenuity on factors that shaped marginal variations. If looting sprang from the need to survive, if making out sprang from the need to compensate for boring work, once set in motion their ideological effects were to conceal their origins and autonomously to generate the ideological conditions for their own reproduction.

Political Effects of the Labour Process

The production of objects is simultaneously the production of relations — relations of competition and interdependence. Under a system of piece rates, competition revolves around the distribution of good and bad jobs,[41] the transfer and promotion of people from one position to another, and the distribution of supplementary wages which supposedly compensate operators for the contingencies not allowed for in the calculation of piece rates. While such competition is to be found in all machine shops, its particular organization reflects and shapes different forms of subordination. Thus, at Allied competition was usually resolved through the application of rules, while at Jay's it was more likely to be resolved through informal bargaining. At Red Star resolution usually came through the arbitrary will of the foreman.

> So everyone is dependent personally on the head foreman who fixes the level of his pay: this is a paradox of piece-rates. The only concern one

worker has for the others is jealous suspicion. Are the others a few fillérs (unit of currency) ahead? Is their hourly rate going up more quickly? Are they getting more of the best 'good' jobs that are going? Such rivalry is equally fierce over all matters in which the head foreman's decision is final: holidays, overtime, bonuses, awards.[42]

There were other sources of competition. Where looting is the secret of survival and its possibility is limited, operators jealously guard their accumulated experience. New operators faced this when they arrived on the shopfloor to be broken in by a senior operator who ran a similar machine. If the novice was prepared to play along with the instructor by turning out lots of pieces to advance the latter's earnings, then he might learn something. But it wouldn't be the angles which made looting possible, or the homemade fixtures which turned a bad job into a good one. These the new operator had to discover for himself by closely watching others, or to elicit through an exchange of favours.

> (The instructor) doesn't let me work on both machines at once, although I'm going to have to do this eventually. He sets up one machine so quickly that I can hardly see how he goes about it, and then he leaves me to put a run through. Meanwhile, he's milling on the other machine himself, and he doesn't utter a single word until I've finished. There's a hint of black-mail in his way of going about things: if I agree to play along, perhaps he'll agree to explain the odd thing to me, now and then. From time to time, he knocks off early and asks me to punch his card for him. In exchange, he's quite prepared to spend half an hour telling me how things work.[43]

An operator really only began to learn the art of looting after his period of training was over and he was plunged into battle. He was left to his own devices not only in operating and setting up his machine, and in competing with other operators seeking the same scarce resources as he was, but in fighting for the cooperation of auxiliary workers as well. He was dependent on these workers while at the same time he was placed in an antagonistic relationship to them. For operators paid by the piece, time lost was money lost; for auxiliary workers paid by the hour, time lost was effort saved. Haraszti soon discovered the meaning of this in his confrontation with the setter (set-up man), who had every reason to lord it over the operator if possible, sending him scurrying hither and yon on futile and unnecessary errands. 'But what is a straight loss for me is a gain for the setter: he's paid by the hour. I begin to hate him.'[44] As a neighbour explained, 'Look, they're just not here to make life easier for you. ... And why should they be any more helpful? If you want to carry on with this, then it's much better to learn how to get by on your own. You've got to, if you want to make any bread.'[45]

The story was similar with the inspector, but with a difference: you couldn't do without him. It was his stamp of approval that decided whether or not you could go ahead and try to make some money. As Haraszti's instructor told him about the inspector:

> His special stunt is never to give his approval to a series straight away. You show him your first piece and he always asks you to tinker with the settings a bit. But don't bother to change a thing. Get the run going, and next time he comes your way, show him another piece. More often than not, he'll stamp your work-sheet at once, because he's ashamed.[46]

Inspectors were so obviously superfluous, so clearly an expression of the system of wage labour, that they had an image of themselves as 'men of quality'. In this role they directly confronted the operator — a man of quantity — as an antagonist.

The petty officials on the shopfloor — neither workers nor bosses — appeared as agents of the company, executors and enforcers of the rules, keepers of the records, and communicators between bosses and workers. Although without power of their own, they were still in a position to humiliate workers on the shopfloor.

> None of this leads to any feeling of solidarity: the piece-rate worker cannot pass insults on to any one else, and suffers enormously when he is kicked around, by those who are not, in principle at any rate, his superiors.
> Besides, any hope of solidarity is excluded by the simple, daily experience that white-collar workers do lighter work and accomplish less. Their work is easier and less intense, they don't clock in at the crack of dawn; they don't eat during working hours; and the coffee machines that simmer in their offices symbolize their stake in power, limited though it is.[47]

At Allied and even more at Geer it was the *cooperation* between machine operators and auxiliary workers that was particularly striking. To be sure, the organization of work structured antagonisms between the two sets of workers, and indeed pressure from management to increase machine operators' output was often translated into a lateral conflict between operators and auxiliary workers (the latter having no interest in the intensification of work). Yet there was no systematic attempt by auxiliary workers to subordinate operators to themselves. On the contrary, they often engaged in illicit activities to facilitate making out by the operators, in what Donald Roy called 'the fix'. Auxiliary workers and machine operators at Allied were all workers together, and there was much mobility between the two groups. The superior status of the auxiliary worker found at Red Star, symbolized by the time spent brewing coffee, gossiping and joking, was absent from Allied. What was the basis of that elevated status? How were the divisions created and reproduced? Why were inspectors, setters and clerical workers more closely allied to the bosses than to the workers on the shopfloor?

The Political Organization of Hierarchy

We have already seen how, at Allied, operators and auxiliary workers were all part of a common internal labour market administered by bidding and bumping rules. Job vacancies were filled by workers filing bids, with seniority as the usual deciding factor. Those vacancies not filled from within the firm were opened to the external labour market. Laid-off workers could bump others with less seniority so long as they could perform the others' jobs. In short, competition for 'promotion' and 'transfers' was determined by rules rather than the personal discretion of the foreman. Although there was a hierarchy of job grades with corresponding differences in basic pay, the hierarchy did not lead anywhere and did not discriminate between workers on the basis of power or allegiance to management.

At Red Star, auxiliary workers earned about the same amount as machine operators, but there was a distinct hierarchical relationship between the two groups. The auxiliary workers had no doubt that their interests lay with the bosses. The role of the party appeared to be critical in ensuring allegiance to management. Promotion to auxiliary work was a necessary if not sufficient step for those seeking a career. But such an advance out of the ranks of the operators was made possible through party membership and party activities. Haraszti's neighbour told him:

> They're all friends of the bosses; that's why they're setters. They are on the way up. . . . (The older setter) was chairman of the local magistrate's court. On full pay, plus all the usual extras, of course. It's the same with the others. The younger one, who only became a setter last year, will be made a trade-union representative or Party secretary by next year, you'll see. The works manager was also a setter in his time.[48]

Inspectors, like setters and foremen, were in a privileged position and obtained their jobs by the grace of the party.

But even if the *meós* (inspectors) were falling over themselves to help us, the bosses would stop them. They are very jealous of their inspectors' reputations and they think that their jobs should be enviable and respected. It's no contradiction that these independent members of the 'jury' have posts on their side, in the union or the Party. Promotion to *meós* should be counted as one of those privileges which can be bestowed on a worker, just as footballers and other sportsmen are often raised up to the level of 'men of quality'.[49]

The party was harnessed to management interests through the creation of a status hierarchy in production. The allegiance of managerial agents of control was guaranteed not by financial benefits (at least not openly), but through privileged positions involving political access criteria. Raised above the lowest ranks and on their way to a career, auxiliary workers had their eyes on those pulling them up, rather than trying to appease the frustrations of those from whom they had come. Auxiliary workers at Allied had no such interest or opportunity, and their allegiance was firmly grounded with the operators. As we shall see, the levelling effect of the trade union at Allied was absent from Red Star.

The Dictatorship of the Foreman

The system of bidding and bumping found at Allied offered employees the opportunity and therefore the threat of transferring to another job if they objected to the piece rates, the foreman, the machine or anything else about their particular job. Workers' power was therefore enhanced in proportion to the amount of training their jobs required. Foremen were careful not to antagonize their subordinates through arbitrary treatment or illegitimate sanctions. At Red Star, by contrast, the foreman was a dictator, not least because he dispensed a wide range of rewards and punishments which at Allied were distributed through administrative rules.

The weakness of the workforce is highlighted when the labour process and the piece-rate system do not uniquely determine relations and activities. Potentially, this could provide an arena of struggle in which workers might recover some of their power. In practice, however, such uncertainty was turned into an arena of absolute power for the foremen. 'They are emperors here. They hold us all in their hands. They dole out favours as they feel like it.'[50] Thus, the fact that there were jobs with good rates and jobs with bad rates — an inevitable concomitant of any piecework system, no matter how 'scientific' — was turned into a power resource for the foremen who distributed the work. The same was true of supplementary payments. Since piece rates could not incorporate the very real contingencies of production — the worn-out drill, the tough material, the warped stock — foremen were entitled to dispense supplementary wages as a recompense for lost time. In practice, operators were reimbursed for only a fraction of the time lost: 'my supplementary wages don't supplement my wages one little bit. Rather, they are a part of my pay on which *they* try to economize.'[51] The crumbs owed to the operator by 'right' were turned into a favour which had to be bargained for, enhancing the foremen's power and wasting the operators' time. 'All the foremen ... do everything to make us feel that supplementary wages are special presents which they hand out to us, for which we give nothing in return.'[52] By behaving as though supplementary wages were a scarce and fixed resource, the foremen promoted jealous suspicion and guarded secrecy among the operators, thus weakening the workers' solidarity even further.

Not content with exploiting uncertainties endemic to the labour process of a piecework machine shop, foremen managed to expand their arena of discretion to include matters which for the most part were out of the hands of Allied foremen, either under different branches of management or subject to administrative rules.

The foreman doesn't just organize our work: first and foremost he organizes *us*. The foremen fix our pay, our jobs, our overtime, our bonuses, and the deductions for excessive rejects. They decide when we go on holiday; write character reports on us for any arm of the state which requests them; pass on assessments of those who apply for further training or request a passport; they supervise trade union activities in the section; they hire, fire, arrange transfers, grant leave, impose fines, give bonuses. Their signatures are essential to authorize any kind of departure from routine. Only information coming from them can be taken as official. They alone have the right to call a meeting.[53]

To be sure, not all workers were equally powerless. Those who managed to make themselves irreplaceable, through monopoly of some skill, knowledge or experience, were in a much stronger position to wheedle concessions out of the foreman than were novices such as Haraszti or others who had nothing special to offer.[54]

More generally, the dictatorship of the foreman fostered an intense rivalry among workers for the crumbs which he chose to dispense. Competition was more formally introduced through the organization of workers into brigades. Twice a year the foreman informed each brigade of its production record and whether it had won some bonus or honorific title, such as 'Socialist Brigade'.[55] Except for the 'good boys who want a political future and are laying the basis of a career',[56] such 'clowning' failed to summon the workers' interest. They were already so divided — first by the labour process and piece-rate system, and second by the personal rule of the foreman — that the organization of brigades had little impact. Finally, workers were further divided by restrictions on their movement around the factory. They obtained no sense of the totality of the production process. Yet, at the same time that these various forms of competition and antagonism split the workers, they also promoted a bitter hostility toward the bosses and their various agents.

Although the labour process, piece-rate system, internal labour market and grievance machinery all promoted a rampant individualism at Allied, this took place within a framework that had a levelling and egalitarian impact on relations among workers. The entrenched informal and formal hierarchies as well as the hostile divisions among Red Star workers could not be found at Allied.[57] The trade union defended the rights and enforced the obligations of its members, and in so doing effectively protected management from itself, from the tendency toward arbitrary domination that would have undermined the consent so essential to the cooperation of Allied workers. When conflict emerged on the shopfloor it was not exploited by the foreman, but was either channelled into the grievance machinery or the triennial collective bargaining between union and management, or was dissipated through resignations or transfers to other jobs. Only rarely did it break out of the institutional mechanisms for its containment. Strikes were most likely to develop when rank-and-file rejected management's proposals for the new collective agreement. Once signed, the contract had the union as its watchdog. In this limited role union officials often excited the animosity of the rank-and-file, which claimed an unholy alliance between their representatives and management. Nevertheless, the factory apparatuses at Allied possessed a certain autonomy, enshrined in legally enforceable rules. This restricted managerial discretion, as well as displacing conflict into channels from which it was less likely to have an adverse effect on production.

At Red Star the factory apparatuses were very much an instrument of despotic rule. As we have seen, in dealing with 'contingencies' the foreman did not appear to be restrained by any regulations or countervailing bodies. To the contrary, all other bases of association existed to enhance his power. Thus, the trade union became an arm of the dictatorship of the foreman. '[W]e look upon [the union official] . . . as a straw man, or a string puppet. If he was a careerist, we would certainly class him as one of *them*. Everyone agrees . . . "The union is our paid enemy." '[58] The union secretary 'is nominated for the job by the head foreman. To put up or vote for another candidate would be a direct provocation of the head foreman. Anyway, what could possibly come of it? After the election, the head foreman fixes the pay of the secretary, who, in any case, has a second master as well: his superior in the union hierarchy, who works from a desk in the factory office building.'[59]

And so the union official strolled about the workshop, promising to put grievances before the head foreman and thereby acting as an effective block on their resolution. He turned up at all meetings, but his presence was a formality, and he was reduced to the status of a spectator.

'There is a collective agreement; almost everyone knows that, but nobody knows what is in it.'[60] After remonstrating with the foreman, Haraszti managed to secure permission to look at a copy of the 'collective', but only under the surveillance of a secretary. It was written in such a way as to confuse, hedging its stipulations with qualifications, and placing the ultimate decision-making power in the hands of the foreman. A fellow-worker put it like this: 'It states everything we have to put up with, except for what it doesn't state.'[61] The collective was merely one more instrument through which the foreman wielded and justified his unrestrained power. 'The "collective" is for them, and not for you,' Haraszti was told.[62] The dictatorship of the foreman was carried out in the name of the dictatorship of the proletariat — in the interests of all. The collective sacrifices, the general revisions of the norms sprung upon the workers, all were stamped with the approval of the workers' representatives — the party and the trade union — and ratified by the workers themselves, after the event, in orchestrated meetings. This is the meaning of bureaucratic despotism.

The Regime of Bureaucratic Despotism

We have been trying to highlight the differences between the politics of bureaucratic despotism at Red Star and the hegemonic regime at Allied. Before extracting the essentials of this comparison I will prepare the ground with the equally important comparison of market despotism and bureaucratic despotism.

Since it appeared to provide a mechanism for the continual intensification of exploitation, Marx regarded the piece wage as the most appropriate form of wage for capitalism. Curiously, management experts in the Soviet Union and Eastern Europe have long claimed that the piece wage is the most appropriate for socialism because it enshrines the principle of payment according to work. It is not surprising, then, that we should discover striking similarities between Marx's description of capitalism and Haraszti's account of Red Star Tractor Factory. Although Marx does not discuss the independent and interactive effects of any specific labour process combined with piece rates, one can infer the following similarities between the two forms of factory politics. In both cases economic survival depends directly on the expenditure of labour. As a result, the labour process combines with the system of piece wages to generate, with a large degree of autonomy, the reproduction of relations in production and relations of exploitation. When these relations are not automatically reproduced, uncertainties in the labour process are resolved to the advantage of management and provide the basis for the dictatorship of the foreman. Finally, the effect of piece rates is to stimulate competition, individualism and the redistribution of hierarchical into lateral conflict.

At the same time, there are fundamental differences between market and bureaucratic despotism, revolving around the use of 'extra-economic' force in the reproduction of relations in production and relations of exploitation. Distinctive to the politics of bureaucratic despotism is the harnessing of the party and trade union structures to the managerial function. The organs of state politics directly enter the regulation of production as instruments for the repression of struggles, in the shaping of everyday relations on the shopfloor, and in the direction, appointment and dismissal of managers. Market despotism is unrestrained but unassisted by extra-economic forces. State politics does not directly enter the reproduction of relations at the point of production; rather it exists to 'support the external conditions of the capitalist mode of production against the encroachments of the workers as well as of individual capitalists.'[63] Except in crisis situations production politics and state politics are separated. Under bureaucratic despotism state and factory politics are continuous, so that struggles which begin in one arena easily spill over into others. They therefore tend to be repressed rather than organized.

Differences between the two forms of factory politics revolve around links between politics of production and state politics. Similarities rest on the bond between an individual's material survival and his or her expenditure of labour on the shopfloor. What happens to the nature of factory politics when this bond is cut, when survival becomes more or less independent of the expenditure of effort? This was the pieceworker's dream.[64] Haraszti asks, 'What would spur us on constantly to increase output if one hundred per cent performance was really feasible, and its corresponding pay satisfactory?'[65] One answer is to be found in the hegemonic production politics at Allied.

In Chapter Three we described a variety of hegemonic regimes. Here we draw together the essentials based on the specific pattern at Allied. With basic survival guaranteed by forms of unemployment compensation and a minimum wage, workers must be persuaded rather than coerced to expend effort on the shopfloor. This is not to say that workers are never fired or made redundant, nor that workers do not fear such eventualities, but that an arena of consent is created, albeit guarded by an armour of coercion. Moreover, the application of coercion must itself be the object of consent — hence management's rule-bound interventions, and access to grievance procedures. The factory apparatuses assume a coherence of their own and cannot be arbitrarily altered by either management or union. The creation of an arena of consent also depends on the concrete coordination of the interests of workers and management, accomplished in two ways. Collective bargaining links workers' material interests to the company's profitability. Wages, vacations, supplementary unemployment benefits and transfers are tied to seniority, so that the longer a worker is with a company the more expensive it is to move and the more committed he or she is to the growth of profits or checking their decline. Such factory apparatuses establish the sufficient conditions for the constitution of the labour process as a game which sucks workers into the expenditure of effort on terms shaped by management.

Such a hegemonic regime of production politics is particulary well suited to the requirements of large, oligopolistic firms which dominate their product and supply markets. For such firms it becomes important to dominate the labour market as well, since there is little point in controlling two sets of markets but not the third. This is accomplished through internalization of the labour market and the setting of limits within which struggles may be waged. Other sectors of the economy, enmeshed in a much more competitive product market, are unable to coordinate the interests of workers and management at the expense of consumers. Here we often find a form of production politics that more closely approximates the market despotism described above, but with important differences — even unemployed workers can secure a minimal existence. And in yet other sectors of the economy, such as construction, we find craft workers retaining control of production despite the existence of a competitive market structure.

Just as the hegemonic regime at Allied is by no means typical of advanced capitalism, so the bureaucratic despotism of Red Star is by no means typical of state socialism. It has to be seen whether the hegemonic regime, in which the reproduction of labour power is independent of the workplace expenditure of labour, has an equivalent in state-socialist societies. In the next section we try to decipher varieties of production politics in Hungary, and in section 4 we explore the ways in which Hungary may differ from the Soviet Union and other East European countries.

3. Varieties of Factory Politics

Under what conditions can we expect to find an approximation of bureaucratic despotism in Hungarian factories? What other forms of production politics can be found, and where? In trying to answer such questions we face a problem of data. There are few published studies on the inner workings of factory life in the Soviet Union and Eastern Europe, let alone Hungary, and even fewer which capture the richness of detail found in *A Worker in a Worker's State*. My approach will be speculative and deductive, raising rather than answering questions. I will try to elicit the specific conditions of Red Star Tractor Factory which gave rise to bureaucratic despotism in its machine shop, and in this way show how other conditions generate different forms of production politics. But here too my approach is handicapped. Haraszti's analysis closes off the workplace from the political and economic context which shaped it. I have therefore tried to reconstruct that context from what I have been able to learn about Hungary at that time, and from the odd reference here and there in Haraszti's account.

The Impact of Industrial Branch

By 1971 Hungary's New Economic Mechanism had reached peak momentum. Red Star was one of its victims. The withdrawal of subsidies aimed to put the enterprise on an independent economic footing. The savage norm revisions were taken as a last resort, a means of survival. They failed to save the factory, which in 1972 was absorbed into a larger enterprise. A Hungarian study conducted in

1968-69 would seem to corroborate such an interpretation of the pressures behind despotic production politics. David Granick summarizes this study of three different enterprises:

> One of the three used an hourly-pay system; the second used piece rates, but with maximum total earnings placed at 100 to 110 per cent of the standard rate; only one used unlimited piece rates, and these were reduced by 20 per cent during a single year with resultant slow downs by many manual workers. Moreover, the third enterprise — the only one in which a genuine piece-rate system was employed — suffered from a most unusual financial squeeze which forced management to attempt to cut costs; its workers were mostly from nearby villages and had less of the solidarity against 'rate busters' than is commonly found among urban workers; and management seemed to have held a peculiarly powerful political position in the region. It seems typical that only such an unusual enterprise was both forced to use piece rates, and was capable of using them, as a means of furthering labour productivity.[66]

The stringent conditions at the third enterprise bear an uncanny resemblance to the experience of Red Star in 1971.

In a state socialist economy, what factors are likely to lead to the application of financial or other pressures to intensify work? And under what conditions would such an intensification be enforced through a despotic regime of labour control? Economic reforms notwithstanding, relations between enterprises and planning authorities determine in large measure the conditions and expectations of performance. Those in a strong bargaining position vis-à-vis the state are more likely to extract concessions and exemptions. These are most likely to be 'key' industries, large enterprises, or branches where there are only one or two enterprises producing a given product. One can conjecture that the more powerful enterprises will be able to secure supplies more easily, as well as bargain for looser targets or performance criteria and larger wage funds.[67] At the same time, simply because the enterprises are more important, central planners are more likely to interfere and to insist on changes in product mix at short notice. Thus, analysing the effects of the New Economic Mechanism on enterprise management, Bauer writes:

> If the relationship between large enterprises (such as Ganz-Mavag or the Hungarian ship-building yards), or large trusts (like in the food and building industries) and central management organs are more reminiscent of the old system, then in the small and medium-sized enterprises of a number of branches of industry (in the engineering industry, in the chemical industry producing household goods, in the pharmaceutical

industry, in the textile and shoe industries) the independence and responsibility of enterprises has risen considerably. . . . Financial concessions and exemptions more rarely affect small and medium-sized enterprises and, in addition, there is less interference on the part of government and political organs.[68]

Although we may conclude that the large and small enterprises are likely to possess different levels of autonomy from the central planners and face different sources and combinations of uncertainty, it is not clear what impact this has on forms of labour control. Are wages lower in the more independent enterprises? But are they also subject to less 'rushing'? Do they have to deal more with local than with national pressures? Is the smaller enterprise better able to coordinate the interests of workers and those of managers and/or planners?

Relations to the state are one set of determinants of uncertainty; the way shortages affect production is another. Where the product is relatively homogeneous and the manufacturing process unchanging, enterprises can place their orders for supplies long in advance. Laki cites the case of a large chemical enterprise which managed to reduce rushing in this way. One might expect fewer supply uncertainties in energy production (mining, electricity and oil). In his work on Soviet metal fabrication and his study of Hungarian enterprise guidance, Granick has shown the importance of vertical integration into supply functions in containing uncertainty. Where enterprises draw their supplies from Western markets, they are subject to less uncertainty in delivery time. But, equally, where production is for Western markets, requiring punctual delivery, this is undertaken at the expense of domestic production, which exhibits intensified forms of rushing.[69]

We can conclude that two sets of conditions determine the pressures on an enterprise. The first is the accountability of the enterprise to the central planners, the vertical relations linking the enterprise to the state. The second is the shortage of supplies, which leads to rushing and forced substitution of both inputs and outputs. What is not clear is how the enterprise deals with these uncertainties as regards the regulation of labour. Under what conditions do economic pressures lead the union and the party to become more visible instruments of managerial repression, and factory politics to move toward bureaucratic despotism? And under what conditions might enterprise management attempt to extract cooperation through rewards rather than punishment, through consent rather than coercion? What resources does it have at its command to pursue either alternative?[70]

Core and Periphery within the Enterprise

The large enterprise of state socialism has not been as successful as the oligopolistic firm of capitalism in stemming the penetration of external uncertainties into the core of production. The anarchy of the plan makes itself felt in three ways: the cyclical intensification of work due to variability in the delivery of supplies; unanticipated and irregular changes in the materials and instruments of production due to forced substitution; and change in products manufactured due to the variability of supplies or of directives from central planners. Just as the competitive sector of the capitalist economy adapts to market pressures through a despotic or craft regulation of work, the same alternatives are found under state socialism, but often in some combination *within* a single enterprise.[71]

Haraszti himself made reference to the existence of senior and experienced workers who obtained more lucrative bargains with management than did newcomers like himself, and in a personal communication he underlined the leadership role of these 'core' workers. It was they who decided to go along with management's intensification of work as a lesser evil than liquidation. But in his book Haraszti dwells almost exclusively on his own experiences as a 'peripheral' worker. A complementary picture emerges from Lajos Héthy and Csaba Makó's studies of what was at the time (1969) one of Hungary's best-run and dynamically developing engineering companies.[72] The specific unit under observation manufactured railway coaches. In 19' it employed about four hundred workers and was subject to gradual reduction in its production. As at Red Star, state subsidies were being withdrawn and management was attempting to intensify production. In 1969 piece rates were cut twice, so that the final wage fell by twenty per cent.

The major investigation focused on the last operation, where sixty men hammered away to level sheets of casings. Although the workers were paid according to a collective piece-rate system, the workshop was divided into two hostile groups: the older and more experienced workers on one side and the younger, less experienced workers on the other. The opposition of interests crystallized around their responses to the payment system. The older workers, having built up a solidary group, staged slowdowns in order to extract monetary concessions or looser piece rates from management. The younger group, rather than fighting for increases in the reward for effort, was concerned to maximize earnings in the short run without regard for possible rate-cutting. The formation of two opposed groups was in part shaped by the wage structure — particularly by the fact that seniority increases in the basic wage stopped after ten or twelve years of service. After the age of about thirty, workers had to deploy alternative strategies to increase wages — namely, fighting for bonuses, overtime and looser piece rates. More significantly, the economic needs of the two groups were very different. The younger workers, starting families, faced heavy expenditures, not least the purchase or, much more likely, the construction of apartments. They could not afford to restrict output, thus sacrificing immediate income for future gain. With major expenses behind them, their children grown and their wives possibly earning wages or other income, and with settled accommodation, the older workers could more easily absorb drastic but temporary cuts in wages in the pursuit of a future windfall.

In the struggle for a unified strategy the solidarity of the more senior workers won the day. Thus in April 1968, even though the work being offered by management had loose rates, the output of the work group as a whole underwent a precipitous decline: average wages fell from 10.1 forints an hour in March to 6.8 forints an hour in April. Tensions between young and old mounted as the latter staged a go-slow and refused to do overtime. Party and trade union entered the fray on management's side in an attempt to restore the original level of effort. When several workers tried to leave the company, asked for transfers or stayed at home on sick leave, management lost its head and intervened ruthlessly, but without much effect on output levels. Only when the bottleneck had developed to such an extent that the entire production of coaches was threatened did management give in and set up special incentive bonuses. The older group now resumed work with intensity, doubling and tripling their output levels and reaching average hourly wages of more than 17 forints. But when, in October 1969, the older workers got wind of impending rate cuts to be based on November and December outputs, they responded with another go-slow and successfully avoided the norm revisions that hit other units.

The factory apparatuses of the coach enterprise studied by Héthy and Makó were very similar to the ones at Red Star. There was no official countervailing power to the monolithic cohesiveness of union, party and management. The union executive had a share in company profits roughly equal to that of top management. The posts of union secretary and president were held by foremen. Not surprisingly, the union fully endorsed management's rate-cutting strategies. All five members of the party committee came from shopfloor supervision. And yet these apparatuses occasioned two very different responses.

On the one hand, the younger workers reacted like operators at Red Star. The payment system tied the well-being of their families to their effort on the shopfloor, and they were not prepared to sacrifice immediate earnings for potential future gains. As a result of their individualist orientation to work and their competitive isolation from other workers, they found themselves defenceless against aggressive and arbitrary managerial interventions. Their future interests were in fact protected by the older workers, who were more experienced, more skilled and less dependent on immediate earnings, and had established solidary social networks. The senior workers took advantage of their irreplaceability and their monopolistic position in the overall production process to hold management to ransom. The three go-slows forced major concessions from management and a retreat from an impending assault on norms.

Héthy and Makó provide a powerful corrective to Haraszti by highlighting the capacity of certain workers to resist managerial offensives and impose their will on other workers who would otherwise have succumbed to labour intensification. The emergent solidarity on the shopfloor is very different from the atomization of Red Star's machine shop. But Héthy and Makó examined other groups in the same enterprise and found that they were much weaker and more defenceless against norm revisions.[73] These groups were either dominated by the younger, inexperienced workers eager to maximise earnings in the short run, even at the expense of future earnings; or they were composed of workers isolated from one another and therefore unable to mount a cohesive resistance.

The development of a core and a periphery within the enterprise is facilitated by the absence of the levelling influence of an independent trade union. It is not simply that unions are dominated by managerial functionaries and are therefore unlikely to take any stance against management, but further, they often support the unequal distribution of power and resources among workers. Thus, party and trade union officials are disproportionately found among core workers.[74] The reproduction of a dual system of production politics within the enterprise is also fostered by central determination either of the average wage level or of the wage fund.[75] This means that concessions granted to one group of workers must be at the expense of some other group.

As we have seen, the New Economic Mechanism attempted to encourage the cooperation of workers and management through profit-sharing schemes at the same time that average wage levels were centrally regulated. In reality the redistribution of profit was so limited and hamstrung by restrictions that it made little difference to earnings. Furthermore, lifting all restrictions on mobility in the context of labour shortage and higher earnings in many of the auxiliary plants of the agricultural cooperatives and small factories made it difficult for state enterprises to hang on to their skilled labour in particular. Thus, unskilled workers would be recruited with the sole intention of bringing down the average wage level so that higher wages could be offered to the more stable skilled workers. More usually, management would manipulate incentive schemes so that, for example, key workers were assigned loose piece rates.[76] In addition, core workers might receive more overtime or their jobs might be redefined to provide compensation for poor working conditions. Whether these concessions are extended in a process of informal bargaining or as bribes to elicit cooperation, they are a recognition of the power of certain key workers in a situation of irregular changes in the form and flow of materials, machinery and manufactured products. And all concessions to the core workers are at the expense of peripheral workers, whose only hope is to leave in search of a better job or to seek promotion to the core.

The Reproduction of Labour Power

The development of a core and a periphery within the enterprise is crucially dependent on the indeterminate and continually shifting character of the labour process, the central control of wage levels and the absence of the levelling influence of independent trade unions. Workers' bargaining strength is significantly affected by location in the production process as well as by skill and experience. But it is also shaped by the dependence of livelihood on performance at work. Thus, older workers, less dependent on immediate earnings, were in a stronger position to withhold effort than were younger workers in need of ready cash. In other words, workers' bargaining strength is critically determined by the extent of enterprise control over the reproduction of their labour power. The more independent the reproduction of labour power is from enterprise control, the greater is the ability to resist managerial offensives.

We have already seen how the transition from early ('liberal', 'competitive') to advanced ('monopoly') capitalism involved the separation of the reproduction of labour power from the labour process. While livelihood outside work came to be guaranteed by benefits allocated by the state independent of performance at work, there emerged rudimentary protection from arbitrary firing, and certain minimum wages were assured independent of the application of effort. This led to a corresponding transition in production politics: from despotic regimes in which coercion prevailed over consent to hegemonic regimes in which consent prevailed over coercion. At the same time, a form of 'market despotism' was created in certain sectors of advanced capitalism where competition among firms impelled dictatorial regulation of work and where the character of the labour force — often women, blacks or migrants — permitted the exercise of such regulation. Can we trace similar transformations of production politics under state socialism? As we shall see, here it is the *liberation* of market forces and the *withdrawal* of state intervention, rather than the regulation and displacement of the market by a growing state intervention, that lead to the separation of the reproduction of labour power from the labour process.

In the period of extensive development, enterprises were more likely to allocate housing and other benefits in addition to wages. Laws regulated the mobility of labour, preventing workers from quitting arbitrarily, and punished 'inexcusable' absenteeism. Households were less likely to have two or more wage-earners, and income from a second economy was more limited. With the transition to intensive development, particularly since the economic reforms, the reproduction of labour power has become increasingly independent of enterprise control. Whereas the state dispensation of housing and social benefits used to be linked to seniority and skill, their present allocation is much less tied to participation in particular enterprises. We also find the burgeoning of family housing built by unskilled and semi-skilled workers on the outskirts of urban areas.[77] Labour was given unlimited opportunities to move from enterprise to enterprise, and legislation during the last decade has been largely ineffectual in limiting labour turnover.[78] Multiple-earner families have increased with the rise in female participation in the wage labour force, so that now workers can either quit or withhold effort and allow earnings to fall without the family being entirely cut off from the state sector. Where before there may have been excess supply of labour, now there is an ever-intensifying shortage, at the existing level of wages, and the vigorous competition for labour leads enterprises to engage in forms of hoarding. Finally, the so-called second economy has been flourishing since the reforms, despite attempts in the mid-seventies to restrict its scope. More recently, since 1980, the state has given the second economy another shot in the arm by explicitly recognizing its benefits and legalizing many of its institutions.

We have little comparative information on the forms of production politics in the two periods, but one would expect the period of extensive development, of primitive socialist accumulation, to be characterized by forms of bureaucratic despotism in which workers' resistance was even more limited than it was at Red Star. The reforms opened up the labour market as a response to the labour shortage, so that from 1968 to 1969 labour turnover increased by 74 per cent.[79] In 1971 many workers had greater opportunities to quit their work at Red Star, despite attempts to punish 'migrating birds',[80] and they were in a better position to obtain income from activities outside the socialist sector than would have been the case twenty years earlier. We must examine the nature of the 'second economy' in greater detail to appreciate its impact on factory politics.

Interest in the second economy was originally stimulated by recognition of the importance of the 'unofficial' economic transactions (the black and coloured markets) operating alongside the socialist sector in the Soviet Union. In the West these were held to demonstrate the irrationality of socialist planning and the superiority of the market as a vehicle for distribution and production. Not surprisingly the concept has been elaborated in greatest empirical detail in Hungary, but it has always been defined in relation to the first economy, often as a residual category: 'By "second economy" we mean the ways in which capacity to work is utilized outside the socialized economic sector as well as the income redistribution processes among the population outside socially organized distribution in their entirety.'[81] This definition directs attention away from the independent dynamics of the second economy, away from the relationship among its different parts and of these parts to different segments of the first economy. However, the data collected by Gábor and others clearly delineate the contours of the second economy and allow us to conjecture its effects on factory politics in the state sector.

According to standard interpretations,[82] the second economy includes legalized private production on agricultural plots and in cooperative enterprises and some retail trade; the unofficial professional services of doctors, dentists, lawyers, teachers and architects; the personal services of housekeepers, cooks, seamstresses and tailors; and the repair services of mechanics, painters, plumbers, electricians and carpenters. All these transactions can take place outside the socialist sector. Within the socialist sector these same service personnel may attract tips, conscience money or bribes; this is also considered part of the second economy. Finally, there are those who illegally use or appropriate state property for their own private economic activities.

In such analyses the critical feature is the differential relationship to the state. Whereas in the first economy the state directs production, in the second economy it regulates only the external conditions of production, limiting among other things the employment of wage labour and the accumulation of capital. In effect the state supplies the conditions and the stimulus for the reproduction of two modes of production subordinated to the socialist sector. On the one hand there is petty commodity production based on self-employment, while on the other hand there is the domestic mode of production where consumption goods which would otherwise have to be purchased are produced by the family units that consume them. Such income which does not derive from labour, including tips and bribes, or what Hegedüs and Márkus call the purchase of good will, and income from appropriated state property, can be regarded as particular modes of *transferring* surplus from the state sector to petty commodity or domestic production.

As we shall see, participation in one or the other of these systems of production, as well as movement between them, shape distinctive responses within the state sector to managerial offensives. Yet these secondary economic activities also depend on the state sector in a number of ways. First, employment in a state enterprise offers workers certain social benefits as well as guaranteed employment that is unavailable to those employed full-time in the second economy. Second, petty commodity and domestic production often depend on the supply of materials from the state sector. Finally, state regulation of the second economy changes so arbitrarily, making illegal and risky what yesterday was legal and safe, that participation in the first economy is essential for security reasons. This also leads to a 'get rich quick' philosophy within the private sector, since long-term investments, innovations and so on become much more risky. One of the consequences is the phenomenon of 'double employment' or *parallel* participation in the first and second economies, with only a few — and during the last decade a diminishing few — *alternating* employment between first and second economies. (Pensioners are an obvious exception to this rule.) Thus, some participation in the second economy is widespread among employees in the first economy. An estimated 75 per cent of families in Hungary participate in the second economy, most broadly defined to include both income and non-income producing activities. It is estimated that those wage earners who participate spend one-and-a-half to two hours beyond the normal eight-hour day in second economy production.

From the point of view of the economy as a whole, petty commodity and domestic production fill gaps in the provision of services and consumer goods. They contribute an estimated 15 to 20 per cent of the gross national product. They are particularly effective in competing with small and inefficient state enterprises. Petty commodity producers are able to supply goods and services at short notice and more cheaply. Because petty commodity production involves working for oneself, reward is proportional to effort and enterprises are cost sensitive — that is, they must be profitable. Estimates suggest that whereas the ratio of labour time expended in the second economy to that expended in the state sector is of the order of 4 to 22, the income ratio is of the order of 9 to 22.[83]

The recognition of petty commodity and domestic production by the state has an effect on the centrally determined wage levels. Inasmuch as wages are calculated on the basis of the cost of reproducing labour power, the second economy acts as a brake on their rate of increase, since it is now assumed that it accounts for at least part of the income of all families. With the renewed expansion of the second economy since 1979, real wages have stopped increasing.[84] At the same time, the expansion of petty commodity production, and in particular its polarization over the last decade, has increased income inequalities despite the growing equalization of wages in the socialist sector.

As we suggested earlier, the existence of alternative incomes has given certain workers in the state sector greater bargaining strength with respect to management, and indeed the stimulus to restrict output (conserve effort), so that economic incentives are less effective. But we should be careful not to generalize for the entire labour force. We must take into account workers' unequal access to the second economy. By no means all workers can engage in petty commodity production, and many workers who are involved in domestic production face an additional drain on income. Although we do not know which sectors of the labour force are active in which segments of the second economy, we do know that only forty per cent of workers in industry and construction have any access to it. What about the remaining sixty per cent? It is possible that other members of their families have access to the second economy. Nevertheless, if wages in the state sector are linked to some national average participation in petty commodity production, then bargaining strength will be increased for some and reduced for others, and economic incentives will be less effective for some and more effective for others.

Who are the workers without access to petty commodity production? We have already discovered variations in participation in the second economy according to life cycle. Young workers face an acute shortage of housing and a system of allocation which discriminates against them. They have no alternative but to begin construction of their own homes, which may take ten years or more.[85] During this time they will also face the costs of bringing up their families, so that every extra fillér counts toward some urgently required commodity. Once their children have grown up and their houses are built, such workers can transfer more of their energies out of domestic production and into petty commodity production. They will then be in a stronger position to withstand managerial offensives. But there is a sizable group of workers who do not and will not have access to petty commodity production but are nevertheless necessarily involved in domestic production, particularly agricultural subsistence production. These are the commuters who work in towns and live in villages.[86] Indeed, half the Hungarian labour force lives in villages — when they come to town they are often housed in large hostels or dormitories. These workers desperately need income from the socialist sector to supplement what they can eke out of the land.[87] They are often confined to lower-paid jobs in the state sector, and the internal labour market bars them from more lucrative positions. Kertesi and Sziráczki refer to this group as internal guest workers;[88] they often make do with unstable employment in road construction, railways and seasonal labour in agriculture. They constitute a distinct segment of the labour force, facing discriminatory labour market allocation mechanisms. Many are in fact women and Gypsies. In short, the existence of flourishing petty commodity production for some actually makes others more dependent on performance at work and therefore more vulnerable to the despotic production politics described earlier.

If my analysis is correct, the expansion of petty commodity production alongside the state sector superimposes further divisions of the working class on those already existing by virtue of position in the labour process, level of skill and experience. To what extent these two sets of divisions reinforce or cross-cut each other has yet to be investigated. But our analysis does suggest that sectoral differences among state enterprises are probably less important than those that develop within the enterprise on the one hand and out of relations to the second economy on the other. The second consequence of petty commodity and domestic production is the promotion of individualism and consumerism as powerful as in advanced capitalist countries. Petty commodity production offers a new channel of mobility, a new mode of acquisition which effectively channels discontent in economic rather than political directions. It has all the effects described by Ely Chinoy in *The Automobile Worker and the American Dream* — above all, blame for failure is attributed to the lack of sufficient exertion on the part of the individual. An obvious question now arises: how representative is Hungary of East European countries? To the extent that atomization, individualism and segmentation are distinctive features of working classes in Eastern Europe and the Soviet Union, how do we explain the extraordinary levels of collective solidarity recently witnessed in Poland?

4. Class Struggles under State Socialism

We have so far considered varieties of production politics in Hungary and their determinants. We must now consider their consequences for class struggles. It is necessary first to map out the meaning of class under state socialism and then to suggest the generic forms of class struggle before embarking on their specific manifestations in different countries. We will finally consider alternative forms of socialism prefigured in the working-class struggles of Eastern Europe.

The Transparency of Class

Under advanced capitalism the existence of unpaid labour is mystified in four interrelated ways. First, labour is paid as though for the entire working day; second, profit is realized in the market; third, profit appears as a return on invested capital; and fourth, ownership of the means of production is separated from the direction of work. The problem for the capitalist is to secure what has been obscured — unpaid labour. Moreover, the success of the operation is known only after the fact — profit is recovered only after the production of commodities and after wages have been advanced. In other words, the process of expropriation coincides with and is thereby masked by the process of production. So without profit workers have no jobs — that is, workers have an interest in capitalist exploitation.

Under state socialism the processes of production and expropriation are separated. Unpaid labour becomes transparent. The exploiters and the exploited are revealed as the class of redistributors and its agents on one side and the direct producers on the other. As workers no longer have a clear-cut material interest in the success of the firm, they must be coerced or bribed into rendering a surplus product. The state is present at the point of production as simultaneous exploiter and oppressor, as appropriator of surplus and regulator of production.

These distinctive features of production politics and state politics under advanced capitalism and state socialism give rise to characteristic forms of class struggle. Under advanced capitalism, enterprise struggles are isolated from one another and organized within limits defined by the survival of the firm. Only under exceptional circumstances do struggles spill over into the wider political arena. Under state socialism, enterprise struggles are immediately struggles against the state, because the factory apparatuses are also apparatuses of the state and because the state is the transparent appropriator of surplus product as well as the redistributor of wages and services and the regulator of prices. Moreover, so long as direct producers are not systematically enjoined to a collective societal interest, their struggles are limited only by the forces of repression or the distribution of concessions.

What can we say about the forms of consciousness that emerge under the two systems? Braverman defined the central tendency of the capitalist labour process as the separation of conception and execution. But he made it clear that he was referring only to the objective moment of production, not to its subjective moment. Under the hegemonic regime the direct producer's day-to-day experience is of the individual bound beneath the domination of capital, whose interests are presented as the interests of all. The direct producer is not inserted into the labour process as a member of one class in opposition to another.

Under state socialism the objective development of the separation of conception and execution becomes the basis of a subjective orientation to society as a whole. Conception and execution become more than categories with which to grasp the development of the labour process or the historical experience of the direct producer. They become the defining elements of class structure. The conceivers or planners are the transparent perpetrators of domination and exploitation, justified by their supposedly superior comprehension of the collective interest. The executors are the direct producers, who can partake in the planning process only by leaving their class and joining the planners. This polarization of classes is as clear on the shop-floor — in the political identification of inspectors, foremen, clerks, and other non-productive workers as agents of redistribution — as it is in the wider society. Thus, Montias refers to one particular but often unarticulated grievance that threads through all accounts of workers' strikes in Eastern Europe. This is 'that the management and the auxiliary bureaucracy that adminster production plants and ship-yards are inflated in numbers, paid too much in relation to workers, and receive disproportionate benefits in the form of vacations, sick leaves and other privileges. One workers' representative at the Szczecin shipyards put this issue in ideological terms, claiming that the authorities by creating different working conditions for blue-collar workers and for white-collar employees and management, were artificially segregating people into classes.'[89]

In his analysis of housing allocation Szelényi notes the same development of class privileges, which place the unskilled workers in a doubly disadvantaged position. The redistributors and their agents not only receive much of the available housing but get it at heavily subsidized prices.[90]

Class struggles bring the executors into direct confrontation with the conceivers. As a result, direct producers become conscious of their function and develop an interest in appropriating the planning function, in taking over the direction of society; they articulate, however inchoately, the principle that 'those who produce the surplus product should dispose over it, not those who claim that they know better how it should be distributed.'[91] This consciousness is heightened by the actual control over production that core workers necessarily exercise as a result of the uncertainties that typically penetrate the shopfloor. Their hostility to the 'bureaucracy' is exacerbated by their knowledge that the supposed conceivers do not appear to conceive anything, this function being actually carried out by the direct producers. Such forms of shopfloor control can only enhance the sense of efficacy of the core workers. Ironically, then, workers are more likely to recover a socialist consciousness and struggle to appropriate control over production and distribution of surplus under state socialism than under capitalism. That is, such control struggles are endemic to state socialism — what must be determined is the form they take in different societies, and at different times.

Varieties of Class Struggle

Whereas a hegemonic regime *organizes* struggles within limits, bureaucratic despotism *represses* open struggle. The form of resistance reflects the form of domination. Haraszti recounts one individualistic response which captures the impetus to recombine conception and execution. In moments grabbed between jobs, workers turned to the production of 'homers', useless but imaginatively conceived objects, shaped (very often with the assistance of others) out of scraps of metal. Homers express an antithesis (and antipathy) to the detail labour of individualized commodity production. They represent what Marcuse calls play: 'The ideas of play and display now reveal their full distance from the values of productiveness and performance: play is *unproductive* and *useless* precisely because it cancels the repressive and exploitative traits of labour and leisure; it just "plays" with the reality."[92] Although such forms of utopian escape play a role under capitalism, they assume a more symbolic and powerful form under more total forms of domination.

More generally, where repression is effective, as it is for the most part in the Soviet Union, resistance is forced into such expressions of individualism. Thus Zaslavsky argues that the repressive atomism of the period of socialist primitive accumulation gave way in the 1950s to new expressions of 'deviance' such as alcoholism, absenteeism and labour turnover.[93] Ticktin refers to the restriction of output and production of waste as marks of struggles to regain control over production.[94] And according to Holubenko, '[T]he right not to work hard at the factory is one of the few remaining rights which the Soviet worker holds. The Soviet worker will resist and "carry on a clandestine struggle", as one Soviet dissident put it, against all efforts to intensify the work pace.'[95]

Despite the pervasive atomization of the working class, strikes, riots and other forms of collective protest do break out in the Soviet Union. Although little is known about them, odd references appear in the Soviet media and the underground press. Not surprisingly, strikes are often instigated by attacks on the general standard of living, such as food shortages or price increases, and attempts to link the 'social wage' to productivity. Thus, such collective mobilization as occurs often springs from norm revisions or inadequate housing.

Holubenko's analysis of the available descriptions of strikes suggests that workers spontaneously direct their hostilities to the seat of power, the local party headquarters; when they get no satisfaction there they target the regional or even national headquarters. The working class is very conscious of the decisive concentrations of power and the organs which shape its daily life. Holubenko's data also suggest that strikes tend to occur more frequently away from centres of power. Peripheral regions are less strategic to the regime and therefore less effectively policed. They are also more likely to suffer from shortages of basic subsistence goods. But strikes can be put down with much greater violence — often including the shooting of workers — since there is less risk that the disturbances will spread. By contrast, when strikes occur in the major centres, the state makes rapid economic concessions to defuse protest. It then follows with a relentless persecution of the strike leaders.

If the development of a cohesive working-class movement is impossible in the Soviet Union of today, the same is not necessarily true where a rudimentary civil society has opened up and workers' organizations have managed to build horizontal ties, a working-class community. Poland and Hungary are examples of countries where such a civil society has opened up, but how do we explain the mobilization of the working class in one and not in the other? The arguments developed in the previous sections suggest that the relationship of the enterprise to the state is critical to the emergence of working-class mobilization. Thus, the greater autonomy of the Hungarian enterprise allows management to combine repression and concessions in such a way as more effectively to divide the labour force and to obtain the cooperation of its most powerful sections. In Poland the much higher degree of centralization left management less room to organize and pre-empt struggles, while establishing a more cohesive opposition to the directing centre. The division of the economy into priority and non-priority sectors was more significant, whereas the bifurcation of production politics within the enterprise was less significant than in Hungary. Centralization generated more acute shortages in the Polish economy, exacerbating tensions between enterprises and entailing that strikes, slowdowns and production failures in one enterprise reverberated through the economy.

In assessing the form of production politics is it sufficient to look at the relationship between factory and state? Are the factory apparatuses in Hungary and Poland so different as to account for class demobilization in the former and rapid class mobilization in the latter? How important are workers' economic activities outside the enterprise? Here there are clear differences. Extensive privatization of agriculture in Poland led to the polarization of rural communities into independent farmers on one side and peasant workers on the other.[96] In 1962 forty-two per cent of rural families obtained less than ten per cent of the value of their agricultural production from wage labour. These families were largely independent of the industrial sector.[97] Peasant workers, on the other hand, were in a much weaker position as they depended on plots of land to supplement income from wage labour. As industrial workers they had lower levels of labour turnover, put in more hours of work over the year, were less absent and drew on welfare facilities less frequently than did urban-based employees.[98] One might surmise, therefore, that the industrial labour force is also polarized between the skilled workers with a weak attachment to the land and unskilled or semi-skilled peasant workers. Could it then be that the skilled workers, precisely because they perform a critical role in production and at the same time are cut off from alternative incomes, are more prone to collective mobilization? In Hungary the dominance of the cooperative, and to a lesser extent the state farm, does not permit the same polarization between farmers and peasant workers. Instead cooperatives encourage all sectors of the labour force to engage in part-time agricultural production, while the state is more tolerant of the expansion of other forms of petty commodity production. The result is that a 'traditional' working class with a powerful collective consciousness never congealed in Hungary as it has done in Poland.

In the above discussions I quite deliberately played down the significance of conventional explanations which revolve around nationalism, the church and popular traditions. I take the opening up of civil society as a necessary but, as the Hungarian case makes clear, not sufficient condition for working-class mobilization. Accordingly, I have tentatively hypothesized that the Hungarian working class is segmented by virtue of enterprise autonomy and atomized by virtue of its participation in other modes of production, while the Polish working class, with more restricted access to other modes of production, seeks advancement through collective struggles rather than individual mobility.

Prefiguring Alternative Socialisms

What does the future hold for Eastern Europe? The most interesting attempts at transition have occurred in the periphery of the Soviet orbit. The political relaxation that was set in motion after 1956 reverberated throughout Eastern Europe, splitting party apparatuses into reformist and old-guard factions. In Poland a new regime was swept into power on a wave of opposition to the repressive policies of the old order and its subordination to the economic and political interests in the Soviet Union. In Hungary protest by students and intellectuals combined with divisions in the party apparatus to fire working-class struggles.[99] The state apparatuses collapsed, leaving a vacuum both at the central administrative level and at the regional and factory levels. The Russian tanks moved in, but not before a situation of dual power had been proclaimed. For a short time workers took control of their enterprises and began to construct rudimentary coordination of enterprises from below. An embryonic system of collective self-management was established, only to be crushed by the overpowering presence of the occupying forces.

The Hungarian factory occupations resulted from the internal divisions and collapse of state power rather than from a mounting working-class movement. The ascending mobilization of the Polish working class from 1956 (or 1944) to 1970 to 1976 and thence to 1980 led in a very different direction. The twenty-one demands made at Gdansk in August 1980 included the satisfaction of material needs, the right to form independent trade unions and to strike, the elimination of party privileges, and the ending of press censorship, but, significantly, they omitted any reference to workers' self-management. Past attempts to introduce workers' councils had shown them to be a sham, a way of cooling off a volatile situation without granting any real concessions, particularly when workers had no means of influencing the central powers. Workers' self-management is meaningless if all the essential decisions are made outside the factory. Moreover, in the first months of its existence Solidarity adopted the formula of a 'self-limiting revolution' which forced the movement into a trade-union corset, refusing to be held responsible for economic decisions and the deteriorating economic conditions. As Staniszkis has argued, Solidarity adopted a fundamentalist rather than a pragmatic orientation to the old regime, failing to develop new institutions which might consolidate and defend any gains made. [100]

Only when the economy appeared to be heading toward catastrophe, the official regime seemed to have run into paralysis and negotiations between Solidarity leaders and the government were deadlocked, did the goals of economic reform and workers' self-management gain support within the movement. But here there was soon a collision with the party over who would control the appointment of enterprise management and to whom it would be responsible. A compromise was struck, forestalling a general strike, but by this time much of the working class was already demobilized and a gap had emerged between the rank-and-file members of Solidarity and its leadership. Efforts at building a system of collective self-management from below received only lukewarm support from the Solidarity leadership, which was threatened by such devolution of power. The horizontal ties, constructed both within the party and among enterprises in the early months of Solidarity, were never effectively consolidated through the radical transformation of factory apparatuses. Not only was this a lost opportunity to construct a system of collective self-management, but it left Solidarity significantly more vulnerable to repression when martial law was declared.

For all its shortcomings, and despite the different outcomes, Solidarity did develop that ascendant dynamic which we saw in operation between the two Russian revolutions of 1917. [101] Although both movements were potentially revolutionary in that they threatened the existing political order, neither was radical at the outset. Beginning with defensive demands for the protection of living standards, the movements only later escalated to demands for the restructuring of state politics. In this way, it became clear that any transformation of production politics required a corresponding transformation of state politics. In both cases the collapse or paralysis of the state was a necessary condition for the further radicalization of the movement, since it offered the opportunity for, and in some cases forced, workers to take over factories. However, once workers assumed responsibility for factory management, the necessity of horizontal linkages, of co-ordination of the economy from below, became apparent. The factory committees in Russia and the Network in Poland took steps to build such horizontal links, beginning to construct from below an alternative society based on the principle of collective self-management. But it was a fragile system as long as there was no state to protect it. And when such a state did emerge in Russia, it quickly developed interests for centralization, opposing the system of collective self-management and the devolution of power.

We find ourselves confronting a number of paradoxes. First, state socialist rather than advanced capitalist societies generate movements for worker direction of society, which in its most developed form leads toward collective self-management. The fusion of production politics and state politics is a necessary if not sufficient condition for the development of socialism oriented toward workers' control. Second, these movements require organizational resources which presuppose the opening up of a rudimentary civil society — that is, institutions outside the economy and outside the direct control of the state. In other words, in order to be effective, struggles for workers' control require the trappings of bourgeois society. But, as we see in the case of Hungary, those trappings may also demobilize and atomize the working class. Third, working-class movements are most likely to develop some muscle in the periphery of the Soviet orbit, where they are infused with nationalist sentiment. But because they take place in peripheral societies they are particularly vulnerable to external and internal repression. Solidarity's 'self-limiting revolution' was a bold and creative attempt to deal with these paradoxes.

Notes

1. Two recent books very sensitive to these issues are Alec Nove's *The Economics of Feasible Socialism*, London 1983, and Ferenc Fehér, Agnes Heller and György Márkus, *Dictatorship Over Needs*, Oxford 1983.

2. See Carmen Sirianni, 'Production and Power in a Classless Society: A Critical

Analysis of the Utopian Dimensions of Marxist Theory', *Socialist Reiview*, no. 59, 1981, pp. 33-82, for an elaboration of this critique of recent theories of the labour process.

3. See, for example, Charles Sabel and David Stark, 'Planning, Politics and Shop-Floor Power: Hidden Forms of Bargaining in Soviet-Imposed State-Socialist Societies', *Politics and Society*, vol. 2, no. 4, 1982, pp. 437-76; and David Stark, 'The Micro Politics of the Firm and the Macro Politics of Reform', in Peter Evans, Dietrich Rueschemeyer and Evelyne Huber Stevens, eds., *States vs. Markets in the World System*, Beverly Hills 1985 (forthcoming).

4. In this section I have been particularly influenced by the class analysis of G. Konrád and I. Szelényi (*Intellectuals on the Road to Class Power*, New York 1979) and M. Rakovski (*Towards an East European Marxism*, London 1978), and the economic analysis of J. Kornai (*Economics of Shortage*, 2 vols., Amsterdam 1980) and T. Bauer ('Investment Cycles in Planned Economies', *Acta Oeconomica*, vol. 21, no. 3, 1978, pp. 243-60).

5. This formula is borrowed from Konrád and Szelényi. But it is important to make the following qualification. Just as capitalists make economic concessions to workers in order to elicit their cooperation, so under socialism similar concessions are made to firms and workers by teleological redistributors. But in neither case do the concessions touch the essential principles based on the search for profit and the central appropriation of surplus.

6. Kornai, op.cit.

7. D. Nuti, 'The Contradictions of Socialist Economies: A Marxist Interpretation', in *The Socialist Register 1979*, London 1979, pp. 228-73, and 'The Polish Crisis: Economic Factors and Constraints', in *The Socialist Register 1981*, London 1981, pp. 104-43; and M. Kalecki, *Introduction to the Theory of Growth of the Socialist Economy*, London 1969.

8. The dynamics of the shortage economy operate independently of the level of development of the forces of production; they are not a product of Hungarian 'under-development', and I found exactly the same dynamics emerging in Allied. Planning in the big corporation faced problems of shortage similar to those I have described for state socialism. Thus, the Allied engine division operated under soft budget constraints. Its relationship to the divisions it supplied was subject to continual bargaining, and its annual plan was continually revised in the light of the changing needs of those divisions. The result was that uncertainty penetrated the shopfloor, exemplified by the 'hot jobs' that appeared from time to time, pre-empting any existing work. Obviously the degree of uncertainty in supplies was less than in the socialist enterprise, since market forces operated in the division's relations with companies outside the corporation, yet still the phenomenon of rushing could be observed.

9. Solomon Schwarz, *Labour in the Soviet Union*, New York 1951, chapter 3.

10. Nuti, 'Contradictions of Socialist Economies'.

11. X. Richet, 'Is There a "Hungarian" Model of Planning?',in Paul Hare, Hugo Radice and Nigel Swain, eds., *Hungary: A Decade of Economic Reform*, London 1981, pp. 23-40; M. Bornstein, 'Price Policy in Hungary', in A. Abouchar, ed., *The Socialist Price Mechanism*, Durham, North Carolina 1977.

12. Charles Bettelheim, *Economic Calculation and Forms of Property*, London 1976.

13. M. Laki, 'End-Year Rush-Work in Hungarian Industry and Foreign Trade', *Acta Oeconomica*, vol. 25, nos. 1-2, 1980, pp. 37-65; David Granick, *Enterprise Guidance in Eastern Europe: A Comparison of Four Socialist Countries in Eastern Europe*, Princeton 1975, pp. 257-316; Bauer, 'The Contradictory Position of the Enterprise under the New Hungarian Economic Mechanism', *Coexistence*, no. 13, 1976, pp. 65-80.

14. I. Szelényi, 'Urban Development and Regional Management in Eastern

Europe', *Theory and Society*, vol. 10, 1981, pp. 169-205.

15. Julius Rezler, 'Recent Developments in the Hungarian Labour Market', *East European Quarterly*, vol. 10, no. 2, Summer 1976, pp. 265-6; István Gábor and Péter Galasi, 'The Labour Market in Hungary Since 1968', in Hare, Radice and Swain, pp. 49-52.

16. Granick, *Enterprise Guidance in Eastern Europe*, pp. 262-9; M. Marrese, 'The Evolution of Wage Regulation in Hungary', in Hare, Radice and Swain, pp. 63-6. Attempts to use capitalist techniques for increasing worker productivity in the Soviet Union have met with little sustained success. Thus, although the Shchekino experiment did score some initial successes these proved to be short-lived (R. Arnot, 'Soviet Labour Productivity and the Failure of the Shchekino Experiment', *Critique*, no. 15, 1981, pp. 31-56). The aim of the experiment was to tie the interests of the workforce to enterprise performance by reducing the number of employees while maintaining the size of the wage fund. The savings obtained by dismissing workers would, with certain limitations, be distributed to the remaining workers. At the original Shchekino plant the released personnel were absorbed into a new plant nearby. Between 1967 and 1974 production grew 2.5 times, the number of workers fell by 1500, productivity increased 3.1 times, and average wages grew by 44 per cent. The very success at Shchekino tells us something of the overmanning in Soviet industry. Yet the experiment was never successfully generalized, for a number of reasons. First, it relied on the creation of unemployment, which is incompatible with the tendencies toward labour hoarding in a shortage economy and with the political imperatives of state socialism. Second, the autonomy of the enterprise to distribute the proceeds of its savings continued to be severely circumscribed by state regulation, particularly control over investment and the determination of plan targets by achieved level. Third, the maintenance of soft budget constraints meant that criteria of profit and productivity could be only weakly incorporated into managerial strategies. The eventual failure of the experiment highlights the distinctive character of the redistributive economy.

17. Harmondsworth 1977.

18. Ibid., p. 134.

19. 'Hungarian Profiles -- An Interview with Miklós Haraszti', *Labour Focus on Eastern Europe*, vol. 2, no. 6, 1979, p. 16.

20. There are a number of problems with Haraszti's study which will emerge in the course of the analysis. Above all it focuses on the despotic character of work at the expense of the ways in which workers cope with their conditions. For example, we are led to believe that it is impossible for workers to restrict output, yet prices are continually being revised downward and output seems to be maintained at a constant level. Second, the book is written entirely from the perspective of an individual machine operator, and therefore reflects the operator's fragmented experience — each chapter is another fragment. Like Haraszti, the reader is never allowed an insight into the totality of the production process, or the pressures on auxiliary workers and on various levels of management. Furthermore, the plant itself is not contextualized. Third, Haraszti himself is not a normal machine operator; he is an intellectual intruding into alien territory. It is possible that his class origins excited hostility from fellow-workers and foremen. More important was the fact that Haraszti was a novice to the machine shop and therefore necessarily found the rates difficult to make and social relations difficult to manipulate. Still, based on my own experience in a similar shop in Hungary, I accept Haraszti's portrait of Red Star's factory regime as unusually despotic. See my 'Piece Rates, Hungarian Style', *Socialist Review* (January, 1985)'.

21. Haraszti, p. 111.

22. Ibid., p. 26.
23. Ibid., p. 25.
24. Ibid., p. 27.
25. Ibid., p. 90.
26. Ibid., pp. 36-7.
27. Ibid., p. 40.
28. Ibid., p. 51.
29. Ibid., p. 49.
30. Ibid., p. 63.
31. Ibid., p. 59.
32. Central Statistical Office, *Statistical Yearbook 1980*, Budapest 1981, p. 140.
33. Haraszti, pp. 56, 57.
34. Ibid., pp. 134, 136-7.
35. Ibid., p. 39.
36. Ibid., p. 58.
37. Ibid., p. 119.
38. Ibid., p. 132.
39. Ibid., p. 114.
40. Ibid., p. 115.
41. Ibid., pp. 53, 66.
42. Ibid., p. 90.
43. Ibid., p. 28.
44. Ibid., p. 31.
45. Ibid., p. 32.
46. Ibid., p. 80.
47. Ibid., p. 76.
48. Ibid., p. 33.
49. Ibid., p. 84.
50. Ibid., p. 86; quote from one of Haraszti's fellow-operators.
51. Ibid., p. 101.
52. Ibid., p. 101.
53. Ibid., pp. 86-7.
54. Ibid., p. 118.
55. Ibid., p. 67.
56. Ibid., p. 69.
57. There were racial divisions among workers at Allied, but since they were not systematically reproduced on the shopfloor they did not break up workers into opposed groups. Only in the white-dominated union local did racial tensions erupt.
58. Haraszti, pp. 93-4.
59. Ibid., p. 42.
60. Ibid., p. 95.
61. Ibid., p. 95.
62. Ibid., p. 97.
63. Engels, 'Socialism: Utopian and Scientific', in Tucker, pp. 605-39.
64. Haraszti, p. 132.
65. Ibid., p. 45.
66. Granick, *Enterprise Guidance in Eastern Europe*, pp. 302-3.
67. Studies of the Soviet Union suggest such a pattern. Thus Granick, referring to the late 1930s, points to the special treatment and closer attention received by firms in key sectors from the *glavki* (planning agencies) (*Management of the Industrial Firm in the USSR*, New York 1954, p. 23). For the same point in the contemporary period see V.

Andrle, *Managerial Power in the Soviet Union*, Lexington, Massachusetts 1976, pp. 22-4. Viktor Zaslavsky highlights the distinction between normal and 'closed' or 'regime' enterprises, roughly corresponding to the cleavage between traditional and advanced industrial sectors ('The Regime and the Working Class in the USSR', *Telos*, no. 42, Winter 1979-80, pp. 16-7). The latter are linked primarily to military and space production. Wages and benefits are higher, modern techniques and machinery are used, but control and surveillance are more intense. W. Teckenberg detects a dualism between large and small firms, with high turnover, low wages, poor working conditions and a higher percentage of women in the latter ('Labour Turnover and Job Satisfaction: Indicators of Industrial Conflict in the USSR', *Soviet Studies*, vol. 30, no. 2, 1978, pp. 193-211). Large enterprises are able to offer not only greater job opportunities but also more social, cultural and welfare services. Literature on Hungarian planning also stresses the greater bargaining power of larger firms which monopolize production of key goods (T. Laki, 'Enterprises in Bargaining Position', *Acta Oeconamica*, vol. 22, nos. 3-4, 1979, pp. 227-46; Kornai, p. 318).

68. 'The Contradictory Position of the Enterprise', pp. 73-4.

69. Laki, op. cit.

70. Basing herself on a study of five Soviet firms, M. McAuley argues that relations between enterprises and the state govern the struggles between management and union at the level of the enterprise *(Labour Disputes in Soviet Russia 1957-1965*, London 1969). The two cooperate in bargaining for as loose a plan and as big a wage fund as possible. Only once the plan is determined does struggle ensue, and then it is shaped by the slack afforded by the targets. A loose plan and a large wage fund give considerable scope for struggle, and the *fabkom* (factory committee of the union) is more likely to attempt to advance the workers' interests. Norm revisions occur only with new machines (McAuley, pp. 99, 177). When the plan is tight the *fabkom* is more likely to be dominated by managerial personnel and struggles more restricted. Under such circumstances management is more likely to unilaterally initiate norm revisions (McAuley, p. 186) and to attempt to regulate production through more despotic means.

71. A number of commentators have noted a similar dualism within the *capitalist* firm. Thus, Friedman distinguishes between managerial strategies toward core and peripheral workers within the enterprise: core workers are governed through 'responsible autonomy' while peripheral workers are subject to 'direct control' *(Industry and Labour)*. Fox highlights the importance of trust for managerial control over those workers whose jobs entail discretion, while more coercive mechanisms can be deployed against workers to the extent that their jobs have been emptied of discretion (A. Fox, *Beyond Contract: Work, Power and Trust Relations*, London 1974). However, the bifurcation of the labour force within socialist enterprises is much more marked because of the penetration of horizontal and vertical uncertainty and the central determination of wage funds or average wage levels. Under capitalism the uncertainty and zero-sum character of the distribution of surplus are experienced and dealt with more at the level of market relations *among* enterprises — that is, the development of 'competitive' and 'monopoly' sectors.

72. Lajos Héthy and Csaba Makó, 'Obstacles to the Introduction of Efficient Money Incentives in a Hungarian Factory', *Industrial and Labor Relations Review*, no. 24, 1971, pp. 541-53; 'Work-Performance, Interests, Powers and Environment', *The Sociological Review Monograph*, no. 17, 1972, pp. 123-50; and 'Labour Turnover and the Economic Organization: Sociological Data on an Approach to the Question', *Sociological Review*, no. 23, 1975, pp. 267-85; and Csaba Makó, 'Shopfloor Democracy and the Socialist Enterprise', University of Turku, Department of Sociology and Political Research, Sociological Studies A:3, 1978.

73. Héthy and Makó, 'Obstacles to the Introduction of Efficient Money Incentives'.

74. György Sziráczki, 'The Development and Functioning of an Enterprise Labour Market in Hungary', *Economies et Societes*, nos. 3-4, 1983, pp. 540-3.

75. Marrese, op. cit. István Gábor notes that state control of average wages in cooperative farms and of the average wage bill in the state industrial enterprises encouraged the latter to subcontract to the former ('The Second Economy and Its "Fringes" in Hungary from the Late Sixties up to the Present', unpublished paper prepared for the International Conference on the Unobserved Economy, Netherlands Institute for Advanced Study, 1982, pp. 23-4). The part of the wage bill saved by such subcontracting was used to boost the earnings of the labour force remaining in the state enterprise.

76. Piece-rate systems are attractive to managers of state socialist enterprises for two sets of reasons. First, they combat the effects of employment security with wage insecurity so long as there is no guaranteed minimum wage and norm revisions are arbitrary. According to Kirsch, both conditions held in the Soviet Union before 1957, so that goldbricking and quota restriction were more or less futile attempts by workers to control the effort bargain (L. Kirsch, *Soviet Wages*, Cambridge, Massachusetts 1972, p. 17). However, Kirsch also refers to annual bouts of output restriction before the customary February norm revisions as workers attempted to maintain old rates (p. 45). Kirsch cites studies that suggest that after the wage reforms of 1957 workers did throw in the towel and not bother to expend much effort when their gravy jobs became stinkers — a pieceworker's nightmare. This was likely to happen to the extent that the state's attempt to centralize norm determination was successful. Central determination of norms seriously threatened to undermine the second function of the piece-rate system. 'The basic reason for and rationale of the greater scope of incentive wages in Soviet industry revolve around the labour market conditions. Relatively "free" local labour markets exist in both economies. In the United States, the individual firm is generally able to adjust wage rates in accordance with local scarcity conditions. A theme that runs throughout this study is that for the Soviet enterprise, such adjustment must be accomplished mainly through the distribution of incentive payments. Thus, the wide application of various incentive systems adds flexibility to an otherwise rigid system of wage administration. The most important source of such flexibility is in the sphere of norm setting' (Kirsch, p. 43). So long as management had control over norm setting, key workers could be rewarded with loose rates and so could easily boost their earnings. The 1957 reforms attempted to replace 'empirical statistical' norms (i.e. norms based on previous levels of fulfilment) with 'scientific technical' methods of norm determination. Attempts were made to standardize jobs so that norms could be scientifically and centrally determined. This encroachment on the autonomy of enterprise management was bitterly resisted. Where centralization had some success, as in the case of machine operators, the resulting scarcity of such workers led to bottlenecks in production and the necessary relaxation of central control. As Bulganin commented on the period prior to the reforms, 'Norms . . . no longer determined earnings, but rather were set at levels that would provide proper levels of earnings' (Kirsch, p. 46).

77. Szelényi, *Urban Social Inequalities under State Socialism*, New York 1983, p. 58.

78. Galasi and Gábor, op. cit.

79. Péter Galasi and György Sziráczki, 'State Regulation and Labour Market in Hungary between 1968 and 1982', paper presented at the Fifth Conference of the International Working Party on Labour Market Segmentation, Aix-en-Provence, 1983, p. 3.

80. Haraszti, p. 16.

81. István Gábor, 'The Second Economy', *Acto Oeconomica*, vol. 22, nos. 3-4, 1979, p. 291.

82. Gábor, 'The Second Economy and Its "Fringes " '; Marrese, op. cit.

83. Gábor, 'The Second Economy and Its "Fringes".'

84. Gálasi and Sziráczki, p. 3.

85. Haraszti, p. 119; Szelényi, *Urban Social Inequalities*, p. 121.

86. G. Konrád and I. Szelényi, 'Social Conflicts of Under-Urbanization', in M. Harloe, ed., *Captive Cities*, New York 1979, pp. 157-74.

87. C. Hann, *Tázlár: A Village in Hungary*, Cambridge 1980.

88. G. Kertesi and György Sziráczki, 'The Structuring of the Labour Market in Hungary', unpublished paper presented at the Oslo Conference of the International Working Party on Labour Market Segmentation, 1982.

89. J. Montias, 'Observations on Strikes, Riots and Other Disturbances', in J. Triska and C. Gati, eds., *Blue-Collar Workers in Eastern Europe*, London 1981, p. 181.

90. Szelényi, *Urban Social Inequalities*.

91. Konrád and Szelényi, *Intellectuals on the Road to Class Power*, p. 224.

92. *Eros and Civilization*, p. 178.

93. Zaslavsky, p. 198.

94. H.H. Ticktin, 'Towards a Political Economy of the USSR', *Critique*, vol. 1, no. 1, Spring 1973, pp. 20-41.

95. M. Holubenko, 'The Soviet Working Class Opposition', *Critique*, no. 4, 1975, p. 22.

96. P. Lewis, 'The Peasantry', in D. Lane and G. Kolankiewicz, eds., *Social Groups in Polish Society*, London 1973, pp. 29-87; G. Kolankiewicz, 'The New "Awkward Class": The Peasant-Worker in Poland', *Sociologia Ruralis*, vol. 20, nos. 1-2, 1980, pp. 28-43.

97. R. Turski, 'Changes in the Rural Social Structure', in J. Turowski and L. Szwengrub, eds., *Rural Social Change in Poland*, Warsaw 1976, p. 53.

98. Kolankiewicz, p. 34.

99. Bill Lomax, *Hungary 1956*, London 1976.

100. Jadwiga Staniszkis, *Poland's Self-Limiting Revolution*, Princeton 1984.

101. Alain Touraine, et al., *Solidarity*, Cambridge 1983; Henry Norr, ' "Quite a Frog to Eat": Self-Management and the Politics of Solidarity', unpublished manuscript, 1983; Staniszkis op. cit.; and Chapter Two of this book.

5
The Hidden Abode of Underdevelopment

Our analysis of production politics under early and advanced capitalism concentrated on factors internal to those societies. Only when explaining differences among them did we turn to international factors, in particular the timing of industrialization relative to the development of capitalism on a world scale. In the last chapter, we saw how global political forces circumscribed changes in the form and inter-relationship of production politics and state politics in Eastern Europe. We now continue our analysis of the limits set by international factors in a study of the transition from colonialism to post-colonialism in Zambia. We will not examine those international constraints in their own right — that task will be left to the conclusion — but rather their 'internalization' as expressed through the Zambian class structure. We will see how the transformation of the class structure accounts for the changing relationship between production politics and state politics.

In January of 1981, the government of Zambia faced two weeks of industrial unrest and strikes following the expulsion of seventeen labour leaders from the ruling United National Independence Party (UNIP) — the only party in Zambia's one-party state. These leaders came from the executives of the country's major unions, including the Zambia Congress of Trade Unions and the powerful Mineworkers' Union of Zambia. The occasion for the expulsion was union opposition to the new decentralization plan of the Zambian government, which would have given more power to the party in the provincial areas. Although it was presented as the extension of democratic control to the people, union leaders saw it as an attempt to subordinate them to the party and thus to the state. Rank-and-file unionists, already facing increasing hardship due to inflation, wage restraint and scarcity, stood by their leadership and staged walk-outs and strikes.

The most significant feature of these strikes was their explicitly political character, at least in their immediate goal. Directed at the state in defence of trade union independence — and not in pursuit of short-run economic demands — they were very different from the organized and sometimes lengthy strikes waged by mineworkers during the colonial era. Even at the height of the independence struggles, these had been dominated by economic or Africanization demands upon the mining companies, and the colonial administration had tried to stay out of industrial disputes.

In the post-colonial era the state has increasingly intervened to regulate relations between capital and labour: to enforce compulsory arbitration, outlaw strikes, detain leaders, monitor union organization, impose wage freezes. The state circumscribes the terrain of class struggle within industry by shaping the institutions that regulate that struggle, the political apparatuses of production. The post-colonial state has sacrificed its independence, becoming ever more closely allied to capital. This was reflected and consolidated in the nationalization of the mines six years after independence. Strikes are directed against the state rather than simply against the companies, and the state has become increasingly concerned with issues of labour discipline, absenteeism and productivity. Once the concern of the companies alone, the labour process itself has become the target of state intervention.

1. Production and Politics in Theories of Underdevelopment

Although there is nothing unusual in the transition to post-colonialism described above, theories of underdevelopment have failed to examine the labour process or its relationship to the state as mediated by the political apparatuses of production. Even when presented in the guise of returning to production, the causes of underdevelopment often remain located in the 'noisy sphere' of the market place, 'where everything takes place on the surface and in full view of everyone'. Theories never accompany the colonial producer into the 'hidden abode of production'.[1] Conventional notions of modernization attribute the failure to recapitulate the trajectory of already advanced capitalist nations to factors indigenous to peripheral societies, such as inappropriate values, the force of tradition or the scarcity of capital. Reacting against this view, Paul Baran and, following him, André Gunder Frank have focused on the plundering of colonies as causing both development in the metropolis and underdevelopment in the satellite.[2] Hence Frank coined the expression 'the development of underdevelopment'. In stressing the size and use of surplus generated in the periphery, its wasteful consumption and its transmission to the metropolises, however, the mode of production of surplus is left out of account.

In explaining the transfer of surplus from periphery to centre, Arghiri Emmanuel claims to throw us back from the sphere of exchange to the sphere of production.[3] In a far-reaching critique of the theory of comparative advantage, Emmanuel tries to show that under conditions of international specialization of products, mobility of capital and immobility of labour, unequal wages lead to unequal exchange between countries. Commodities produced in the periphery, where rates of exploitation are higher (or, which amounts to the same thing for Emmanuel, wages are lower), exchange at prices below their value, while commodities produced in high-wage countries exchange in the international market at prices higher than their value. Even though he appropriates Marx's schemes for the transformation of values into prices, Emmanuel never actually enters the hidden abode of production, for he treats wages as an independent variable determined outside production. Samir Amin's elaboration of Emmanuel's model loosens some of its assumptions, in particular those of international trade in specific commodities and the exogenous determination of wages. Amin claims that unequal exchange occurs 'when the differential between rewards to labour is greater than between productivities'.[4] Growth of wages in the centre is determined by the conditions of 'autocentric accumulation' — that is, by the productivities in the production of the means of production and of the means of consumption — whereas wages are held down in the periphery through processes of marginalization, including rising levels of unemployment, subsidies provided by pre-capitalist modes of production, and repression.[5] For all the talk of productivity, there is still no attempt to come to terms with the labour process in peripheral societies.

The same can be said of Amin and Emmanuel's critics, such as Charles Bettelheim and Geoffrey Kay, who return us to the law of value and wages as the value of labour power.[6] We now discover that rates of exploitation are *lower* in the periphery than in the centre. 'A lowly paid worker barely able to make ends meet, illiterate, poorly housed, unhealthy, and poorly equipped, is much less productive than a highly paid worker who is educated, well fed and well equipped. It takes him much longer to produce the equivalent of his wage, and therefore the proportion of the working day he is able to give away free is much lower. The more productive highly paid worker, on the other hand, produces his wage in a much shorter time and is therefore able to perform much more surplus labour. By implication, therefore, affluent workers of the developed countries are much more exploited than the badly paid workers of the underdeveloped world.'[7]

A great deal separates the perspectives of Kay and Bettelheim from those of Emmanuel and Amin, particularly in their opposing conceptions of the labour process. However, in neither case do they attempt to support their assertions with any empirical analysis.

A break with 'underdevelopment theory' comes more forcibly from those who throw us back to 'production' and to Marx's original conception of capitalist development as spreading evenly through the world.[8] In a powerful polemic with stagnationist conceptions which root backwardness in the transfer of surplus between countries, Bill Warren insists on very real capitalist developments taking place in peripheral countries. Particularly since World War II, they have achieved a measure of autonomy sufficient to attract capitalist investment.[9] Warren's return to production and his debunking of the conventional wisdom of underdevelopment theory are refreshing, but he never reaches into the specificity of 'the forces of production' — that is, into the production processes that are advancing in different parts of the world. Instead, these processes are reduced to levels of industrial or manufacturing output and to their contributions to gross national product.

Warren does, however, recognize the heterogeneity of the so-called periphery. Here we also find the fashionable interest in 'modes of production' and their 'articulation'.[10] Underdevelopment is no longer attributed exclusively to integration into a world capitalist system. Instead the point of departure becomes the reproduction of precapitalist modes of production, which, rather than being destroyed, are reshaped and subordinated to capitalist modes of production that are often transnational. On closer examination many of these formulations tend to reduce the mode of production to relations of exploitation — that is, the mode of appropriating surplus — without considering relations in production, that is, the relations of the labour process. For example, in his important critique of the so-called modes-of-production analysis, Jairus Banaji distinguishes between relations of exploitation and the broader relations of production, which concern the relations among enterprises.[11] The latter ultimately determine the rhythm of underdevelopment, and the enterprise is of only secondary interest. And where the distinction between capitalist firms and enterprises such as haciendas, plantations, and independent peasant production becomes central to the analysis, the varieties of capitalist firms and in particular of the capitalist labour process are never examined.[12] It is presumed that the capitalist enterprise is much the same in the periphery as in the centre, and that only the relative preponderance of non-capitalist enterprises is significant.

As the labour process is left out of these studies of modes of production, it is not surprising that the struggles over its relations — the politics of production — are ignored as well. Indeed, some even claim that there are no such struggles. 'The absence of this struggle in underdeveloped capitalism is also the absence of a tendency internal to it that leads to the constant revolutionizing of the forces of production.'[13] And when a politics of production is recognized, it is dissociated from struggles over state power. 'A study of working-class politics ... would have to go beyond the unions to the shop floor and examine the various forms that the struggle of labour against capital took. Such detailed research is not within the scope of this book. Also, inasmuch as this struggle was not about the question of state power, we feel justified in leaving it out of our analysis of the principal contradictions that informed the politics of Uganda up to 1972.'[14]

In a celebrated article on the post-colonial state in Tanzania, John Saul examines the indeterminacy of state intervention springing from struggles within the state between different fractions of the yet unformed class of the petty bourgeoisie.[15] As Leys points out, Saul's account does not consider the external limits on state intervention posed by class struggles outside the state. But Leys himself does not tell us how to conceptualize those struggles or their relationship to struggles fought within the state.[16] Above all, he does not specify those day-to-day struggles over relations in production and relations of exploitation, whether in the villages or the factories. As Poulantzas has suggested, once we recognize state apparatuses as a terrain of class struggle, we must also recognize that not all power is congealed there. It also materializes in institutions outside the state, such as factory apparatuses.[17] The relationship between struggles within the state and those outside it must be understood as shaped by the relations between the corresponding apparatuses.

One reason for the neglect of struggles outside the state lies in the prevailing conception that the post-colonial state plays a central role in development and possesses a certain 'autonomy'.[18] First, it inherits an overdeveloped structure from its colonial predecessor, which had to subordinate all indigenous classes and corresponding modes of production. Second, the post-colonial state plays a prominent economic role, appropriating a large proportion of the economic surplus. Third, the post-colonial state plays a critical ideological role in establishing 'hegemony', binding the subordinate classes to the nation-state. Under attack from Leys and others, Saul's attempt to substantiate the centrality and autonomy of the post-colonial state falls apart at the seams.[19] But we are left with little sense of the post-colonial state vis-à-vis metropolitan or colonial states.

In all these treatments of underdevelopment, the lack of any notion of production politics has political and theoretical consequences. The reduction of politics to state politics — to struggles over or within the state — and of the labour process to a technique of production easily slips into a distinctive conception of socialism as a strategy of development orchestrated by benign technocrats operating within the state.[20] Socialism is no longer a form of society in which unavoidable conflict is institutionalized through organs of popular control that guide public policy, a society in which local (production) politics takes on a form of collective self-management that is not subordinate to state politics.

Our alternative approach focuses on the relationship between production politics and state politics, so that neither 'overdevelopment' nor 'relative autonomy' occupies such a central place. Instead, we examine the functions of the colonial and post-colonial states as they are reflected in the relations between apparatuses of the state and those of the economy — industry or agriculture. My argument is simple. The colonial state was indeed an interventionist, although not necessarily a strong, state whose 'function' was to establish the supremacy of the capitalist mode of production. It was concerned with primitive accumulation in two senses: the separation of direct producers from the means of production in generating labour supplies for industrial capital, and the extraction of surplus from pre-capitalist modes of production by merchant capital. The relative importance and precise articulation of these two forms of primitive accumulation varied from colony to colony and, over time, within each colony.[21] Thus, the colonial state was concerned not with production per se but with the orchestration of relations among modes of production in such a way as to secure the ascendancy of the capitalist mode. Once the dominance of the capitalist mode of production has been established and other modes subordinated to its requirements, the *raison d'être* of the colonial state disappears. A new form of state emerges, concerned with the expanded rather than the primitive accumulation of capital, with the extraction of relative surplus value from production rather than of specific surplus labour through exchange, and with the production of specific types of labour power rather than the generation of labour supplies. The granting of formal political independence is but a symbol of the transition from the colonial to the post-colonial state.[22]

In the next section it will be shown that although studies of Southern African labour history have examined the processes of primitive accumulation, they have neglected the way these have been shaped by the specific economic and political requirements of expanded accumulation in the mining industries. Subsequent sections will turn to the hidden abode of production itself, examining the nature of the labour process under colonialism and the political conditions for its regulation. We will then see that with the eclipse of colonialism, in some instances the labour process itself has changed, while in others, where technological constraints inhibit such changes, the conflict continues between production apparatuses and the labour process. In the final sections of this chapter we shall analyse how the relationship between production politics and state politics is limited by the labour process on one side and international forces on the other.

2. From Primitive Accumulation to Expanded Reproduction

Capitalism's genesis must be distinguished from its reproduction. In the first stage, primitive accumulation, capital is initially accumulated and brought together with labour, which is dispossessed of the means of production and turned into a commodity: labour power. In the second stage, expanded reproduction, capitalism has already been established, and the focus of analytic attention becomes the capital–labour relation itself and the accumulation of capital based on the search for higher rates of profit. In *Capital*, Marx takes the *historically specific* form of primitive accumulation as it occurred in England through the ravages of merchant capital and the enclosure movement and juxtaposes it to a *general theory* of the reproduction and dynamics of capitalism. Primitive accumulation is thus dissociated from expanded reproduction. Marx does not theorize how the form of primitive accumulation may shape the extraction of absolute and relative surplus value — that is, the capitalist labour process.

Trotsky, however, appreciated the connection between the origins and the expansion of capitalism by underlining its combined and uneven development: 'The laws of history have nothing in common with a pedantic schematism. Unevenness, the most general law of the historic process, reveals itself most sharply and complexly in the destiny of the backward countries. Under the whip of external necessity their backward culture is compelled to make leaps. From the universal law of unevenness thus derives another law of combined development — by which we mean a drawing together of the different stages of the journey, a combining of separate steps, an amalgam of archaic with more contemporary forms. Without this law, to be taken of course in its whole material content, it is impossible to understand the history of Russia, and indeed of any country of the second, third or tenth cultural class'.[23]

In Russia, primitive accumulation skipped the early phases of handicraft production and small industry and thrust a 'backward' proletariat, recently torn from feudal estates, into the crucible of the modern factory based on advanced technology imported from the West. Sponsored by the state and dependent on foreign capital, the Russian bourgeoisie was too weak to contain the volatile proletariat it had created. And the absolutist state, compelled to compete economically and militarily with modern European nations but lacking a modern economic base, could only limp from crisis to crisis. Thus, Trotsky drew out the implications of different forms of primitive accumulation for the relationship between the proletariat and the state.

Marx insisted on not only a theoretical but also a historical rupture between primitive and expanded accumulation: the former was the prehistory of the latter. Rosa Luxemburg fundamentally challenged this formulation in *The Accumulation of Capital*,[24] arguing that capitalism's continued expansion rested on the incorporation of non-capitalist modes of production. Yet she retained the orthodox view that this necessarily led to the dissolution of non-capitalist modes of production. Hence capitalism destroyed the very conditions upon which its continued expansion depended. As history has shown, however, pre-capitalist modes of production are by no means automatically dissolved by the advance of capitalism. More often they are recreated and restructured in accordance with the needs of the dominant capitalist mode of production. The history of Southern and Central Africa demonstrates particularly well the conservation/dissolution tendencies among the pre-capitalist modes of production, as orchestrated by the state.

Although there are now many excellent accounts of primitive accumulation in Southern Africa, Giovanni Arrighi's study of labour supplies in Southern Rhodesia (Zimbabwe) continues to be the most theoretically important.[25] Arrighi distinguishes four periods. In the first, 1890-1904, African peasants responded to a growing demand for food from the emerging towns and industries by voluntarily entering into production for the market; no extra-economic force was necessary to stimulate agricultural production. Even though there was increasing demand for wage labour, Africans were able to increase their incomes without entering the labour market. In the second period, 1904-23, a combination of economic and political forces compelled Africans to sell their labour power. As they became increasingly dependent on the exchange economy for basic requirements, the colonial administration inaugurated forced labour, taxation and land expropriation. Africans were pushed into 'Native Reserves', where declining productivity and increasing transportation costs combined with falling prices to reduce their earnings from agriculture. White settler farmers, given preferential treatment by the colonial government, increasingly gained a monopoly on food production for the market. This was a period of genuine primitive accumulation, in which political mechanisms were used to subordinate the African peasantry to the requirements of capital accumulation.

In the third period, 1923 to the 1940s, market mechanisms accelerated the peasantry's demise. Overcrowding and soil erosion in the reserves made it increasingly difficult to produce a surplus, let alone compete with white farmers. The Land Apportionment Act of 1931 and the institutionalization of separate African and white price systems for maize only consolidated these trends. Africans were compelled to enter the labour market in increasing numbers, selling their labour power for a wage calculated on the basis of maintaining a single worker in town. Children, the old, the sick and the unemployed were cared for in the rural reserves. The connection between the maintenance of direct producers and the renewal of the labour forces was guaranteed through a system of migrant labour based on limited residence rights in the town and remittances to the rural areas to supplement the bare subsistence obtained there.

A similar story can be told for Zambia (Northern Rhodesia). When the British South Africa (BSA) Company took over the administration of the territory in 1889, it was empowered by the British government to exploit all available resources. Although little was found in the way of minerals, the BSA Company did open the territory to international market forces and develop a basic infrastructure to facilitate trade. Copper was mined only intermittently until the second quarter of the twentieth century, when the discovery of rich underground sulphide ores and new processing techniques made commercial exploitation feasible. Until then Northern Rhodesia had been a labour reserve for the mines and industries of Southern Rhodesia, South Africa and, after 1910, Katanga. In order to facilitate labour recruiting and to boost its own revenue, the BSA Company imposed taxes on the African population as early as 1900. In 1902, 69 per cent of its administrative revenue came from that source.[26] As in many other parts of Southern Africa, Africans responded to taxation by producing food for the market. They began supplying maize for a growing urban population in Northern Rhodesia as well as for the Katanga mines. Fearing a loss of labour to the south, the BSA Company began alienating the most fertile land along the line of rail for white settlers. This and other preferential policies combined to undercut African peasant agriculture's competitiveness with European agriculture, forcing greater numbers of Africans into the labour market. By 1921 an estimated 41 per cent of able-bodied males were working for wages, almost all outside the territory.[27] Of course, these were migrant labourers who would periodically return to their villages and eventually resettle there.

As the BSA Company drew substantial capital into Northern Rhodesia, it created new classes — the white settler population of farmers, traders and skilled workers — whose interests were opposed to the strict profit criterion of the BSA Company. Moreover, the rise of indigenous classes of migrant workers and peasant producers required a state administrative apparatus. Yet as an instrument of metropolitan capital, responsible to its shareholders, the BSA Company could not be responsive to these interests, so essential to the development of its territory. Thus, in furthering the development of capitalism, the BSA Company guaranteed its own demise. In 1924 it was replaced with a more stable form of colonial administration that was subordinate to the Colonial Office and, to a certain degree, responsive to indigenous and settler classes.[28]

The colonial administration pursued a cautious policy toward the Northern Rhodesian copper mines when they began to be developed commercially in the late 1920s. The administration was reluctant to cut off or control the flow of labour to other territories, for state revenue depended on the migration of African labour to other employment centres in Southern and Central Africa.[29] It would not extend priority to the copper mines until they had proven themselves viable. However, under pressure from the mines and the white settler population, the administration did establish a system of reserves in 1929 that both enhanced the protection of white farmers and generated labour supplies for the Copperbelt. When the Depression hit in 1931, copper prices tumbled from 24 cents per pound in 1929 to 6¼ cents at the end of 1931, and cutbacks in production reduced the African mine labour force from a peak of nearly thirty-two thousand in September 1930 to less than seven thousand at the end of 1932. During the succeeding years African peasants faced even greater obstacles to food production, as pricing policies gave a virtual monopoly to white farmers. So Africans became increasingly dependent on wage labour, and many found it in the Copperbelt, where industry expanded rapidly before and during the Second World War.

Let us now turn to Arrighi's fourth period of labour supply, characterized by the rise of multinational corporations with their capital-intensive investments. Arrighi describes the result in terms of the replacement of unskilled migrants by semi-skilled 'stabilized' workers. Multinationals, with higher wages, encouraged migration of families, and an 'aristocracy' of labour began to form. Here Arrighi makes his closest approach to the hidden abode of production. He accounts for the capital-intensive techniques of large corporations by reference to the 'logic of capital'. Although his main arguments involve technological considerations, managerial expertise and the financial resources of international capital, he does suggest that the skill requirements of a mechanized production process — 'semi-skilled and high-level manpower' — are more suited to colonial labour supplies. Such a 'capital logic' argument, however, pays little attention to the different ways in which the colonial context might shape that logic. Thus, Arrighi dismisses Baldwin's claim that since the Second World War the wages of Africans and Europeans working on the Copperbelt 'have been raised by monopolistic actions to levels considerably above the rates necessary to attract the numbers actually employed. The consequences of this wage policy have been the creation of unemployment conditions in the Copperbelt towns, especially among Africans, and widespread substitution of machines for men in the industry.'[30] Instead, Arrighi accepts the conventional wisdom that migrant workers have limited capacity to engage in effective industrial struggles, and argues that African trade unions, formed since the Second World War, have 'played a dependent role in the spiral process of rising wages and mechanization.'[31]

This fourth phase represents a curious shift in the focus of Arrighi's analysis, from a concern with the *political* mechanisms that generated labour *supplies* to the *economic* forces behind the *demand* for labour. In the first three periods the state stimulates and compels primitive accumulation, but in the last period it drops out of the picture. In omitting from his analysis the changing forms of state intervention, Arrighi fails to note that the colonial state, which organized primitive accumulation, has given way to a 'post-colonial' state, whose concern is the regulation of the expanded reproduction of capitalism. The formal declaration of political independence may either precede or follow this transition. If the colonial state is not primarily concerned with the expanded reproduction of capital, the consequence is not that expanded reproduction does not take place but that alternative institutions take over its regulation. As we shall see, these are the apparatuses of the company state — the compound system of the mines of Southern Africa, which closely monitors the day-to-day life of African workers.

A further weakness in Arrighi's analysis is that he introduces the demand for labour only in the final period of the ascendancy of the multinational corporation. In the first three periods he pays little attention to the labour needs of the industries and mines to which African peasants migrate, and thus misses the way in which proletarianization is itself shaped by the requirements of capital accumulation. It is to this that we turn next.

3. The Labour Process and the Colonial Legacy

Charles Perrings's excellent study of mineworkers in Northern Rhodesia and Katanga moves beyond Arrighi, consistently interpreting the supply of labour in terms of the conditions of capital accumulation. Perrings shows how geological constraints, the state of technology and the price of copper determined the range of production techniques open to any given mine. Thus, the labour strategies of the various mines were shaped primarily by the specific technical conditions of production, not by managerial style, nationality of directors or corporate policies, as had previously been argued.

The very different ore bodies in Katanga and Northern Rhodesia led to distinctive types of mines: those in Katanga were usually open-cast, while those in Northern Rhodesia were underground. This had immediate implications for labour requirements, underground mining being more arduous and dangerous and requiring more skills. In Katanga desertion was therefore less of a problem, and it was more feasible for the *Union Minière du Haut Katanga* to pursue a policy that settled miners and their families in the mine compounds for longer periods of employment. The conditions underground in Northern Rhodesia, on the other hand, were such that Africans would undertake only relatively short stints of work. This restricted any policy of stabilization, although there was variation from mine to mine. The higher level of skills required in underground mining drew a larger contingent of white workers to the Copperbelt than to Katanga, and the devaluation of the franc made it very expensive to attract white miners from sterling areas to the Congo. The advancement of Africans into skilled or even semi-skilled jobs was powerfully blocked on the Copperbelt by the presence of white workers; while in Katanga African Advancement required substantial investment in training which further predisposed management to a policy of labour stabilization. Also crucial to the different labour strategies in the two regions were the options available to potential African mineworkers. Whereas in Northern Rhodesia settler farmers had taken over food production, forcing Africans into the labour market, the absence of settler farmers in Katanga allowed Aftricans to produce cash crops for the mines. This led to a recurrent shortage of labour, which encouraged the mines to improve working conditions and monetary compensation and to introduce stabilization policies to promote a deeper commitment to wage labour.

For Perrings, then, geology and technical knowledge impose limits on the techniques of production, levels of mechanization, and so forth. The characteristics of the labour supplies and the form of proletarianization not only are determined by but also select the prevailing production techniques. Unlike Arrighi, Perrings consistently takes the issue of capital accumulation as a point of departure in understanding the process of proletarianization. Like Arrighi, however, he reduces the labour process to a production technique that gives rise to a corresponding skill requirement. In so doing he confuses labour power with the labour process. It is one thing to produce or recruit a particular type of labour power, but quite another to turn labour power into labour. The labour process involves relations and practices that must be regulated and therefore require certain political apparatuses of control. These in turn depend on the existence of certain state apparatuses. Perrings reduces capital accumulation to production techniques of economic efficiency and ignores production apparatuses of political regulation. He reduces capital requirements to the reproduction of labour power and excludes the reproduction of the relations of the labour process, relations *in* production.

Having said all this we immediately come up against a methodological problem: how do we examine these relations in production and their mode of regulation? Unfortunately we do not have the rich case studies of the labour process that have defined the heritage of industrial sociology in Europe and the United States. Indeed, data on the organization of work during the colonial period are virtually non-existent. We must rely on hearsay, on occasional comments in evidence before commissions of inquiry, or on the recollections of participants. What follows, then, is but a first landing on new terrain.

The reconstruction of the colonial labour process is based on participant observation and interviews conducted by myself and three Zambian students at a single Zambian mine in 1971, seven years after political independence. The mine at which we worked was one of six concentrated in the Copperbelt, which lies in the northwest of the country, near the Zaire border. In 1971 approximately fifty thousand people were employed by the six mines. Of these, twenty per cent were expatriates who continued to control the mines through the operation of the colour bar principle: no black should exercise authority over any white. Expatriates earned six times as much as Zambian mineworkers, who earned twice as much as other Zambian industrial workers.

In terms of the overall production of copper we can delineate three types of operation: the actual removal of ore, the processing of the ore into a refined product, and the performance of various services and infrastructural work necessary for the functioning of the mine as a whole. In order to provide a firmer basis for generalization, we shall first take a labour process that belongs to the processing of copper ore, then move on to one from the service division, and finally examine a work situation in the mine itself.

Copper Anodes

The more relations among workers are limited by technology, the less likely they are to be affected by changes in political regime — or so it might seem. The first work situation to be examined, casting copper anodes, is organized on the principle of the assembly line, while the second, tracklaying, involves gang labour under personal supervision, with few technological constraints on relations and activities.

The casting section of the smelter converts molten copper matte into anodes ready for transportation to the refinery. The matte is poured from the furnace onto a huge 'spoon', which is operated by a caster seated in a cage on an elevated platform. Copper is ladled from the spoon into the moulds of a casting wheel. The wheel, with its twenty-two moulds, continuously rotates at a speed controlled by the caster. After the copper has been poured into a mould, it passes under a water cooler. The lug man then removes the 'stoppers' holding the copper anodes in place. A little further on, the take-off attendant removes the anode with a mechanical contraption that grips the corners of the anode and lifts it out of the mould. Additional operators then clean and dress the mould before copper matte is again poured into it.

The anode wheel differs from an assembly line in that its speed is controlled by the operators themselves. Although the caster actually operates the wheel, the take-off attendant dictates the speed; when he becomes weary, he conveys this to the caster, who then either slows down the wheel or takes a break. If the caster decides not to go along with the take-off attendant's demands, the latter can simply allow an anode to pass him by, and the wheel must then be stopped and reversed.

All the workers in 1971 were Zambians. Their relations at work were largely governed by their position in the production process. Steam and noise made communication difficult, and the operators had developed an elaborate sign language in which they conveyed the condition of the moulds, the impending appearance of the foreman, their previous night's activities, and anything else they chose. The dominant conflict was between the take-off attendant and the caster, over the speed of the wheel. The most senior operator was the caster, a position which had previously been held by a European. Presumably before the Zambianization of the position, the caster would almost unilaterally dictate the speed of the wheel, and the other operators — the take-off attendant, mould cleaner, mould dresser, lug man and spoon attendant — would have to try to keep up. In 1971 the caster could no longer draw on any colonial status to impose his will on the rest of the gang. Indeed, he was now subject to their control. The transition from colonial to post-colonial production relations (relations *in* production) led to the reversal of power relations between the positions in the labour process.

Although the technology of casting anodes was well suited to colonial production relations, in a post-colonial society it led to friction among operators, which impeded its functioning. Workers, rather than management, now controlled the speed of the machine. Technology is not neutral: it is a product of the political relations extant at and outside the work point. One might say that there are colonial and post-colonial technologies, and that the persistence of the former into the period of the latter undermines managerial control. As the example of casting anodes reveals, Zambianization facilitated the transition to post-colonial production relations. The Zambian caster could no longer command the support of management to maintain the authoritarian hierarchy of the colonial context. Even when the supervisory positions are not Zambianized a similar situation develops, as our next example shows.

Tracklaying

Tracklaying is part of the engineering department of the mine. The transportation section, which includes tracklaying, keeps the various shafts and plants supplied with the materials they require. There are approximately forty miles of track and six gangs to service it. Each gang includes six men and a ganger, who is responsible to a Zambian assistant foreman. The assistant foreman is supervised by an expatriate plate-laying foreman, who in turn reports to a sectional engineer. Each gang is responsible for maintaining a certain stretch of track, although the gangs come together in the event of an emergency or a particularly big job.

The gangs must maintain old track and build new. Maintenance involves searching for broken rails, cleaning up, oiling points, and replacing worn rails. In replacing or laying new track the most important tasks revolve around lifting and packing the rails so that their elevation and gradient are correct, particularly the relative height of parallel rails. Tracks are raised or lowered by 'packing' more or less ballast — small stones — under the sleepers. This is a strenuous job, and workers are expected to lift and pack about eight sleepers on one shift. Building new track involves cutting and bending track to size and shape, bolting rails to sleepers and, most difficult, getting the track into the correct position. At ninety-one pounds a yard, this may involve all the concerted effort of thirty men. In short, all the tasks of tracklaying are labour-intensive, and most are extremely arduous. Cooperation among the gang members is essential.

In 1971 the gangs were largely self-regulating groups of workers who established and enforced norms of effort. Using a wide range of mechanisms, day-shift workers made continual and successful attempts to limit output in order to obtain overtime and sometimes Sunday work; responding to management efforts to cut back on overtime, they restricted their output until it had to be restored. When younger workers began working too hard, older ones instructed them to slow down; if conflict broke out, the older workers would draw on their greater powers of witchcraft to instill fear into the rate busters. Tribal slurs were often used to bring workers back into conformity with the norms laid down by the experienced workers, so that the group presented a united front to the ganger.

The gang mobilized resources against the ganger more often than against one another. When the supervisor began pushing his subordinates too hard, the younger workers started arguing in English, which the ganger had difficulty understanding. They also used

English, when necessary, to persuade the foreman James, who spoke only English, that they were not at fault. When gangers tried to press charges for lack of discipline, they were in a weaker position than the educated younger workers. The older, experienced workers, for their part, would threaten the gangers with witchcraft. Frequently the shop steward would enter the fray and threaten to bring in the union. Workers would also play off one ganger against another, casting aspersions on those who tried to imitate colonial bosses and praising those who were more relaxed in their supervision.

The organization of the labour process made the gangers' position untenable. Tracklaying depends on the cooperation of several unskilled workers. Management can regulate the group either through a militaristic and punitive system or through a wage system based on some form of bonus. In Zambia the coercive system of the colonial era gave way to post-colonial production relations without an incentive scheme. Under colonial production relations, white foremen and assistant foremen were in a position to impose stringent controls through the use of coercive sanctions, and even black gangers had more power to regulate their gang's output than they did in 1971.

In the transition from colonial to post-colonial production relations, the foreman remained an expatriate but his powers were considerably diminished. The transition was brought to a head in one of many incidents that occurred for a number of years after independence. In 1969 the expatriate foreman Marshall, nicknamed Kafumo because of his potbelly, came under attack from the tracklayers for his racist and insulting behaviour. He was still trying to uphold colonial production relations. All the tracklaying gangs struck, brought in both the United National Independence Party and trade-union officials, and refused to return to work until Marshall Kafumo had been replaced. The assistant foreman James, also an expatriate, took over from Marshall. Learning from the incident, James's leniency earned him the nickname *Polepole*, 'easy'. But his leniency in the face of recalcitrant gangs of workers made the position of his Zambian assistant and, in turn, of the gangers very weak. They had recourse to few sanctions with which to combat group regulation of output and distribution of overtime. If workers sat around, took a rest in the bushes or engaged in heated political discussion, gangers could either stand and watch or give vent to their wrath by working by themselves.

Colonial production relations could not be reproduced by the post-colonial system of managerial authority, and in this instance were overturned through struggle. A new set of relations was introduced, although the foreman was still white. Just as the Zambian caster could no longer draw on managerial support to enforce the compliance of the take-off attendant, so Polepole could not dictate work norms to the tracklaying gangs. Irrespective of the colour of the supervisor, the old forms of regulation based on racial domination were no longer tenable. Thus, as in the case of anode casting, workers in the tracklaying gangs enhanced their control of the labour process as a result of the way it had been organized under the regime of 'colonial despotism'.

4. The Rise and Fall of Colonial Despotism

What distinguishes industrial production under colonialism is not the labour process, for the same relations in production could as easily develop under other political and economic conditions.[32] Rather, the particular mechanisms through which production relations are regulated — the particular political apparatuses of the mine — are the distinctive factor. I call this form of production regime colonial despotism: despotic, because force prevails over consent; colonial, because one racial group dominates through political, legal and economic rights denied to the other. It is very different from the despotisms of nineteenth-century Britain, where coercion stemmed from the economic whip of the market. Although a colonial labour market obviously existed, Africans' survival did not depend on the sale of their labour power, for they always had access to some kind of subsistence existence in the rural areas. The arbitrary power exercised by the dictatorial 'Bwana' (white boss) was based on the control of life outside work. An overt and explicit racism was the organizing principle behind these production apparatuses.[33]

Colonial Despotism

What was the nature of the power exercised by white bosses over African mine labourers? Physical violence was the rule rather than the exception, especially in the early years. It was even noted by the Russell Commission, which otherwise tried to whitewash the conditions that precipitated the Copperbelt strikes of 1935. Working from the disciplinary records of one mine, George Chauncey concludes:

"Though there were frequent instances of physical brutality in the compounds during the early years of the industry, its use in the enforcement of workplace discipline underground was pervasive. Any sign of disrespect, slowness in obeying orders, or improper work was liable to be punished on the spot. A lashing worker reported in 1934 that "fumes were coming from the stuff we were lashing so I went close by to wash my face, but as I moved off my Bwana hit me twice on the face and kicked me three times, and I fell down . . . The Bwana then handed aa length of belting to No. 8590 and told him to beat me." Another worker in 1935 reported that his supervisor beat him after accusing him of being too slow; two years later a common labourer complained, "I took one of the machines back to the Bwana but he said that I had brought him the wrong one, and he did not want it. The Bwana was angry and he kicked me with his boots and hurt me." A file at the Roan Antelope archives contains literally hundreds of such examples.'[34]

Although violence in the compounds, where it was particularly visible, may have soon diminished, it continued to be normal in the mine, despite the introduction of 'native supervisors' who were to look into grievances. Africans were more likely to desert mine employment altogether than to risk lodging a grievance against their Bwana. Moreover, despite a few notable exceptions, management was reluctant to discipline those European bosses who were reported for brutality.

White bosses also controlled a system of bonuses and fines, which further enhanced their power. They distributed so-called efficiency bonuses to obedient and cooperative workers and levied fines on others, charging them with insubordination, coming to work drunk, sleeping on the job, laziness or absenteeism. The 'ticket' system of payment opened further channels of abuse. Africans were paid only on completion of a 'ticket', which required thirty shifts of work to be performed within forty days, usually in five six-day working weeks. Leaving the mines before completion of one's ticket meant forfeiting one's pay. The system also encouraged workers to bring forward their pay day by working every possible shift, even on weekends.[35] Until the mid-1930s, if the European supervisor refused to sign the ticket, a worker would lose both a day's pay and the day's food rations.[36] White bosses could also manipulate the dangers of underground work in order to secure active acquiescence from their African workers. 'In this context, the various "Safety First" programmes launched by the companies can be seen as serving the dual purpose of encouraging safe work habits and emphasizing the importance of obeying orders. The company emphasized the dangers of the work environment and of straying from the supervisor's area on the first day a man went underground by giving him a tour of the most dangerous areas. And once underground the supervisor had enormous power over his workers. In the many dark tunnels of the mines where no electric lights had been installed, supervisors took on enormous power simply because they were the only ones with lanterns.'[37] Moreover, the

European supervisor had complete discretion over the distribution of safe and dangerous work among the members of his gang.

The Rise of the Company State

In the late 1920s, when construction work on the mines was at its height, much of the labour was recruited and controlled by contractors. The despotism of the Bwana emerged in the early thirties. Thereafter, however, some of the white bosses' power was withdrawn and centralized in the compound offices. Domination at the point of production was linked to the mining company's control of the compounds where miners lived. Increasingly, survival outside work became tied to subordination at work through means other than the cash nexus, arbitrary firing and the system of bonuses and fines. In the thirties and forties the regulation of all facets of African life came to be vested in the 'company state', personified by the compound manager, who reigned as supreme dictator over 'the natives' in compound and in mine.

The compound system was adapted from South Africa, where it was first developed at the Kimberley Diamond Mines in the 1880s. In Southern Rhodesia and then on the Northern Rhodesian Copperbelt, a more open version of the South African system, with more relaxed surveillance, was adopted.[38] Whereas in South Africa single black mineworkers were kept prisoner in a barrack-like system, on the Copperbelt they had greater freedom of movement, and between 30 and 60 per cent shared their cramped quarters with their immediate dependants.[39] One of the mining companies, Roan Selection Trust, encouraged workers to live with their wives, arguing that 'in general, women give a fair amount of trouble but this is offset by the care they take of their husbands, and we have found that the presence of the woman gives the man a sense of responsibility so that he hesitates to jeopardize his billet by some senseless trouble-making.'[40] Since rations were distributed according to the number of certified dependants living with the miner, and huts for married workers were bigger than those for single ones, the advantages to be gained from such stabilization entailed higher economic costs — costs that could be borne by the Northern Rhodesian copper companies but not by the South African gold mines, where profit margins were usually much lower. Because workers automatically lost their compound accommodation when they were fired, this system enhanced their subordination at work.

The compound system facilitated almost totalitarian surveillance of the workforce. The compound offices kept close watch on activities through the mine police. When a miner was reported absent, the mine police were sent out to find him.⁴¹ Visitors were expected to register with the company, a regulation enforced by midnight house-to-house searches and the eviction of anyone not holding a pass. After several unsuccessful experiments, the companies devised an invidious system of identification. '[T]hey fastened metal wristlets bearing the appropriate mine number to the wrist of every worker and dependant in the compound. "Tickets and Identification Certificates can be stolen and given to a friend," a compound manager pointed out, "but wristlets with Mine Numbers stamped on are all fastened with ACME fasteners." By means of the wristlet, police could distinguish visitors from workers at a glance, and could immediately identify and ascertain the mine number of anyone caught breaking company rules. Workers despised the system, and their attempts to tear off the wristlets were the single most frequent cause for their being fired. "We couldn't take it off ourselves," remembered one worker. "We would sleep with it, work with it, die with it." '⁴²

The compound manager also used a system of tribal elders to keep him informed of the happenings in the compound and possible disturbances or even strikes. The tribal elders, who were respected representatives of the various tribes living in the compound, adjudicated disputes among Africans in the urban context and were regularly consulted by management.⁴³ The strikes of 1935 and 1940, however, dramatically demonstrated that the tribal elders were ineffective for industrial conciliation and unreliable for social control. Both strikes took the companies unaware, for they were organized by associations that Africans had built independently of compound management and its network of informants. In the 1940 strike, in particular, the tribal elders were pushed aside as representatives of the workforce, and at Mufulira the miners elected a negotiating committee composed largely of 'boss boys', the immediate supervisory assistants of European workers.

True to the paternalistic impetus behind the compound system, the companies extended their control into recreational activities. In an attempt to regulate beer drinking, they constructed beer halls and outlawed home brewing. They encouraged dancing societies and supervised religious groups. But the very form of the compound and the 'corporate' labour strategies of the companies consolidated the unitary structure of the mining community and encouraged the development of class consciousness.⁴⁴ The more stabilized and skilled workers could pursue their interests within the industrial context only by mobilizing the unskilled and temporary migrants. Furthermore, the compound provided powerful encouragement to working-class solidarity across ethnic, language, skill, and sometimes even racial boundaries. Africans turned out to be adept at shaping their own cultural institutions to their class purposes. Thus, the Mbeni Dancing Society and the Watchtower Movement became the political bases from which struggles against the companies, particularly strikes, were launched. In the absence of legitimate channels of protest and organs of industrial struggle, such as trade unions, these clandestine and subversive institutions were much more difficult for the companies to control.

The mineworkers' capacity to create a world of their own limited direct supervision by the company state. So too did the duration of employment. Although the mines encouraged *stabilization* by allowing longer periods of service and building married quarters, they did not encourage *proletarianization* — that is, the severing of all ties to the rural areas. Although the day-to-day maintenance of the black mineworkers was to take place under the direction of the company state, the renewal of the labour force — the creation and recruitment of new miners and the care of the old — was to take place in the villages. Neither the mines nor the colonial administration was prepared to countenance the political and economic costs of proletarianization. Accordingly, there was no provision for education, health services or retirement once workers left the mines.[45] Most workers, for reasons of economic security, had to maintain contact with their home villages through frequent visits and the remittance of savings.

The Decline of the Company State

The supremacy of the company state began to be questioned after the strikes of 1935 and 1940. The Colonial Office investigated the shootings of Africans and pushed for the establishment of a labour department within the colonial government.[46] The colonial administration of Northern Rhodesia opposed such an apparatus, fearing that it might undermine the concordat between government and mines over their respective spheres of influence. The Forster Commission, which reported on the 1940 strike, also highlighted grievances of black mineworkers, which included not only wages and working conditions but also the explosive issue of African Advancement.

In 1936, the white miners had formed a union to defend their monopoly of certain jobs. During the war, the Northern Rhodesian Mineworkers' Union was able to blackmail the companies into procrastination. In 1947, however, the Colonial Office sent out trade unionist Bill Comrie to set up African trade unions, and in 1948 the mining companies were forced to cooperate in establishing the first African Mineworkers' Trade Union. As it developed strength, the union adopted increasingly militant tactics, striking in 1952 and again in 1955 and 1956 over increased wages and the companies' willingness to recognize a rival union, the Mines African Staff Association. Any such recognition would have divided the black miners along class lines, depriving the union of many of its leaders.

All these developments eroded the supremacy of the company state. White bosses could no longer arbitrarily determine earnings or fire workers. Survival in the compound was less directly linked to productivity in the mines, and regulations on the flow of labour were relaxed. It was now a matter not of stabilization but of full-fledged proletarianization. And as opportunities in the towns expanded, workers became less subservient to the whims of their white bosses.

Under these conditions it was no longer possible for compound officials to act as a unitary authority in both compound and mine. Compound life was being absorbed into a wider urban environment, and a breach was being forged between work and leisure. The company state had to break down, and in 1955 the compound offices split into two sections. Industrial relations controlled hiring and firing, acted as judge and jury in all disciplinary cases, and dispensed loans; community affairs organized housing, welfare, recreation and other aspects of compound life. Both sections were run by white officers. In the townships Africans were represented by tribal representatives until 1953, when these were abolished. At the mine they were represented by trade union officials, although it would be some time before an active shop organization developed.[47]

Bureaucratization of Industrial Relations

The split in the company state and the rise of the mineworkers' trade union reshaped the mechanisms through which production relations were reproduced and struggles were regulated.[48] The worst abuses inflicted by white bosses on black labour were eliminated, and the white departmental African personnel officers, who were stationed at the work sites, became more active in the control of black labour. However, discriminatory treatment of employees and colonial production relations were still evident in the existence of a separate departmental European personnel officer to handle the problems of European labour. Only in 1962 did both positions amalgamate into the single departmental personnel officer.

With independence around the corner, the mining companies began planning for an accelerated 'Africanization' or Zambianization programme, and the personnel department had top priority. Accordingly, a number of younger Zambian school leavers were recruited and, together with the more 'promising' African members of the personnel department, were trained for new positions. Not until 1966, two years after independence, however, did the head offices in Lusaka dictate the speed at which Zambianization should take place. In 1967 the community affairs and industrial relations departments were brought together, again under a single white personnel manager. The department was then reorganized so that the personnel manager became the 'staff development adviser', a new position created to look after expatriates, Zambianization, training and manpower services. A Zambian became personnel manager and took responsibility for industrial relations as they affected Zambian employees and for community affairs in the townships.

This reorganization considerably reduced the personnel manager's authority. His dealings were now confined to African workers, and he lost control over manpower services, training, work study, and odd attachments such as parks and gardens. The decline in status was reflected in the personnel manager's subordination to the mining manager, and his loss of direct access to the mine's general manager. The staff development adviser was a surrogate personnel manager with direct access to the general manager, and he was frequently consulted over issues that were rightly in the personnel manager's domain. At the level of the corporation, the new personnel manager also lost status. Previously the personnel managers of the different mines belonging to the two mining corporations would work out common policy and participate in industry-wide negotiations with the various unions. Now a new position, the group industrial relations manager, was created to perform this function, and it was filled by an expatriate who in most cases had previously been a personnel manager.

According to the plan, the staff development adviser would be phased out as the Zambian personnel manager reabsorbed some of the old personnel functions. Although the adviser was eliminated in 1971, the personnel department remained weak, for most of the adviser's functions were farmed out to other departments.

The lack of trust in the personnel manager and his diminished power weakened the personnel officers' ability to resolve conflicts, to influence line management, and to deal with the union and settle workers' grievances. Personnel officers are now clerks who process disciplinary cases, leave requests and clothing requirements, and participate in union works committee and safety meetings. The power to enforce sanctions against employees, impose fines, grant loans and dispose of other resources has been withdrawn.

There are a number of explanations for this devaluation of the personnel department. Throughout the mining industry, Zambianization took place without upsetting the colour bar principle that whites should not be subordinated to blacks. What changed was the colour bar's position — and even then the change was often only formal. Not only were new jobs usually created for the displaced expatriates, but the Zambian successors to the old jobs were not granted the support from their expatriate supervisors that their white predecessors had had, and were therefore unable to command the same authority over their subordinates. In many cases resources were formally withdrawn from the Zambian successor. In short, the devaluation of supervisory authority lay in the very process of Zambianization.

In the case of the personnel department, Zambianization was particularly rapid, and those who were responsible for training the new incumbents were the very people losing their jobs. They had no incentive to work themselves out of lucrative employment, and often promoted their own interpreter-clerks into positions for which they were obviously not equipped. The rapid succession to personnel manager provided expatriate management with a justification for appropriating many of the essential functions of the personnel department. This further weakened the Zambian personnel manager, who became even more dependent on expatriate management. At the same time, hostility between the successor and his white supervisor drove a wedge between them, which forced the personnel manager into passivity and isolation. This confirmed the prejudice of management that Zambians were not to be trusted.

The personnel manager's apparent spinelessness made life difficult for the personnel officers — which in turn created rifts in the department, often cast in the idiom of tribalism. Personnel officers were only too conscious of their diminished role and of the contempt with which line management regarded them. Zambian workers were also quick to point this out and had little faith in the personnel and industrial relations officers. In short, the very mechanisms of Zambianization, the retention of the colour bar, the rapidity of the process, the Zambian personnel, the threat these posed to expatriates, and the opportunity for expatriates to reallocate managerial authority in an upward direction — all these combined to reduce the power of that department in comparison with that of its colonial predecessor.

The diminished capacity of the mine's political apparatuses and the development of administration through rules also weakened the position of trade-union officials. While colonial despotism had fallen away, the bureaucratic apparatuses that the union dealt with from day to day protected centres of power that had shifted to the higher reaches of mine organization, such as the group industrial relations manager in Kitwe or even the head of industrial relations in Lusaka. To confront those powers, more drastic actions, such as strikes or walk-outs, were necessary. But this was to court the direct and sometimes repressive intervention of the state, as we shall see in the next section. No union official would openly advocate such a tactic.

Not surprisingly, trade union leaders directed much of their resentment over their loss of power toward Zambian representatives in the industrial relations apparatuses. The personnel officers were branded as 'stooges' who were selling out their fellow Zambians to white management. Workers shared this opinion. Zambians had not yet accustomed themselves to a post-colonial production politics that divided racial groups along class lines. Although personnel officers, including the personnel manager himself, were hostile to expatriate management, the function they performed placed them in clear opposition to workers and, to a lesser extent, to trade union leaders. As if to emphasize their new position, personnel officers began to adopt a patronizing attitude toward union officials, regarding them as 'uneducated' people who failed to appreciate the new common interest between workers and employers.

At the same time, the weakness of the mine apparatuses was an opportunity for the union to impose constraints on managerial discretion. In the early years of independence, the union officials, aided by the party, were often able to change colonial production relations. They intervened to remove racist supervisors and to eliminate the abuse of workers. Even though their activities were severely curtailed by the government, their potential power was feared by both expatriate and Zambian management. Trade union and personnel officers intervened less and less in the direct regulation of the labour process, but their very presence acted as a deterrent to the restoration of colonial production relations.

I have described some of the changes in the political apparatuses of the mines. In the first phase, power was concentrated in the hands of the company state, and the offices of the compound manager were mobilized as a despotic power over workers. In the second phase,

Africans became effectively organized, and the links binding compound life to work activities were severed. The company state fragmented and lost its monopoly of power. In the final phase, it was replaced by the weaker and less extensive personnel department. While Zambianization was the occasion and the excuse for the deflation of the mine apparatuses, this transformation dovetailed with the growing intervention of the state apparatuses in the regulation of industrial relations.

5. The Disjuncture between Labour Process and Production Apparatuses

As colonial despotism gave way to a weaker and more bureaucratic administrative apparatus, adjustments were made in the labour process, often in the direction of greater worker control. Coercion became less dominant in day-to-day work activities, and consent more important. In other work situations, however, the labour process could not be so easily reshaped, either because of technological constraints inherited from the colonial period or because of managerial attempts to regulate work in the old ways. These factors operated among the hand lashers, our next case study, where the struggles engendered by the organization of work were in continuous tension with the regulative capacity of the mine apparatuses.

Continuity in the Organization of Work: The Case of Lashing

In mining an ore body, sections of rock ('stopes') are excavated. Main-level development provides the tunnels that carry the trains transporting the ore blasted out of the stopes, and sub-end development enables drills to gain access to the stopes so that blasting charges can be placed. Blasting on sub-end development takes place by day, and the ore is removed ('lashed') at night. The sub-ends are so small that lashing must be done by hand.

Just as the compound is the distinctive institution in the regulation of the colonial labour force, hand lashing is the prototypical colonial labour process. It gained currency in the South African gold mines and then spread to all the mines of Southern Africa. It is distinguished by its simplicity and arduousness. Underground lashing involves shovelling broken rock in a cramped space into a wheelbarrow and carrying it to a tip. In other countries this is done by mechanical loaders. According to Baldwin, 'one mechanical loader in Northern Rhodesia handling 250 tons per day and working six days a week would cost (in 1959) $54 per day including spares, maintenance, and amortization. This is equivalent to the cost of 39 labourers. In the United States the daily cost for the equipment would be $60, or an amount equivalent to the cost of less than four labourers. The loader can do the work of about ten workers, so that it is highly profitable in the United States but a dead loss on the Copperbelt.[49]

However, Baldwin captures only one aspect of the colonial legacy: supplies of cheap labour power. He misses technological constraints that prevent mechanization; and, even more important, his narrow 'efficiency' criteria ignore the political requirements of lashing. We can appreciate the importance of these requirements by looking at the experiences of the British coal mines, where the labour process is generally organized around self-regulating and relatively autonomous work groups. These enforce their own output norms and develop their own informal leadership, while management provides services and equipment, ensures safety, allocates work, and administers the system of remuneration. Attempts to mechanize British coal mining after the Second World War led to a fall in productivity and resistance from the miners, since the new methods broke down the self-regulating groups and introduced a hierarchical division of labour based on the fragmentation of tasks. Trist, Higgin, Murray and Pollock concluded that, owing to the uncertainty and danger inherent in mining, production could be organized either through the self-regulating group, paid according to some bonus scheme, or through a system of coercion, which they claimed was 'impractical and unacceptable' to British miners.[50] But what was 'impractical and unacceptable' to British miners has been the basis of mining in the colonial context of Southern Africa. Lashing is just a small part of the coercive system there, which depended not only on the availability of cheap labour power but also on a system of managerial control capable of enforcing colonial production relations. What happens to lashing when the external political regime is transformed, with 'independence'?

In some ways the problems of lashing are similar to those involved in tracklaying. Both draw on unskilled labour to perform heavy manual work. Yet where tracklaying approached self-regulation, lashing continued to be organized on a strictly coercive and bureaucratic pattern. In the present study there were approximately fifteen workers in a lashing gang, supervised by a Zambian section boss (ganger) with the assistance of a crew boss. The next two layers of management, the shift boss and the mine captain, were also Zambians by 1971. At the beginning of the shift, workers were allocated to particular ends in groups of two, three, four or more, depending on the size of the end, the footage to be advanced, and the distance to the tip. When the section boss or crew boss had come to 'water down' the end and make sure it was safe, the lashers could begin work. They were usually expected to complete the assigned end by 2:00 a.m., in which case they would share a bonus calculated on the basis of the amount of ore removed, usually amounting to about a fifth of their earnings. If they had not finished by 2:00 a.m., they were normally expected to work into overtime until they did finish.

Confronted with their end at the beginning of the shift, a group of lashers would estimate their chances of cleaning it up before 2 o'clock. If they thought they could do this without becoming totally exhausted, they would try. If it looked too big or the tip was too far away, they would take it as easy as possible and hope they would not be forced to finish in overtime. In short, the lashers tried to minimize the time they spent underground, and when this was not possible they minimized the expenditure of energy. Why were they so different from the tracklayers, who tried to maximize overtime by restricting output during the normal shift? First, the tracklayers were generally older and more experienced workers who had family responsibilities and therefore needed more earnings, while the lashers tended to be young, single workers, who treasured their time more than their money. Second, tracklayers were more able to take it easy during the day in order to conserve energy for overtime, whereas lashers were invariably worn out by 2:00 a.m. They could not relax during the shift, for they were subjected to much more stringent supervision than were the tracklayers.[51] In general, the underground night shift was an altogether more unpleasant experience than daytime surface work.

The third difference between the two systems of regulating the labour process — namely, the use of bonuses — was also the least important. Indeed, it was so ineffective in regulating lashing output that it might as well not have existed. A bonus system is effective only if workers have some measure of control over the labour process. Management's failure to provide the necessary conditions and its arbitrary punitive interventions systematically thwarted such control. The allocation of workers to ends was usually dictated by the shortage of labour rather than the amount of work involved. Workers often had no chance of completing the assigned task by the end of the shift. There were frequent shortages of equipment, such as wheelbarrows. Lashers might have to wait up to four hours before their ends were checked and they could begin work. From time to time a breakdown in the air-cooling system would bring all work to a halt.

Because the bonus system was less than effective in eliciting what section and shift bosses considered an adequate amount of work, the bosses intervened with threats of disciplinary charges, overtime and an even worse allocation of ends the following night. By using its power to intensify effort controls, management made the lasher's life even more unpredictable and the bonus system even more ineffective. Yet the coercive system was not particularly successful, and section and shift bosses no longer had the support of colonial sanctions and apparatuses. To be sure, they had the power to allocate work and enforce overtime, but lashers were able to resist by manipulating the work situation, feigning illness, and so forth. A situation of continuous struggle ensued, leading to spontaneous walk-outs and sometimes wildcat strikes.

Why did lashing, unlike tracklaying, continue to be organized on the basis of colonial production relations? And what happened when shift bosses and mine captains were Zambianized? As in other situations, the Zambian successor did not inherit all the power of his predecessor. The jobs were fragmented, and a new layer of supervision was created for the displaced expatriate. The number of shift bosses and mine captains increased while their span of control diminished. From the labourer's point of view this meant closer supervision and even fewer opportunities to control conditions and earn bonuses. In short, Zambianization advanced the division of labour and bureaucratization while withdrawing the supervisors' power to enforce the division of labour. Moreover, these changes coincided with mounting worker resistance to that mode of organizing the labour process. The result could only be intensified struggle at the point of production.

There were other reasons why hand lashing persisted into the post-colonial era. Management often defended its continuation on technical grounds, arguing that the small sub-ends on which excavation was based made machine lashing unfeasible. Hand lashing was thus the legacy of a time when cheap labour power was in easy supply and coercive production relations could be enforced. To redesign the mine in accordance with the transformed production apparatuses would be unprofitable.[52] However, this cannot have been the whole story, because one mine did manage to eliminate hand lashing.

Equally significant is lashing's relative unimportance in the overall mining process. It rarely created a production bottleneck, so that only strikes could draw management's attention to the problem. Furthermore, management was able to exploit the supposed necessity of hand lashing. All employees entering the mine, whether on the surface or underground, had to engage in a spell of lashing. Even Zambian shift bosses and mine captains (although not their expatriate counterparts) had to do their stint. Lashing thus served two functions for management: it provided a labour reservoir for the rest of the mine, and disciplined workers for the arduous work on the mines. Those who could not make it through their stint of lashing were rejected as mineworkers. In Erving Goffman's terms, new recruits were stripped and mortified in preparation for their service to the mining industry. According to expatriate management, this was particularly important in light of the increasing recruitment of school leavers, who 'thought tough and dirty jobs were beneath them'. Since compulsory lashing was introduced only after independence, it must be seen as a managerial attempt to uphold or restore the colonial regime of labour in a post-colonial period. Thus, rather than change the technology, which would have been costly, management attempted to impose coercive relations in production with a view to intensifying labour discipline. Class struggle ensued. Its outcome was shaped not only by political apparatuses that regulate relations at the point of production, but also by the apparatuses of the post-colonial state.

The Lashers' Wildcat Strike

A year before our study, there had been a mine-wide strike of lashers.[53] The events began when four lashers who went underground at 6:00 p.m. only reappeared on the surface at 11:00 the next morning. Despite their seventeen hours underground, they were charged for failing to complete their ends. The next day all the lashers at this shaft refused to go down the mine, complaining about the non-payment of bonuses and overtime and the excessive charges for uncompleted ends. After a three-day strike these lashers returned to work, whereupon lashers at a second shaft came out on strike for a week. The reasons given were the transfer of seven lashers from day to night shift, the fact that the periods on lashing were longer than at the other two shafts, and the non-payment of overtime. The day after lashers at the second shaft struck, those at the third shaft came out in sympathy for the duration of the week. During the strike, management dismissed nine lashers.

In its public statements and its negotiations with management, the national leadership of the Mineworkers' Union of Zambia sympathized with the lashers' grievances but condemned them for striking, and exhorted them to return to work. The union maintained that the bonus for completing an end was an insufficient incentive to work hard, that section bosses were being allocated fewer men than the tasks warranted, and that section bosses, for fear of being disciplined themselves, were forcing lashers into unpaid overtime. The union claimed that the four men who had spent seventeen hours underground 'had completed their initial end and were charged for not completing an additional end. They had started late, not because of loafing, but because they had no tools.' The union also suggested that part of the problem lay with the mine's policy of employing only Zambians with four or more years of schooling.

In its response, management denied any responsibility for defective equipment or inadequate staffing levels, maintaining that the lashers' failure to clean the ends was caused by their working slowly. It referred to work-study investigations that had established what an average man could accomplish in eight hours, but naturally the union insisted that the conditions prevailing underground were very different from those that provided the basis for work-study investigations. Management specifically laid the blame for the strike on irresponsible troublemakers who 'thought they were highly educated and expected to rise to a high position overnight. They were not prepared to work under less educated supervisors who had many years of mining experience which these youngsters lacked.' Management lambasted the new type of worker that was appearing in the mines: 'The quality of the lasher had to be considered too. What was considered a fair amount of work as done by lashers some time back was suddenly too much for lashers today. It was quite obvious that their attitudes toward work must change.' In short, it was not that previous management was excessively coercive but that previous lashers were well disciplined. By holding up the 'colonial' lashers as the paragon of virtue and castigating the new lashers as 'undisciplined' and 'without respect', management was denying the political gains of the post-colonial order and trying to reassert a colonial regime of production.

Although the union recognized the legitimacy of the lashers' grievances, it concurred with management that there was a general problem of discipline in the mines and that 'the problem of educating today's youth in the facts of life was real, and they would continue their struggle to make them realize that paper qualifications alone did not make them useful citizens.' Thus, the union also failed to recognize the significance of the transition from colonial to post-colonial production politics. It merely reiterated the government view that striking workers were undisciplined and irresponsible. The cabinet minister for the Copperbelt Province reportedly said 'that the government fully supported management's action in dealing with strikers.' The secretary general of the Zambian Congress of Trade Unions attacked the striking lashers in parliament: 'In the first place both the Mineworkers' Union of Zambia and the Zambian Congress of Trade Unions do not support the strike of young people on the mines. It is unconstitutional, it is irresponsible.' After the strike, he stated publicly that 'disciplined members are an asset to the union, just as disciplined soldiers are an asset to the commander. . . . But undisciplined members cannot expect protection.' The government not only identified its interests with those of the mining companies but also upheld a despotic regulation of production akin to the colonial pattern. And it was precisely this endeavour that was at the root of the strike.

6. From Production Politics to State Politics

The repercussions of strike activity may serve to illuminate the relationship between production politics and state politics. From the lashers' standpoint, the strike was a struggle over the organization of production relations. The government, however, defined the strike as a concern of the state. The union was caught straddling state and production politics, upholding the legitimacy of the lashers' grievances while condemning the use of a strike as a bargaining weapon. Although on this occasion the government did not directly participate in the repression of the strike, its support was essential in management's moves against the strike leaders. By mobilizing public opinion against the lashers and ignoring their actual grievances, the Zambian state became a more direct instrument of the 'exploitation of wage labour by (mining) capital' than its colonial predecessor had been.

Similar observations were made by Bruce Kapferer in his 1966 study of a garment factory in Kabwe.[54] In waging struggles with management, workers tried to prevent the intervention of the union and party while the manager sought to call them in. So long as struggle was confined to the factory, workers were in a strong position to extract concessions; but as soon as their actions attracted the attention of the party or the union, let alone the government, their chances of victory were slim. In the colonial period, by contrast, although an enlargement of the field of struggle was difficult to achieve, it stood a good chance of strengthening the workers' position. Why should this be?

The Separation of Production Politics and State Politics

The *raison d'être* of colonial rule, established in 1924, was to replace the administration of the British South Africa Company with a state that would possess sufficient autonomy from the dominant economic interests to secure capital accumulation. The company state arose alongside the colonial state. It provided the conditions for the immediate production of surplus value, for the regulation of the labour process through colonial despotism, and for the maintenance of migrant workers through the compound system. The colonial state sought to generate labour supplies for various industries in Southern Africa through rural taxation. Because the mining companies required a stable labour force in order to remain profitable, and the provincial administration was dependent on revenues from a migrant labour force, the two clashed over labour policy. 'The Government's policy on migrant labour was formed by the economic pressures of the depression and from consideration of native policy in a rural rather than an industrial context. Lack of faith in the future of the copper industry, fear of the expenses of large-scale urban administration, devotion to Indirect Rule, and a wish to circulate money in the remote and poor country districts away from the line of rail led the Government to discourage the creation of a large class of settled workers.'[55]

The colonial administration sought the mines' assistance in the regular repatriation of workers to the rural areas. It tried unsuccessfully to persuade the companies to reintroduce labour recruitment from the hinterland, a system that had been discontinued in 1931, and, through deferred payments, to compel workers to return home periodically.[56] So long as the mines did not have to bear the costs of urban administration outside the compounds, their interests were best served by the development of a reserve army of labour on the Copperbelt.

However, for the most part the mining compounds and the colonial administration recognized the legitimacy of their separate jurisdictions. The government maintained a non-interventionist role in the copper mines' industrial relations, and the companies did not directly shape colonial policy. To be sure, there were occasions when the colonial state intervened in rash and reactive fashion, as when defenceless blacks were shot in the mine strikes of 1935 and 1940, or when union leaders were arrested following the rolling strikes of 1956. But these were tantamount to declarations of weakness and in-experience in the handling of industrial struggles, and were the exception rather than the norm. Generally, the government restricted itself to setting up commissions of inquiry or appointing arbitrators. The industrial relations legislation itself allowed little scope for government intervention. When the Colonial Office began pushing for the creation of a labour department, the colonial administration dragged its feet, claiming that district officers could perform the job equally well. In practice the district officers rarely entered the mines, and were regarded with much suspicion when they did. The mines themselves were equally opposed to the appointment of labour officers, who might deem it their duty to interfere with the operation of the company state.[57]

Even when the mines sought the colonial administration's intervention, they often failed to secure it. In the post-war period the mining companies pushed unsuccessfully for more repressive labour legislation. Similarly, the administration remained silent when the mines asked it to take a stance on African Advancement. This issue, touchy even before the war, became much more sensitive as African labour militancy increased and the political power of the white settler population became more entrenched. Rather than legislating against the colour bar, the government insisted that, as Africans had their own trade union, African Advancement was an industrial, not a political, issue. It maintained this position in the face of successive commissions that recommended that the European union transfer jobs to the African one. Only a risky initiative by Roan Selection Trust in 1954, threatening to withdraw recognition of the European union, broke the deadlock.

Orthodox Marxism has regarded colonialism as a means of generating super-profits (Lenin) or of resolving crises of accumulation (Luxemburg). Such theories portray the colonial state as an instrument of transnational capital. As we have seen, however, the colonial state possesses a distinct autonomy from international capital, so much so that the latter has to create its own 'company state' to guarantee the extraction of surplus value. How can we explain this anomaly? The distinctive function of the colonial state is to organize primitive accumulation so as to maximize the transfer of surplus to the metropolis. Merchant capital requires the colonized populations to produce for the market (for example, cocoa farmers in Ghana), whereas industrial capital requires proletarianization (for example, Southern Africa). The revenues of the colonial state emerge from and thereby reproduce the forms of primitive accumulation. The economic base of the colonial state is as weak as the surpluses it helps to generate are inaccessible to it. It is a limited state that cannot afford the costs of extensive infrastructure and urbanization. And so there is a separation of powers between the company state and the colonial state.

The Convergence of Production Politics and State Politics

The very success of the colonial state in generating labour supplies leads to its demise, as capitalist relations of production become self-reproducing. With the stabilization of the towns and the degeneration of the rural areas, the colonial state can maintain its reason for existence only through the coercive reproduction of a system of migrant labour. A new form of state necessarily arises, responsive to the needs of expanded capital accumulation in a social formation dominated by a capitalist mode of production. It retains an increasing proportion of the surplus in order to build an infrastructure, to reproduce specific forms of labour power, and to foster indigenous capital accumulation. The new form of state, which in the post-war period was a settler-dominated administration, stands in opposition to the metropolitan state.[58] As the colonial state becomes less effective as a political mechanism for securing the transfer of surplus back to the metropolis, the latter relinquishes its control.

From where do the pressures for a settler state come? Baylies has analysed in great detail how primitive accumulation led to the formation of new classes, in particular settler farmers, settler entrepreneurs and white workers.[59] In alliance these classes managed substantially to increase their political power in the Legislative Council after the Second World War. They pushed through increased taxation of the mining companies and of the BSA Company's royalties, thus redirecting surplus toward the construction of a more self-sustaining economy.[60] The Federation of Rhodesia and Nyasaland, which lasted from 1953 to 1963, was designed to further independence from the Colonial Office and to establish a more integrated economy. For Northern Rhodesia the federation proved to be an economic disaster, because huge copper revenues flowed to Southern Rhodesia, and a political disaster, because it galvanized the opposition of African nationalism. During this period, the mining companies exercised little direct influence over the state except through the dwindling powers of the Colonial Office. Although the federal and territorial governments were subject to immediate pressures from the settler classes, they were at the same time becoming increasingly dependent on revenues from the copper mines. Accordingly, the Northern Rhodesian government was prepared to intervene in the industrial relations of the mining companies in exceptional circumstances. In 1956, for example, it arrested strike leaders and proceeded to neutralize the African Mineworkers' Union as a political force.

Just as the settler state reflected an expanding accumulation of capital, with surplus being reinvested within the territory, political independence and majority rule formalized reintegration into a world capitalist economy. Surplus was now transferred back to the metropolis via *economic* mechanisms, while external political constraints became internalized as class forces. International capital developed ties to local capital through either joint or para-statal enterprises.[61] The post-colonial state concerned itself with making the ex-colony attractive to foreign investment. Expenditure on infrastructure, such as roads, railroads and energy, rapidly increased along with the education and welfare budget. Nationalization of the mines in 1969 merely cemented the growing coincidence of interests between international mining companies and the Zambian state. It was announced along with a wage freeze, an official ban on strikes and an appeal from President Kaunda to Zambian miners to work harder and give up their colonial habits now that the mines were 'theirs'.

New relations developed between state politics and production politics. Because the company state was fragmented and the new production apparatuses were weaker, less extensive, and more autonomous from management, the state itself intervened to narrow the scope of purely industrial struggle. It introduced industrial legislation that protected the rights of workers, but within ever narrower limits. The Industrial Relations Act of 1971, for example, established works councils whose scope and power were so limited as to render them largely ineffectual as a means of collective self-management. They were a mechanism for the regulation and absorption of class struggle at the level of the firm. The new legislation also aimed to stamp out strike activity by making collective bargains legally binding and subject to ratification by a newly created Industrial Court. The implications for class struggle are clear. Under the colonial order the development of primitive accumulation led to the insulation of production apparatuses from state apparatuses and, as a consequence, the separation of production politics from state politics. Under the constraints of late development, expanded accumulation of capital led to the interpenetration of production apparatuses and state apparatuses and the rapid transformation of industrial struggles into struggles against the state.[62]

7. Transitions in a Capitalist World Economy

Earlier I drew attention to the failure of development literature to analyse the labour process and therefore to consider its relationship to politics and the state. But one exception stands out. Immanuel Wallerstein attempts to link what he calls modes of labour control and forms of state as they appear in different zones of the world capitalist system. He summarizes his argument thus:

> Why different modes of organizing labour — slavery, 'feudalism', wage labour, self-employment — at the same point in time within the world economy? Because each mode of labour control is best suited for particular types of production. And why were these modes concentrated in different zones of the world-economy — slavery and 'feudalism' in the periphery, wage labour and self-employment in the core, and as we shall see share-cropping in the semiperiphery? Because the modes of labour control greatly affect the political system (in particular the strength of the state apparatus) and the possibilities for an indigenous bourgeoisie to thrive. The world economy was based precisely on the assumption that there were in fact three zones and that they did in fact have different modes of labour control. Were this not so, it would not have been possible to assure the kind of flow of surplus which enabled the capitalist system to come into existence.[63]

As both Skocpol and Brenner have stressed, Wallerstein's 'model' of the world system rests on a mechanical reduction of state apparatus to class structure, of class structure to mode of labour control, and of mode of labour control to technical possibilities and opportunities afforded by position in the world market.[64] Underdevelopment is the product of primitive accumulation, understood as the transfer of surplus from the periphery to the core made possible by the relative strength of states. These relative strengths in turn are dependent on the international distribution of modes of labour control.

Yet there is a certain plausibility to Wallerstein's logic, a logic we have in broad outline followed. We have argued that location in the periphery of the world capitalist economy generated cheap labour supplies based on a system of migrant labour and led to specific forms of the capitalist labour process whose reproduction required a particular set of production apparatuses. These in turn presupposed a particular form of state, to facilitate the transfer of surplus back to the core. Indeed, this was our mode of exposition, which started from the labour process and moved to the level of the state via the political apparatuses of production.

But such a functionalist logic does not explain how the various structures (labour process, production apparatuses and state apparatuses) come into being and change over time. Synchronic functionalist teleology is no substitute for diachronic causal analysis. Thus, the world market and technical possibilities cannot explain the change in production politics (mode of labour control?) from colonial despotism to bureaucratic rule, nor the transition from a colonial to a post-colonial state. Rather, these can be understood only as a result of class struggles, which were internal to the social formation and which led to the completion of primitive accumulation and the consolidation of self-reproducing capitalist relations of production as the dominant mode of production. Furthermore, such internal struggles reshaped, within limits, the form of the capitalist labour process (leading, for example, to the diminution of coercion and a corresponding increase in consent) and the form of international relations (away from direct political control and the repatriation of profits to direct economic subordination through forms of unequal exchange). Wallerstein's combination of teleological determinism and economic reductionism must be supplemented with causal-historical analysis. The relationship between production politics and state politics and the form assumed by each selects, at the same time that it is limited by, the labour process on one side and international forces on the other.

We saw how the attempts in January 1981 to subordinate production politics to state politics beyond the existing 'corporatist' arrangement foundered on the powerful collective resistance of labour, resistance nurtured by a production politics that stemmed from the labour processes of the copper mines. In neighbouring Tanzania, by contrast, state politics could impress itself on production politics more easily. There factories were smaller and labour less well organized during the colonial era, so that the Tanganyika African National Union (TANU), the single party of the one-party state, and the National Union of Tanganyika Workers, the government-controlled trade union, could forge a direct link between apparatuses of production and those of the state. As a result, workers were even more sensitive to state policy than in Zambia, and the socialist ideals of the Arusha declaration provided ideological weapons for workers to extend class struggle. In particular, Mwongozo (the TANU guidelines for 1971) was the occasion if not the cause of a rash of strikes, leading in some instances to workers taking over and running factories.[65] These were either directly suppressed by the state or allowed to dissipate of their own accord.

Tanzania represents a top-down control of production politics by the state through the party and trade union — that is, a movement toward bureaucratic despotism. By contrast, the unusual situation in Algeria between 1962 and 1964, after the evacuation of the settler population, represented a movement toward collective self-management or *autogestion*. However, within five years *autogestion* had become a dead letter. In hindsight the outcome might appear as a foregone conclusion.[66] First, *autogestion* affected only those marginal sectors of the economy that had been run by the *colons*. Worker control never touched the nationalized industries, such as the oil fields, nor many of the larger estates. Second, the success of worker control depended on protection and guidance by the state. Facing competition from large-scale private, often international capital and a legacy of debt left behind by the *colons*, worker committees became increasingly dependent on the government for finance and marketing as well as raw materials. This necessary centralization of resources provided the state bureaucracy with the opportunity to appropriate and distribute surplus in its own interests and thus to undercut worker control. The preservation of a colonial administrative structure, often staffed with colonial personnel, only accelerated the demise of *autogestion*. Finally, the workers and peasants themselves were economically, politically and ideologically unequipped to withstand the state's encroachments. Inasmuch as worker control brought few if any material benefits, it lost its initial appeal.

The destiny of *autogestion* was sealed by the workers' and peasants' failure to extend their control beyond the small businesses and farms they had inherited from the *colons*. In certain sectors the *comités de gestion* successfully controlled relations *in* production, but this was rendered meaningless by their inability to control the relations *of* production, at the level of relations among enterprises and between enterprises and consumers as well as of surplus distribution between the enterprise and the state. The conquest of the apparatuses of production becomes meaningful only in conjunction with the conquest of the apparatuses of the state. But when moves are made in that direction, as happened in Chile, for example, Third World governments always have the invited or uninvited support of international capitalism's political and economic sanctions.

Thus, we see that the labour process and the international economic and political orders are the inner and outer limits on transitions between systems of production politics and state politics. Hitherto, attention has focused almost entirely on international constraints and modes of production. This chapter has suggested the importance of penetrating the mode of production to the hidden abodes of production, the organization of enterprises, the relations *in* production, and the constraints these pose for production politics and their relationship to state politics.

Notes

1. Karl Marx, *Capital* Volume 1, Harmondsworth 1976, p. 279.
2. Baran, *The Political Economy of Growth*, New York 1957; Frank, *Latin America:Underdevelopment or Revolution*, New York 1969, chapters 1, 2.
3. *Unequal Exchange*, New York 1972.
4. 'The End of a Debate', in *Imperialism and Unequal Development*, New York 1977, p. 217. For a critique of Emmanuel and Amin, see Alain de Janvry and Frank Kramer, 'The Limits of Unequal Exchange', *The Review of Radical Political Economics*, no. 11, Winter 1979, pp. 3-15.
5. See Amin, *Unequal Development*, New York 1976.
6. Bettelheim, 'Theoretical Comments', in Emmanuel, *Unequal Exchange*, pp. 271-322; Kay, *Development and Underdevelopment*, New York 1975.
7. Kay, p. 54; see also Bettelheim, p. 302.
8. There is now an extensive literature critiquing 'underdevelopment theory' for inverting 'modernization theory' and thereby retaining many of the latter's assumptions. See, e.g., John Taylor, *From Modernization to Modes of Production*, London 1979; Lorraine Culley, 'Economic Development in Neo-Marxist Theory', in Barry Hindess, ed., *Sociological Theories of the Economy*, London 1977, pp. 92-117; Henry Bernstein, 'Sociology of Underdevelopment versus Sociology of Development', in David Lehmann, ed., *Development Theory*, London 1979, pp. 77-106; and Robert Brenner, 'Origins of Capitalist Development', *New Left Review*, no. 104, London 1977.
9. Warren, *Imperialism: Pioneer of Capitalism*, London 1980. For a critique of Warren's controversial work, see Emmanuel, 'Myths of Development versus Myths of Underdevelopment', *New Left Review*, no. 85, May–June 1974; and Philip McMichael, James Petras and Robert Rhodes, 'Imperialism and the Contradictions of Development', *New Left Review*, no. 85, May–June 1974.
10. See, e.g., Mahmood Mamdani, *Politics and Class Formation in Uganda*, New York 1976; Colin Leys, *Underdevelopment in Kenya*, Berkeley and Los Angeles 1975; Leys, 'Captial Accumulation, Class Formation and Dependency: The Significance of the Kenyan Case', *Socialist Register*, 1978, pp. 241-66; Ernesto Laclau, *Politics and Ideology in Marxist Theory*, London 1977, chapter 1; and Harold Wolpe, ed., *The Articulation of Modes of Production*, London 1980.
11. See Banaji, 'Modes of Production in a Materialist Conception'; and Banaji, 'For a Theory of Colonial Modes of Production', *Economic and Political Weekly*, no. 7, 23 December 1972, pp. 2498-502.
12. See, e.g., Norman Long, 'Structural Dependency, Modes of Production and Economic Brokerage in Peru', in Ivar Oxaal, Tony Barnett and David Booth, eds., *Beyond the Sociology of Development*, London 1975; and Harriet Friedmann, 'World Market, State and Family Farm: Social Bases of Household Production in the Era of Wage Labour', *Comparative Studies in Society and History*, no. 20, October 1978, pp. 545-86.
13. Mamdani, p. 145.
14. Ibid., p. 282.

15. John Saul, 'The State in Post-Colonial Societies: Tanzania', *Socialist Register*, pp. 249-72.

16. Leys 'The "Overdeveloped" Post-Colonial State: A Re-evaluation', *Review of African Political Economy*, no. 5, January-April 1976, pp. 39-48.

17. Poulantzas, *State, Power, Socialism*, NLB, London 1978.

18. Hamza Alavi, 'The State in Post-Colonial Societies: Pakistan and Bangladesh', *New Left Review*, no. 74, July-August 1972, pp. 59-81; and Saul, 'The State in Post-Colonial Societies'.

19. Leys, 'The "Overdeveloped" Post-Colonial State'; W. Ziemann and M. Lanzendorfer, 'The State in Peripheral Societies', *Socialist Register*, 1977, pp. 143-77.

20. Such an emphasis underlies Amin's conception of socialism as 'self-reliance' and Clive Thomas's *Dependence and Transformation*, New York 1974.

21. Thus, Kay's emphasis on the role of merchant capital reflects his experience in Ghana, while those who write on Southern Africa, such as Arrighi, emphasize the importance of industrial capital. Reflecting the history of Kenya, John Lonsdale and Bruce Berman examine the changing relationship between the two forms of primitive accumulation ('Coping with the Contradictions: The Development of the Colonial State in Kenya, 1895-1914', *Journal of African History*, no. 20, 1979, pp. 487-505; and Berman and Lonsdale, 'Crises of Accumulation, Coercion and the Colonial State: The Development of the Labour Control System in Kenya, 1919-1929', *Canadian Journal of African Studies*, no. 14, 1980, pp. 37-54).

22. The position adopted here is similar to Leys's view of 'neo-colonialism' as 'a system of domination of the mass of the population of a country by foreign capital, by means other than direct colonial rule' *(Underdevelopment in Kenya*, p. 27). The transition to post-colonialism corresponds to the reproduction of capitalism as the dominant mode of production without direct political subordination to a metropolitan country. A similar set of conceptions is implicit in the work of Emmanuel, Amin and Mandel, and in Fernando Cardoso and Enzo Faletto's *Dependency and Development in Latin America*, Berkeley and Los Angeles 1979. This is not to say that political relations among states are not important, but that they assume less significance with the consolidation of the capitalist mode of production in peripheral social formations. Apart from the work on Africa cited in this chapter, see, e.g., Peter Evans, *Dependent Development: The Alliance of Multinational, State and Local Capital in Brazil*, Princeton 1979; and David Collier, ed., *The New Authoritarianism in Latin America*, Princeton 1979.

23. Leon Trotsky, *The History of the Russian Revolution*, London 1977, p. 27; see also Trotsky, *The Permanent Revolution and Results and Prospects*, New York 1969, pp. 29-68.

24. See also Rosa Luxemburg and Nikolai Bukharin, *The Accumulation of Capital — An Anti-Critique: Imperialism and the Accumulation of Capital*, New York 1972.

25. 'Labour Supplies in Historical Perspective: A Study of the Proletarianization of the African Peasantry in Rhodesia', in Arrighi and Saul, eds., *Essays on the Political Economy of Africa*, New York 1973, pp. 180-234. Other studies of primitive accumulation in Southern Africa include Charles van Onselen, *Chibaro*, London 1976; Colin Bundy, *The Rise and Fall of the South African Peasantry*, Berkeley and Los Angeles 1979; Maud Muntemba, *Rural Underdevelopment in Zambia: Kabwe Rural District, 1850-1970*, Ph.D. dissertation, University of California, Los Angeles 1977; and Charles Perrings, *Black Mineworkers in Central Africa*, New York 1979.

26. Carolyn Baylies, *The State and Class Formation in Zambia*, Ph.D. dissertation, University of Wisconsin, Madison 1978, p. 148.

27. Ibid., p. 123.

28. I am here following Baylies's important argument, ibid., chapter 2.

29. Elena Berger, *Labour, Race and Colonial Rule*, London 1974, chapter 3.

30. Robert Baldwin, *Economic Development and Export Growth*, Berkeley and Los Angeles 1966, p. 105.

31. 'International Corporations, Labour Aristocracies, and Economic Development in Tropical Africa', in Arrighi and Saul, p. 124.

32. It would be interesting to compare, for example, the labour process under colonial despotism with the one in the Scottish coal mines under conditions of slavery.

33. This is recognizable even in the account of the compound system by one of its practitioners: F. Spearpoint, 'The African Native and the Rhodesian Copper Mines', supplement to the *Journal of the Royal African Society*, vol. 36, July 1937.

34. George Chauncey, Jr., 'African Work Culture, Resistance, and the Evolution of Management Strategy for Labour Control in the Zambian Copperbelt, 1925-1945', paper presented to the Southern African Research Program, Yale University, 29 November 1979, pp. 12-13. See also Jane Parpart, *Labour and Capital on the Copperbelt: African Labour Strategy and Corporate Labour Strategy in the Northern Rhodesian Copper Mines 1924-1964*, Ph.D. dissertation, Boston University Graduate School, Boston 1981, pp. 98-99.

35. Chauncey, p. 16.

36. Ibid., p. 16. See also Parpart, p. 67.

37. Chauncey, p. 17. See also Perrings, pp. 202-3.

38. Van Onselen, op.cit.

39. Parpart, chapter 2; Perrings, chapter 7.

40. Spearpoint, p. 38. As both Parpart and Perrings make clear, the different levels of stabilization reflect the different ore bodies and therefore techniques of production; see, e.g., Parpart, pp. 48-51.

41. On the role of the police in labour control, see Parpart, pp. 64-70.

42. Chauncey, p. 26.

43. See A.L. Epstein, *Politics in an Urban African Community*, Manchester 1958.

44. I am here following Parpart's convincing analysis, which opposes both the official views attributing the early African strikes to outside agitators and subversive millennarian movements, and the more scholarly views that give prominence to Bemba tribal leadership or the effects of dual dependence on two modes of production.

45. The mines adopted a variety of strategies to encourage stabilization without proletarianization. Workers were permitted to take long leaves without losing their jobs and even to take leaves without pay. The pension scheme paid retired miners enough to live comfortably in a rural economy, but discouraged them from remaining in the towns, where living costs were much higher. See Baldwin, pp. 138-9.

46. See Berger, chapter 5.

47. The African Mineworkers Union was constructed from the top down. It was highly centralized, with initiatives coming from the leaders, reflecting the centralization of mining operations. Attempts to introduce grievance machinery and a system of shop stewards came to nought until 1963.

48. This section is based on a detailed study of the personnel department at one mine over a period of two years. It involved participant and non-participant observation as well as extensive interviewing of personnel officers and line management.

49. Baldwin, p. 92.

50. Trist, et al., pp. 66-7.

51. This is the reverse of what Alvin Gouldner reported in *Patterns of Industrial Bureaucracy*. There Gouldner shows how the self-regulating groups appeared underground while on the surface bureaucratic patterns prevailed. This only highlights the importance of examining the political context of the development of the labour process.

52. Perrings, pp. 234-5.

53. The information on the strike comes from newspaper accounts and the minutes of the four meetings held between management and the union.

54. *Strategy and Transaction in an African Factory*, Manchester 1972.

55. Berger, pp. 40-1. See also Helmuth Heisler, *Urbanization and the Government of Migration*, London 1974, chapter 4.

56. Perrings, pp. 113-4.

57. See Parpart, pp. 182-90.

58. Behind the claims that the colonial state is an instrument of international capital lies the assumption that the colonial state is an instrument of the metropolitan state. We have already questioned orthodox Marxism's first assumption; we are now questioning the second. For an elaboration of this argument, see Emmanuel, 'White-Settler Colonialism and the Myth of Investment Imperialism', *New Left Review*, no. 73, May-June 1972, pp. 35-57.

59. Bayliess, part 2.

60. Until 1935 the Northern Rhodesian government's income from 'Native Taxes' was greater than its income from the mines (ibid., p. 250). In 1947 taxes paid by the mining companies made up only 27.7 per cent of total government revenues, but by 1952 this had already risen to 57.5 per cent (Berger, p. 8).

61. Baylies (chapters 7-9) explores in great detail the changing relationship between international, national and state capital.

62. For an account of the relationship between trade-union and nationalist struggles in Northern Rhodesia, see Ian Henderson, 'Early African Leadership: The Copperbelt Disturbances of 1935 and 1940, *Journal of Southern African Studies*, no. 2, October 1975, pp. 83-97; and Henderson, 'Wage Earners and Political Protests in Colonial Africa: The Case of the Copperbelt', *African Affairs*, no. 72, July 1973, pp. 288-99. The divergence between union and nationalist struggles has been explained in a number of ways. Thus, Epstein refers to the 'unitary' structure of the mine compounds and the 'atomistic' structure of the locations where the African National Congress was strong (pp. 188-93). But such an argument does not explain the convergence of industrial and political struggles after independence. Parpart argues that the 'decision to keep the union outside politics emerges as a pragmatic solution in an oppressive colonial context, rather than proof of the absence of political consciousness' (p. 256). There is little evidence to suggest that the colonial state was any more oppressive than the post-colonial regime. It was more the insulation of the company state from the colonial state than actual colonial oppression that structured the separation of struggles irrespective of political consciousness.

63. Wallerstein, *The Modern World System*, p. 87.

64. Theda Skocpol, 'Wallerstein's World Capitalist System: A Theoretical and Historical Critique', *American Journal of Sociology*, no. 82, March 1977, pp. 1075-89; R. Brenner, 'Origins of Capitalist Development', *New Left Review*, no. 104, London 1977, pp. 25-92.

65. For accounts of the relationship between production politics and state politics in Tanzania, see Henry Mapolu, ed., *Workers and Management*, Dar-es-Salaam 1976; Paschal Mihyo, 'Industrial Relations in Tanzania', in Ukandi Damachi, Dieter Seibel and Lester Trachtman, eds., *Industrial Relations in Africa*, London 1979, pp. 240-72.

66. I am here relying on Ian Clegg, *Workers' Self-Management in Algeria*, New York 1971.

Conclusion:
Toward a Global Perspective

We began with production; we must end with politics. What should we mean by politics? This is itself a political question. Definitions are not innocent.

Throughout this book I have distinguished between the labour process, as the economic moment of production, and the apparatuses of production, as crystallizing the political moment of production. By politics I understand struggles over or within relations of structured domination, struggles that take as their *objective* the quantitative or qualitative change of those relations. What then is the relationship between politics and apparatuses? Originally I wanted to claim a one-to-one correspondence between apparatuses and politics, such that apparatuses guarantee the production of a distinctive set of relations. In particular, the apparatuses of the state should guarantee the relations *of* production, while the apparatuses of the workplace should guarantee the relations *in* production. This, however, is patently not the case, as the apparatuses of the workplace are involved in struggles over wages and benefits — that is, relations of exploitation which are part of the relations of production. A better approximation might be that production apparatuses regulate struggles over the labour process and the valorization process — relations in production and relations of exploitation — while state apparatuses regulate struggles over relations of *re*production. Yet this departs from reality, as the state can be actively involved in the regulation of wages, benefits, working conditions, and even technology, and production apparatuses may regulate struggles designed to transform relations of *re*production, as when wage negotiations are tied to public control of investment.

Considering that there is at best a weak correlation between apparatuses and the relations they regulate — that is, there is not a one-to-one mapping between the two — we must choose between politics defined as struggles regulated by *specific apparatuses*, politics defined as struggles over *certain relations*, and the combination of the two. In the first, politics would have no fixed objective, and in the second it would have no fixed institutional locus. I have therefore opted for the more restrictive third definition, according to which politics refers to struggles within a specific arena aimed at specific sets of relations. Thus, family politics are struggles waged within the family over patriarchal relations. Production politics are struggles waged within the arena of production over relations in and of production and regulated by production apparatuses. State politics, on the other hand, are distinctive in that they cannot be characterized by struggles over any particular set of relations. A given set of relations may or may not be the object of struggle within the arena of the state. This varies historically. What is distinctive about the state is its global character, its function as the factor of cohesion for the entire social formation. The state not only guarantees the reproduction of certain relations but, more distinctly, it is the apparatus that guarantees all other apparatuses. State politics include as their core the politics of politics. The characteristic effects of state apparatuses are to protect and shape family apparatuses, production apparatuses, community apparatuses, and so on.

Our alternative understanding of politics critically engages two tenets in the Marxian tradition. First, as we have just seen, it refuses to accept the reduction of politics to state politics and of state politics to the reproduction of class relations. Second, it challenges the reduction of production to economics, so that history can no longer be viewed as unfolding in accordance with a fixed set of economic laws. Economics, politics and ideology are inextricably interwoven within the sphere of production. In this concluding chapter we shall consider how the case studies in this book point to an alternative conception of history — in relation, first, to the development of particular modes of production and, second, to the transition from one mode of production to another. But first we must elaborate the critique of fixed laws of history.

For Marx the hallmark of capitalism, distinguishing it from all pre-capitalist societies, is the separation of state and civil society. Civil society is inhabited by atomized, privatized and above all depoliticized individuals, whereas the state is the locus of political community. In his later writings Marx specifies the separation of state and civil society, so that the former is the arena in which classes become organized into parties, form alliances and struggle, while the latter is the site of laws of development of the capitalist mode of production, the concentration and centralization of capital, and the tendency of the rate of profit to fall. These laws operate behind the backs of their agents. In this perspective there is little theoretical room for self-conscious collective action at the level of production. Indeed, Marx could only 'discover' these laws of capitalism by suppressing any theorization of the politics of production.

Whatever ambiguities remain in Marx's writings are brushed aside in the self-confident scientific Marxism of Engels, Kautsky and Luxemburg. Here the economic base is the locus of inexorable laws driving capitalism to its final collapse, while the superstructure is the locus of working-class organization into a party with the aim of ensuring that socialism rather than barbarism rises from capitalism's ashes. The base is again the realm of laws acting through atomized agents, while the superstructure is the realm of subjectivity, of purposeful collective action. The idea of a politics of production, and of political apparatuses of production, undermines this perspective by insisting that the arena of production contains political and ideological institutions as well as a purely economic organization. Now both 'base' and 'superstructure' are realms simultaneously of subjectivity and objectivity. There are no longer any objective laws of development of the capitalist mode of production: different political apparatuses of production lead to different struggles and thus to diverse patterns of accumulation. Our perspective dovetails well with the game–theoretic approaches where objective limits on subjective choices link micro–indeterminacy to macro–determinacy but without indicating any unique pattern of development.

If the idea of production politics undermines the essential premisses of scientific Marxism, it also directly challenges the two classical Marxist responses to that tradition: Leninism and evolutionary socialism. Both restrict politics to state politics, so that different types of politics are defined by their *goals* rather than their arenas. Theorists of social democracy distinguish, for example, between legal, political and social rights; political, social and economic democracy; and consumption politics, mobility politics and production politics; and in each case politics is restricted to state politics.[1] Furthermore, in repudiating economic laws such theorists follow Bernstein in postulating alternative political laws — the tendency for the expansion of rights, the progressive movement from political to economic democracy, from consumption to production politics. These predictions are at best statistical extrapolations of a putative past into a speculative future. There is no attempt to provide any mechanisms for the unfolding of this progressive movement.

We must think not only of the politics of production but also of the production of politics. Just as production cannot be reduced to a purely economic component but is a 'base' with its own 'superstructure', so the state cannot be reduced to its political effects. We must go beyond statements about the necessary functions of the state to an account of how those functions are performed.[2] We must now look at the state as an ensemble of apparatuses with their own distinctive 'labour processes', which, rather than producing commodities (although some, such as nationalized industries, do so), produce and reproduce relations (police, law), provide services that socialize the costs of the reproduction of labour power (welfare, education) and of accumulation (postal service), or regulate struggles within the state (representative apparatuses). Thus, state institutions have their own productive component and their own politics of production as well as certain global political *effects*. Just as the politics of production undermine the possibility of fixed economic laws, so the production of politics by state labour processes is entangled with diverse forms of struggles which preclude any developmental laws of state politics.

The lack of any serious theoretical consideration of production politics is reflected in the practice of social democracy, most notably in the recent socialist governments of Sweden, France, Spain, Chile and Britain. Socialist governments have distinguished themselves by their attempts to contain or even strangle organs of popular control. To be sure, in each case the initial weakness of the working-class base compelled an accommodation to forces hostile to socialism. But it is also clear that without forms of popular control the state is largely ineffectual when faced with the mobility of international capital. By themselves the apparatuses of the state cannot inaugurate socialism in a capitalist work economy.

Leninists, of course, come to the same conclusion but by following a very different argument. For them the root of the problem lies in the character of the state itself. Social-democratic parties become prisoners of the capitalist state — a state that is structured to reproduce capitalism irrespective of the political aims of its personnel. Production politics is a distraction from the real goal of transforming the capitalist state. Thus, the salient distinction is not between production politics and state politics but between reformist and revolutionary (state) politics. The transformation of production apparatuses is condemned as an infantile disorder, so that in the practice of state socialism forms of collective self-management are eliminated in favour of centralized direction. The blindness is compounded in Lenin's own brand of speculative evolutionism, akin to that of Bernstein: the natural movement from the dictatorship of the proletariat to communism through the withering away of the state. Lenin provides no mechanisms that might guarantee such a withering away. Indeed, he eliminates the very organs of popular control that would be essential to such a devolution. Furthermore, because he reduces all politics to state politics Lenin embraces the idea that politics themselves will be abolished. The end of politics — that is, the coincidence of the particular interest and the general interest — not only is a mythical impossibility but also lays the ideological ground for a coercively imposed collective interest. Thus, we see how both social democratic and Leninist traditions, while differing in their conceptions of transitions beyond capitalism, reduce politics to state politics and implicitly or explicitly reject economic laws in favour of political laws. These political trajectories are as erroneous as the economic tendencies they replace.

For all their differences, classical Marxisms, whether scientific, evolutionary or Leninist, subscribed to historical materialism — the Marxian meta-theory of history in which historical progress is assured by the expansion of the forces of production. According to this theoretical framework, any given set of relations of production first accelerates the development of the forces of production and then fetters them so that they can no longer expand, whereupon the old relations of production are overthrown, a new, higher set is installed, and the productive forces are given a renewed impetus. So capitalism follows feudalism and socialism follows capitalism as surely as night follows day. Although this meta-theory has recently been awarded a daring and rigorous defence,[3] it has been the *bête noire* of Western Marxism, in both its structuralist and its critical theory variants.

In the structuralist account of history, there is a radical discontinuity between modes of production so that the origins of a new mode are separated from the dissolution of the old.[4] Whereas we can theorize about the development of a given mode of production, about its *dynamics*, we cannot theorize about its *genesis*. There is nothing necessary about the appearance of a new mode of production; rather, it is the product of conjunctural circumstances. In other words, we cannot theorize a diachronics — a necessary transition from one mode of production to another; only the internal development and decline of a mode of production can be formulated in terms of laws. Just as there is nothing necessary about the rise of capitalism, so there is nothing necessary about the subsequent rise of socialism. In short, the unilinear and deterministic conception of history marked by the expansion of the forces of production is abandoned in favour of an indeterminate perspective on the future, a voluntaristic picture in which class struggle suddenly enters as the arbiter of history.

We shall return to the question of class struggle. Here I want to underline how the rejection of a telos to history also called forth a reconceptualization of the forces of production. In the structuralist account these are no longer a collection of objects — instruments of production, raw materials and labour power — but a set of relations to nature. A mode of production becomes a double set of relations: appropriation of nature and appropriation from humans. However, to characterize the forces of production in this way raises a question that structuralists repressed: namely, the problem of their reproduction, and thus of a specific politics — the politics of production.[5] Thus, we see how the concept of production politics first emerges from a concept of history that rejects any unilinear succession of modes of production. But, as I suggested above, once one systematically incorporates the idea of production politics, not only are there no clear diachronics but there are no longer any fixed dynamics either. We have dispensed with all laws.

If structuralism insists on dispensing with the idea that the expansion of the forces of production is the guarantor of progress toward socialism, critical theory has usually taken a much stronger position. It has condemned capitalist forces of production as irrevocably tainted by capitalist relations of production or simply by the domination of nature — so much so that they are inimical to socialism. Capitalist technology and the capitalist labour process, far from posing a challenge to capitalist relations of production, far from being the seed of socialism within the capitalist womb, are effectively shaped by those relations in order to reproduce them. Far from being neutral, the productive forces are a major obstacle to the transition to socialism, both stifling and integrating class struggle within the parameters of capitalism, and impeding the development of collective self-management under socialism. I do not embrace this position here. The distinction between the labour process and the apparatuses of production suggests a distinctive form of socialist production politics that is fused with state politics. But it remains an open question whether a labour process developed under capitalism is or is not compatible with such a system of politics. It is quite possible that certain labour processes are compatible while others are not. The answer will also depend upon the specific form of socialism — that is, the specific form of unity of production politics and state politics — that we are considering.

We have now examined one arm of historical materialism: history as the contention of the forces of production and the relations of production, leading to a particular succession of modes of production. This contention plays itself out in the realm of the 'superstructures', in the form of class struggle. Indeed, the second arm of historical materialism is history as the history of class struggle. But what does this mean? Is it any more than a tautology in which class struggle refers to struggles which affect classes, and that history should be seen as the accumulation of such class effects? Or are Marx and Engels making a stronger claim, that the decisive struggles in history have been between classes? The latter interpretation is the most common and the more easily refuted, since struggles between groups other than classes or struggles within rather than between classes have often been decisive in the transformation of societies. In particular, the transition from capitalism to socialism, it is argued, cannot be reduced to a struggle between capital and labour. To the contrary, the working class can only develop interests in the reproduction of capitalism; it does not develop radical needs that point beyond capitalism. Thus, those originally committed to the working class as the saviour of humanity, the agent of emancipation, now throw up their hands in despair and, feeling let down by the proletariat, abandon it for social movements forged in civil society outside the economy, or embrace avant-garde forms of popular struggle outside, or sometimes even inside, the electoral arena. It turns out that the rejection of one metaphysical imputation evokes its opposite: that the working class never has and never will decisively enter the historical arena. We were, in short, deceived from the beginning.

Here I have adopted a more cautious approach, replacing philo-sophical speculation with sociological analysis. Rather than abandon-ing the working class for the peasantry, for a new class of intellectuals or for new social movements, I have sought to examine the conditions under which it has intervened and might continue to intervene in the historical process. Furthermore, I have retained the Marxist ortho-doxy that the critical arena shaping the working class is the process of production itself, understood as a political regime. But in reducing the burden forced upon the working class I have left the tracks of history (the contention of the forces of production and the relations of production) in disarray, and the engine of history (class struggle) spluttering. What remains? Here I can only begin a reconstruction based on the case studies contained in this book.

We must return to the question of 'laws' of history and what it may mean to reject their existence. It certainly does not imply that any-thing is possible. Even in the limited exposition of this book we have seen how the state, the reproduction of labour power, and market forces all shape the form of production apparatuses, which in turn set limits on the nature of the struggle. Nor does the absence of laws imply that there are no patterns of historical development — such as the transition from despotic to hegemonic to hegemonic-despotic regimes — but only that they are themselves historically contingent. The patterns we discover in history are not immutable, nor are they tendential toward some ultimate 'true' pattern; they are continually reconstructed as part of the historical process. History is always coming into existence. To be sure, we build upon earlier reconstructions, we perhaps build a tradition of reconstructions, but they are all relative to the time and place of their theorization, whether or not we acknowledge this. There is no final reconstruction, if only because history does not suddenly cease. That is to say, we do not stand outside history watching it from afar; we are at its centre, continually looking back for pointers to the future. Just as we change with history, so history changes with us and our conception of future horizons expands and contracts.

Laws cannot anticipate what history continually throws up: surprises. They cannot entertain the fundamentally new. Laws can only freeze history into a mould shaped according to the specifications of a particular time and place. They take as given what at the moment of their inception appears unproblematic, what appears eternally fixed and natural, but which subsequently becomes variable and problematic. Thus, Marx did not take the international economic system as problematic, as an object of study in his formulation of the tendency of the rate of profit to fall, so that Mandel, responding to the global dimensions of the second slump, reconstructs the history of capitalism as a series of long waves. But Mandel's reconstruction remains rooted in the orthodoxy which locates laws of development in the base and political struggles in the superstructure. From a different vantage point I have argued that such laws of development can be constructed only by repressing the political component of production, whose variations, I claim, are a necessary part of any explanation of the fate of working-class movements during the last century.[6]

The tradition of reconstructions becomes the reconstruction of a tradition, continually problematizing what was earlier taken for granted. I too must follow this route. In what follows, I reverse the direction of causality predominant in the preceding chapters. There I sought out the conditions of existence of factory regimes and the way those regimes then shaped struggles. Now I want briefly to attend to the more complicated question of the extent to which those struggles in turn shaped different factory regimes. I will problematize the forces that shaped factory regimes by examining how they are determined by struggles. In this way I want to highlight the interdependence of factory regimes, between now and the past, between here and elsewhere, so that changes in particular regimes can be linked to changes in other regimes as a result of the struggles they promote.

We reconstructed the history of capitalism as a sequence of factory regimes: despotic regimes (patriarchal, paternalistic, and market despotism), followed by hegemonic regimes, which in turn are beginning to give rise to hegemonic despotism. The first transition can be understood as the separation of the reproduction of labour power from the process of production. Under despotic regimes survival outside work depended on performance at work. The bond rested on the partial or complete expropriation of labourers from the means of subsistence, and was mediated through the family, the employer, the labour market, or some combination of these. Subsequently, survival outside work came to depend more on the state and less on performance at work, although the latter never lost its predominance over the former, and some fractions of the labour force were better off than others. The rise of the welfare state, however rudimentary, compelled management to rely less on coercive practices and to expand the scope of consent.

How can we explain this transition? Since it has been so widespread in capitalist societies, a general rather than a nationally specific explanation is necessary. I have argued that the pressure came from two directions. First, it came from large-scale capital, seeking the regulation of the labour market through its internalization and of class conflict through its institutionalization — the containment of uncertainty in product and supply markets requiring commensurate regularization in management–worker relations. Moreover, as it faced crises of overproduction stemming from the very success of earlier despotic regimes, collective capital had an interest in reconstituting the norm of working-class consumption and tying it to profitability levels. The second source of pressure, exacerbated by cyclical economic crises, was the drive of labour to establish minimal levels of security in unemployment as well as in employment. It was the convergence of these interests that underlay the consolidation of social insurance and guarantees against arbitrary managerial domination. Different states with different capacities and interests, responding to different constellations of forces, reshaped production apparatuses and reorganized the reproduction of labour power in different ways. But in all advanced capitalist countries minimal levels of security at work and outside work did eventually become the norm, so that management was forced to temper despotism with various forms of hegemonic regime.

The relaxation of despotism in advanced capitalist countries and the turn to hegemonic regimes did not entail a similar transition in peripheral societies. Indeed, despotic regimes continued to be implanted there, often under the auspices of colonial rule. Inasmuch as they were an extension of the metropolis, colonial economies, such as the one we examined in Zambia, served to supply raw materials for the advanced capitalist economies at the lowest price and with the greatest profit. The colonial state orchestrated the supply of cheap labour, while the company state imposed colonial despotism at the level of production. There was no attempt to boost the purchasing power of colonial working classes to offset tendencies toward overproduction in the metropolis, or to establish demand for the products produced in the colonies themselves. Such colonial economies were indeed 'enclave' economies, extensions of the central economy into a sea of deepening underdevelopment. Or in Amin's words, autocentric development in the centre entailed hegemonic regimes of production, while disarticulated development in the periphery entailed despotic regimes.

Nevertheless, dominant classes in the colony do develop interests independent of, and then opposed to, those of the dominant classes in the metropolis. As we saw in the case of Zambia, a settler population emerged seeking to develop the Zambian economy beyond its enclave, trying to establish a domestic market and threatening the political dominance of the copper mines, so that the colonial state was forced to reorient some of its policies toward the interests of indigenous classes. The embryonic settler regime was soon swamped by the rising African nationalist movement, itself a product of economic development. The new African government only cemented the process of autonomization from the metropolis that had been developing since the beginning of colonial rule. The mining corporations had to dispense with their distinctive apparatuses of production as the settler and post-colonial states proved incapable of providing the conditions of their reproduction. The substitution of bureaucratic rule for colonial despotism, and the corresponding material concessions to the working class, escalated the costs of production of copper — at a time when it was being replaced by other materials in the industrial production of the advanced capitalist countries. The declining importance of their raw materials devastated the post-colonial economies, and the survival of peripheral countries came to depend on the re-imposition of coercive regimes of production to attract new forms of capital from the core countries. But this must also be understood in terms of further changes in the core countries themselves.

The hegemonic regime sowed the seeds of its own destruction. It established constraints on the deployment of capital, whether by tying wages to profits or by creating internal labour markets, collective bargaining and grievance machinery which hamstrung management's domination of the workplace. The recomposition of capital was made difficult, and deeper crises threatened to ensue. Yet at the same time, technological developments, particularly in communications, facilitated capital mobility and the segmentation of a single labour process among different countries. A new periphery, epitomized by the export-processing zones, emerged. Thus, while the old extractive industries of the Third World were relaxing their despotic regimes, other countries of the Third World were installing new regimes of despotism. Manufacturing, particularly of consumer goods, from clothes to automobiles, footballs to radios, moved to peripheral countries, seeking not only reservoirs of cheap labour but also political orders which would nurture repressive factory regimes. Most usually the new reservoirs of labour were made up of young, single women, presumed to be supplementary income earners and paid very low wages. High levels of turnover, at least in the beginning, were an effective means of containing any resistance. Peripheral states created a distinctive powerlessness among this new army of workers, so that forms of patriarchal, paternalistic and colonial despotism could be imposed. Just like they did in the past, these regimes generated their own working-class opposition, strongest in the older export-processing zones, such as South Korea, and in the larger 'industrializing' countries of the semi-periphery, such as South Africa and Brazil.

These industrializing countries of the semi-periphery combine elements of the old periphery — the extractive industries such as gold mining in South Africa — with new export-processing zones in textiles or electronics. A third distinctive feature is the creation of consumer goods for domestic consumption — the prototypes being the auto industries of Brazil and South Africa. We can see different production regimes in the different sectors — the continuation of colonial despotism in extractive industries, the patriarchal or, more likely, paternalistic despotism in export substitution, and new forms of despotism in the auto industry, combined with limited trade-union representation. South Africa and Brazil today are the loci of powerful working-class movements centred on such import-substitution industries, and in both countries the state has sought the insulation and regulation of struggle rather than its repression. Given the nature of their repressive orders, however, it is not clear to what extent such struggle can be confined as it was in the United States, since basic political rights necessary for the defence of working-class organizations, such as trade unions, are still absent. Working-class movements quickly recognize the importance of such rights, so that struggles at the point of production, far from being contained, easily spill over into the wider public arena.

The movement of substantial amounts of manufacturing capital from the core to the periphery, and the transfer of capital within core countries to new industrial areas often reliant on cheap imported labour, effectively undermined the hegemonic regime. Thus, in the remaining manufacturing industry and in allied service industries there emerges what I have called hegemonic despotism. This is a new form of despotism — built on the basis of the erstwhile hegemonic regime — which, rather than creating antagonistic interests (as the early despotic regimes did), begins to construct a coordination of interests around despotic rule. Collective bargaining is now a means of extracting concessions from workers, faced with the threat of plant closures or lay-offs. Fractions of the working class compete with each other to retain capital's 'allegiance'. Moreover, the intensification of competition is also made possible on the one hand by the erosion of the popular roots of working-class organization through the previous hegemonic regimes, and on the other by the withdrawal of the state as an arena in which struggles between capital and labour can be fought out. The possibility of constituting a hegemonic despotism becomes a major attraction to capital as it faces widening struggles in peripheral and semi-peripheral countries.

If hegemonic despotism is ascendant in the old core industries with entrenched unions, what is happening in the new industries such as electronics or the so-called service sector? Here too we can detect major changes in the relations of production, making advanced capitalist countries once more attractive centres of investment. The growth of part-time and temporary work, particularly among women, orchestrated by specialized agencies, enhances the separation of relations of production from relations in production, mystifying the former while effectively subordinating workers to the latter. On one side relations of production often revolve around the temporary work agency. The worker relates to her employer as an individual, receiving assignments by telephone and driving to them in an automobile. Unions are barred and fellow employees unknown. Moreover, the worker is sucked into this oppressive isolation not only by her material circumstances but also in the name of enhanced autonomy — greater 'freedom' to balance domestic work and low-paid wage labour. On the other side, she moves from one set of relations in production to another, unless she should prove herself 'worthy' of a permanent job. She has no security of contract, receives no fringe benefits, and cannot bargain over wages. She is at the mercy of her supervisor, who reports back to her employer — the temporary agency. There is no clearly defined job ladder, and the distribution of jobs is clouded in mystery.[7]

Capital's attraction to temporary or part-time work, as well as to various forms of subcontracting, does not stem merely from the cheapening of labour costs. Through the creation of an atomized and vulnerable labour force,[8] the conditions of an advanced capitalist economy intensify subordination without struggle to the whims of management. For, in export-processing zones of the Third World, workers, usually single women, live together in dormitories or go home together in buses, forge communities of solidarity and present employers with escalating resistance. To maintain a flexible deployment of labour requires brutal coercion at the point of production, whereas the creation of a new hegemonic despotism in core countries effects silent submission. The car and the telephone, artifacts of advancement, potential instruments of collective solidarity, in the hands of capital become the instruments of atomization.[9]

If the private capitalist firm is backing into regimes of hegemonic despotism, how does this relate to changes in state socialism? Although the effects are difficult to isolate, the trajectory of capitalism both stimulated and then reshaped the development of state socialism. Thus, the incapacity of the Czarist state to compete with more advanced capitalist nations in trade and war set the conditions within which the Russian revolution unfolded. Moreover, the backwardness of Russian capitalism instigated various experiments in accelerated industrial development, leading eventually, if not inevitably, to a coercive regime of accumulation framed by five-year plans. Primitive socialist accumulation, like its capitalist counterpart, operated through coercive production regimes based on the unity of the reproduction of labour power and the production process. Survival outside work depended on adequate performance at work, monitored by party, trade union and management. Whereas under capitalism despotism rested on the autonomy of firms linked to one another through a market, under state socialism it operated through the coercive arm of the state at the point of production. Hence, I called it bureaucratic despotism.

Just as the variants of capitalist despotism — market, patriarchal, paternalistic — gave way to hegemonic regimes as the state *intervened* partially to separate the reproduction of labour power from the process of production, so corresponding processes can be discerned under state socialism. There the reproduction of labour power became more independent of the enterprise as the state began to *withdraw* from production, so that housing, employment security and social benefits were increasingly dispensed directly by the state, independently of performance at work. Management, party and trade union became less important in superintending individual workers' lives outside the factory, so that bureaucratic despotism gave way to bureaucratic bargaining. But this has been an uneven transition, varying, as we have seen, both within and between enterprises. Indeed, superimposed on the secular shift have been cyclical changes tied to the expansion and contraction of the second economy and the increase or decrease of enterprise autonomy within the state. The opening of the second economy and the limited expansion of market relations provide alternative sources of income which enhance individual workers' independence from arbitrary control by management. Enterprise autonomy gives management more flexibility in bargaining with different interests within the enterprise. But these moves toward the second economy and enterprise autonomy have generally set in motion political counter-pressures from industries directly dependent on the state and corresponding fractions of the party apparatus. Even in Hungary the reforms of 1968 suffered reversals in the mid-seventies.

More generally, the central direction of production through the fusion of production apparatuses and state apparatuses generates pressures for enterprise autonomy. The demand for decentralization may appear as a demand for some form of worker participation in management, as in Yugoslavia and Cuba, or for increased efficiency, as in Hungary.[10] As centralization begets pressures for decentralization, conversely decentralization creates pressures for recentralization. These cyclical movements are particularly clear in the case of Yugoslavia, in part because it is less affected by Soviet hegemony. There is, however, a second dynamic of state socialist societies, a product less of the fusion of production and state apparatuses and more of the class character of these societies. The principle of centralized appropriation and redistribution of surplus in the name of a putative and 'scientifically' determined societal interest generates an alternative conception of socialism in which direct producers control the surplus they produce. Inasmuch as central coordination is still necessary, it takes the form of planning from below. Workers' control is not confined to production apparatuses but is institutionalized in the central directing organs of society. This is a system of collective self-management. It began to emerge in embryo in Poland in 1981, when the existing order proved incapable of running the country. It also began to emerge in Hungary in 1956, after the regime collapsed and before the Soviet Union reasserted its control. In both cases, it was global politics that established the limits of national transformations. Indeed, the idea of 'the self-limiting revolution' which informed the practice of Solidarity is an explicit recognition of the decisive character of international political relations.

The experience of state socialism has a definite bearing on advanced capitalist societies. As under state socialism, there is an analogous fusion of production politics and state politics in the public sector of advanced capitalism, although the linkage operates chiefly through management — there is no party or trade union binding workplace regimes to the state. Thus, struggles at the workplace are implicitly and sometimes explicitly struggles against the state. No matter which workers they are — medical or postal workers, police, or workers in nationalized industries — their struggles can assume a political character. Just as there are variations both within and between state socialist societies as to the propensity toward collective struggles, so there are similar variations both within and between the state sectors of advanced capitalist societies. Externally, the various apparatuses of the state are situated in different ways with respect to one another, while internally each develops a different form of production politics.[11]

What is the economic basis of the distinction between public and private sectors? We can say, as a first approximation, that in the private sector exchange value dominates use value. The pursuit of profit in the market establishes the framework within which struggles are carried out. Questions of use value, of supply and demand, are relevant only in relation to the pursuit of present and future profit. In the same way, we can say that in the state sector, on the other hand, use value dominates exchange value — although the extent and character of that domination will vary from apparatus to apparatus, and will itself be subject to struggle. The state's *raison d'être* is the provision of 'social needs'. Whereas the logic of profitability is defined by competition in the market, the logic of social needs is defined by political negotiations within the state. But through what processes are those social needs to be determined? Citizens can be excluded only if state managers appoint themselves as the arbiters of the collective interest, making such judgements by virtue of their supposedly superior knowledge and expertise, their monopoly of a scientific rationality.

However, this principle has never been supreme, and the definition of social needs continually bursts into public discourse. The capitalist state deals with this in different ways, shaped partly by the nature of the threat and the character of the apparatus, and partly by the balance of class power both within and outside the state. On the one hand, it can open up struggles by state workers to limited public debate in which questions of social justice define the ideological terrain. The state may seek to defend a particular 'social contract' and isolate a given set of workers as pursuing their narrow self-interests at the expense of others. Workers, for their part, may defend their own position by appealing to public sympathy, seeking alliances with consumers and other fractions of the working class.[12] On the other hand, the state can refuse to enter into any public discussion about 'social justice' and instead try to privatize state apparatuses, applying criteria of efficiency to their operation. But even in the case of nationalized industries, which are easier to put on a commercial footing, the substitution of profitability for the satisfaction of social needs is a contested political process. As in the case of state socialist societies, the profitability of a state enterprise is arrived at through a series of political negotiations over subsidies, taxation, pricing and labour policies.[13] For this political process to be mystified behind market criteria requires effective control over the media. The state must suppress discussion of the social needs implicated in state workers' struggles.

This second strategy of restricting public debate has been pursued by the British and United States governments. However, as the private sector becomes enshrouded in a hegemonic despotism, questions of the provision of social needs, inescapably focused on the state, will continue to bubble forth. The very blockage in the private sector forces questions of socialism into the public sector. This calls for ever more repressive mechanisms from the state to contain those demands, not least the confinement and control of civil society. And this, of course, is precisely why in state socialism civil society has been so restricted. In a society that claims to operate on the principle of the satisfaction of socially defined needs, class divisions can be preserved only by repressing public discourse and movements for the creation of an autonomous civil society — that is, by a 'dictatorship over needs'.[14] Vistas of socialism or barbarism can be attenuated by opening up a private sphere, made up of a second economy, a second culture or, more generally, a second society.[15] But can this privatization of the pursuit of social needs be more than a temporary expedient?

Notes

1. W. Korpi, *The Working Class in Welfare Capitalism*, London 1978; John Stephens, *The Transition from Capitalism to Socialism*, London 1979; J H Marshall, *Citizenship and Social Class*, London 1980.

2. See Göran Therborn, *What Does the Ruling Class Do When It Rules?*, NLB, London 1978.

3. G A Cohen, *Karl Marx's Theory of History*, Princeton 1978.

4. See, for example, Etienne Balibar, 'The Basic Concepts of Historical Materialism', in Louis Althusser and Etienne Balibar, eds., *Reading Capital*, NLB, London 1970, pp. 199-308; Barry Hindess and Paul Hirst, *Pre-Capitalist Modes of Production*, London 1975.

5. To be sure, structuralists were very concerned with the general problem of the reproduction of social relations, but not with the specific problem of the reproduction of relations *in* production.

6. Let me clarify the philosophical basis for rejecting fixed laws of development. There are both epistemological and ontological reasons. First, I am quite convinced by the arguments of such philosophers as Duhem, Quine, Lakatos, Hesse and Feyerabend that theories are underdetermined by data. Although the empirical world may set limits on our theory of history, it does not uniquely determine it. We have to reconstruct history in the light of the standpoint of the present — and even then different paths are open. For example, our reconstruction in terms of politics of production is only one of a number that make sense of the past in a way that also responds to the metaphysical pathos of the present. Second, there are ontological reasons for rejecting fixed laws of history. These should not, however, be construed as a denial of real mechanisms that explain empirical events. At least in this respect I follow such realists as Harré and Bhaskar. But social events are distinctive in that they provoke social responses, struggles, that change those underlying mechanisms. The mere fact that there are limits to the transformation of those mechanisms, at least as long as one remains within one mode of production, does not mean that they do not change. History, then, is the product of changing mechanisms, and we are forced to reconstruct history in the light of the newly emergent mechanisms.

7. See Heidi Gottfried, 'The Value of Temporary Clericals: The Production and Reproduction of a Vulnerable Workforce', unpublished manuscript, 1983.

8. See Vicki Smith, 'The Circular Trap: Women and Part-Time Work', *Berkeley Journal of Sociology*, vol. 28, 1983, pp. 1-18.

9. Soon Kyoung Cho, 'The New Phase of Capital Mobility and the Dilemmas of Export-Led Industrialization', unpublished manuscript, 1984.

10. See Ellen Comisso, *Workers' Control under Plan and Market*, New Haven 1979; Linda Fuller, *Changing Politics of Workers' Control in Cuba: 1959-82*, Ph.D. dissertation, University of California, Berkeley, 1985.

11. See, for example, the study of two branches of the British Post Office by Eric Batstone, Anthony Ferner and Michael Terry, *Consent and Efficiency*, Oxford 1984.

12. See, for example, Paul Johnston, 'Democracy, Public Work and Labour Strategy', *Kapitalistate*, no. 8, 1980, pp. 9-26.

13. Batstone, Ferner and Terry, op. cit.; Tony Manwaring, 'Labour Productivity and the Crisis at BSC: Behind the Rhetoric', *Capital and Class*, No. 14, 1981, pp. 61-97.

14. Ferenc Fehér, Agnes Heller and György Márkus, *Dictatorship over Needs*, Oxford 1983.

15. For the concept of second society see Elemér Hankiss, 'A Második Társadalom', unpublished manuscript, 1984.

Index

270

272